CRICKETING ALLSORTS

CRICKETING ALLSORTS

Stephen Chalke

FAIRFIELD BOOKS

Fairfield Books
17 George's Road, Bath BA1 6EY
tel: 01225-335813

First published 2018
ISBN: 978 1 9996558 3 9

Printed and bound in Great Britain by
CPI Antony Rowe, Chippenham, Wilts

Introduction

In 2008 I published a collection of 105 articles that I had written for *Wisden Cricket Monthly* and *The Wisden Cricketer*, plus a few for *The Times*. The book was called *The Way It Was*, subtitled *Glimpses of English Cricket's Past,* and it was chosen as the Cricket Book of the Year at the National Sporting Club's British Sports Books awards.

The pieces in *The Way It Was* were all of a similar length, and almost all focused on the memories of former cricketers. A paperback edition, published in 2011, added a further 13 pieces.

Cricketing Allsorts is a sequel, collecting articles that did not appear in the original hardback of *The Way It Was*, though a few are among those added to the paperback. It is a more varied collection, featuring pieces of different lengths drawn from a wider range of publications.

Between 2010 and 2016 I wrote obituaries for *The Independent*, and this book contains these, together with some that I wrote for other publications. In one or two cases, I have amalgamated two obituaries on the same subject to make a fuller piece for this book.

The article on cricket in World War Two appeared in the *Wisden Cricketers' Almanack* so will have been widely read, but other pieces such as the one on Rupert Webb – for a limited-edition booklet produced by the Sussex Cricket Museum – had a much smaller circulation. The opening article on the resumption of cricket in 1919 has been written specially for this book.

I have included the speech I gave at Keith Andrew's funeral, a foray into ghost-writing on Bomber Wells' sofa, even a chess column that I wrote for a local newspaper long before I started writing about cricket.

The result is a less unified collection than *The Way It Was*, but I hope that nevertheless it provides pleasure. In their different ways these 53 pieces are all celebrations of cricket – even the one about chess!

Stephen Chalke

September 2018

Note: For the most part the pieces are left as written at the time. As a result they contain a small number of statements, such as the one on page 60, written in 2000, that Somerset's third place in 1958 remains the highest position in the county's history, that are no longer true.

CONTENTS

MISCELLANY

OBITUARIES

SLICES OF HISTORY

A ZEAL FOR RECONSTRUCTION

How English Cricket resumed after the First World War

This has been written specially for this book.

On the afternoon of Monday 16 December 1918, five weeks and a day after the signing of the Armistice, fifteen of cricket's first-class counties – all except Worcestershire – sat down in the Midland Hotel, St Pancras to discuss arrangements for the summer of 1919.

Back in August 1914, when war was bringing an early end to the first-class schedule, there had been a sense of crisis in the game. Most of the county clubs had fallen into debt, with at least two – Gloucestershire and Worcestershire – on the brink of withdrawing from the county championship. What had been a tight-knit competition in 1894, with nine counties all playing each other twice, had mushroomed by 1905 into a sprawling structure involving 16 counties, each of which was free to arrange from 12 to 30 fixtures. A programme of 72 matches in 1894 had become one of 192 by 1914, and there were simply not the spectators to pay for it all.

The Times put it bluntly in May 1914:

> Unfortunately at the present moment there does not seem to be the same "county spirit" that there used to be. Perhaps it is owing to the fact that people have to work more strenuously than they had to 20 years ago. They are still keen to know how the cricket of the day is going, but they do not turn up in numbers, and numbers mean gate-money, and gate-money means everything to a county, stoutly though the authorities may deny it.

As it transpired, the war eased the financial crisis. Many members continued to pay subscriptions and, with little expenditure, most clubs found themselves in better shape than in 1914. Somerset's 200 loyal members turned a pre-war debt of £600 into a surplus of £93. Hampshire cleared the £950 they owed, Leicestershire similarly went into the black, and Nottinghamshire, thanks to a Special Appeal by the Duke of Portland, not only reduced their debt from £6,000 to £672 but purchased the freehold of their Trent Bridge ground. By contrast Gloucestershire only achieved solvency by selling their Bristol ground.

Little serious cricket had been played since 1914, with almost a million young men dead and many more wounded. So, when the county clubs gathered in the Midland Hotel, there was a prevailing sense that the game could not pick up from 1914 as if all had been well back then and nothing had happened in the intervening years. In the straitened circumstances of post-war Britain, would people find time to watch cricket? And could the counties afford the expense of putting on a full programme? The cost of living had risen markedly; rail fares were up 50% and an Entertainment Tax, introduced in 1916, would slice into the monies taken at the gate.

Then there was the challenge of raising teams. Of the eleven Warwickshire men who had left the field after the last match of 1914, five were gone – dead, injured or retired; another would hardly play again, and three more were past their 44th birthday. When the county's committee met in November, the Secretary Rowland Ryder wrote, 'It was more or less groping in the dark, with a little ray of light here and there, somewhat dim and ill-defined maybe, but sufficiently luminous to make possible the first few steps in the new road that must be trod.' He was reassured by the realism of expectations when one committeeman asked him, "Can you rebuild the team in five years?"

In the words of Worcestershire's Fred Root, 'The war had an almost devastating effect upon cricket. Promising youngsters were killed; old hands were made aged and weary; and when the Armistice came, first-class cricket needed building up again.'

All the counties were eager to establish a programme of matches but, in the jubilation that followed the end of the war, perhaps a meeting barely five weeks after the Armistice allowed too little time for reflection. Looking back in early February, *The Times* was scathing about the occasion:

> Many counties sent two and even three delegates, there was a good deal of desultory conversation, and the Midland Hotel, St Pancras, where the meeting was held, lacked the calm and the judicial atmosphere of the Committee Room at Lord's. One county put forward eight different proposals which had not been circulated beforehand.

Several counties, concerned about costs, proposed reducing matches to two long days. Some, wanting to avoid paying for weekend accommodation, called for an end to games starting on a Saturday. Then there were the counties, all in the south and midlands, who argued for a cap on the number of professionals in a team. Sussex proposed no more than four, Leicestershire no more than five.

Lancashire and Yorkshire both wanted to increase the length of the over. Lord Hawke, chairing the meeting, cited an experiment at Headingley that showed how an eight-ball over would add the equivalent of an extra hour to a day's play. George Hirst and Wilfred Rhodes, the county's two great all-rounders, were both in favour of eight balls, he said.

The newspapers were full of letters advocating reforms, all intended to speed up and brighten the game: a simpler lbw law, out if the ball would hit the wicket, to eliminate pad play; a ban on newspapers publishing averages more than once a month; a less prominent seam on the ball, a shortening of boundaries, a penalty for playing out a maiden over, even a ban on left-handed batsmen. The *Yorkshire Post* regarded this talk as 'the creations of the faddists' while others argued that the counties' undertaking in May 1913 to make no changes for four years still applied as only two of those years had taken place.

In the *Sunday Times* the young novelist Alec Waugh was against all reform, wanting cricket to resist the commercialism that he felt was beginning to erode the culture of the game:

> The public is just as much to blame as the cricketers. During the years before the war it had been fed on sensationalism and clamoured for excitement. It wanted to find on the cricket field the mingled dash and speed of a football match or a cinematograph.

'A Cricketer' in the *Manchester Guardian* took a more balanced view:

> It was evident before the war, from the financial statements of too many clubs, that the game was losing its attractiveness with the average man. The lover of cricket need not take fright at this zeal for reconstruction; cricket may well be all the better for a public inspection and overhauling. All one asks is that the scrutiny shall be conducted in the right spirit, on the understanding that national games, like constitutions, are grown rather than made.

On the one hand, the writer argued, the two-day game would make it easier for amateurs to make themselves available and would 'abolish slow scoring'; on the other hand, 'you will increase the speed of cricket only at the expense of much of its variety and beauty.' Or, as the Middlesex captain Pelham Warner put it, there was a danger that the speeded-up two-day game would become 'too much of an American hustle'.

Despite strong opposition from Surrey and Yorkshire, the Midland Hotel meeting voted 10-5 in favour of two-day matches in 1919: 11.30 to 7.30 on the first day, 11 to 7.30 on the second. There would be no tea interval, just refreshments brought onto the ground, and there would be no Saturday starts. Some counties argued for the freedom to make their own arrangements – whether two- or three-day fixtures, Saturday starts or not – but the decisions were binding on them all. How else, it was argued, could the county championship have any coherence?

In the emotional aftermath of war this show of central authority led some who had been outvoted to protest that they were 'being Prussianised'. The

Wisden editor Sydney Pardon thought the counties were making a 'fetish' of the championship. He called the switch to two days a 'lamentable blunder', predicting that most spectators – in need of their evening meals – would be gone long before the 7.30 close. 'To my thinking it would have been far better to drop the championship entirely for one year.'

Some reforms were not accepted. A proposal for seven-ball overs was defeated by one vote, and there was little support for a restriction on the number of professionals. If the main intention of this proposal was to reduce costs, it was – in the opinion of *The Times* – entirely misguided:

> Are professionals more expensive than amateurs? The payment of the amateur's out-of-pocket expenses, hotel bills and first-class railway fares would certainly in these days exceed the fee allowed to the professional, who received £5 or £6 a match according to whether his side lost or won and had to pay his own expenses, including hotel bills and travelling.

Soon enough there developed a groundswell of unease about the outcomes of the meeting. Middlesex, for one, wanted to retain the option of three-day matches with Saturday starts against neighbouring counties, and in mid-January the MCC General Committee suspended confirmation of all the decisions, setting up a second meeting for Wednesday 5 February, this time to be held at the Sports Club in St James's Square.

Meanwhile, great crowds were flooding into all sporting events, regardless of their standard – football, racing, rugby, billiards – often to the point of extreme discomfort and with many spectators having almost no view of the action. Perhaps cricket did not need to be so pessimistic about its future.

Of all the counties Worcestershire were in the most parlous state, coming close to winding up in 1917. Before the war, with too few home-grown players of sufficient standard, they had recruited out-of-county professionals, some of whom were paid during their two-year residential qualifications, and they did not have the income to sustain the practice. They did not attend the December meeting, announcing in January that there would be only two professionals in their eleven and that they hoped to arrange fixtures with six counties who would constitute their teams on similar lines. They failed in this and did not compete in the 1919 championship, contenting themselves with a programme of friendly fixtures.

When the counties met at the Sports Club in February, five southern counties – Middlesex, Surrey, Essex, Hampshire and Somerset – pressed unsuccessfully for flexibility on the question of two- and three-day matches, but the counties of the north and midlands countered that a championship with such variation would not be taken seriously. Surprisingly Kent voted with the north but only, Lord Harris explained, because they were totally opposed to the shorter game and thought that "one season of two-day cricket would finish it." There was, however, some concession to flexibility: tea intervals of up to 15 minutes could be taken, at the captains' discretion, and counties were free to arrange Saturday starts.

The fixture list was now in a mess, with the added complication that nobody knew whether the Australians would, as hoped, be sending a touring team. In this confusion Warwickshire found themselves playing two fixtures on the same two days in early August: a championship match against Derbyshire and a friendly against their traditional bank holiday rivals, Worcestershire. Remarkably, for a team who had not won a game up to that point, they beat Derbyshire by ten wickets and gained first-innings lead in a high-scoring draw against Worcestershire.

With too few key players available, the Australian tour was abandoned, but it re-emerged in the form of a 15-strong party of ex-servicemen already in Europe who played as Australian Imperial Forces. They stayed all summer, drawing great crowds in a mixture of two- and three-day games.

Amid the post-war reconstruction another great issue came to the fore: the playing of sport on Sundays. War work, either at home or on the frontline, had not been suspended on Sundays, and in France, when hostilities were not at their peak, men had played organised games after the church services. Traditionally some sports, such as golf and tennis, were deemed private and thus allowed on Sundays, though this led to some deception by the newspapers. When tennis staged important public matches on Sundays, *The Times* and *Daily Telegraph* drew a veil over this, reporting that they had been played 'during the week-end' or even on the Saturday.

The *Manchester Guardian*, seeing the inequity between the sports of different social classes, called for it all to be 'put on a proper footing':

> Before the war it was not a really healthy and comrade-like thing, as between one kind of man and another, to have golf clubs in full use on Sunday, lawn tennis played in gardens instead of at clubs, and rowing clubs practising for Henley without their club colours, while the youth of many villages were confined on their Sunday afternoons to such substitutes for exercise, athletic or devotional, as loafing in groups on bridges and expectorating joylessly over the parapet. There will be more health, more equity, more friendliness and good-humour, and more fair play for religion in an England in which the word rest is better understood.

Support for this cause came from Pelham Warner who in April presided over a meeting to form a Sunday Games' Association. 'After church hours he failed to see that healthy recreation was different from reading or smoking,' reported *The Times*. 'We must get rid of our puritanical ideas of Sunday and give the boys a chance.' He went on to say that Sunday sport 'would result in a better, happier, more healthy and more contented nation, with Socialism, Bolshevism and the various other "isms" gradually dying out.'

With raw material and labour in short supply, there was a dearth of new sports equipment, with much of the available stock being exported to the British Army of Occupation. A newly created cricket league around Cologne was reported to have received entries from almost 100 teams, with 'grounds extemporised from the most improbable beginnings'.

At Taunton the county ground had to be converted back from its wartime uses as a regimental base and a poultry and pig farm. The scoring apparatus, left open to the elements, had rotted while a section of seating had been pulled up and used for firewood.

At The Oval £2,000 was needed for painting and repairs while the pavilions at Old Trafford, Trent Bridge and Derby had to be restored from their use as hospitals. Late in the war the Old Trafford pavilion had taken in a boatload of men from the southern states of America, many of whom had fallen victim to a flu epidemic on the voyage and were dying of pneumonia. In the words of one employee, 'the home of cricket was more like the home of death.' When the Red Cross departed in February, the building was fumigated, then painted and decorated.

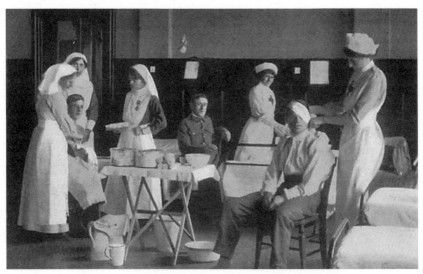

The Red Cross hospital in the Old Trafford pavilion

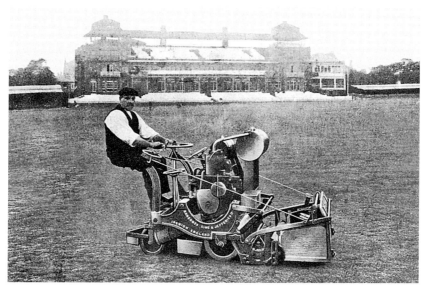

Cutting the grass at Lord's

On Friday 16 May, at Lord's and The Oval, the championship programme finally got under way and, despite a doubling of admission charges from sixpence to a shilling, large crowds gathered. Earlier in the month the weather had been unseasonally wintry, with shortages of coal exacerbating the sense of chill, but the sun was out in time for the county cricketers. At Lord's, *The Times* reported, 'the famous ground looked all the better for its long rest, and not for a very long time can the turf have been in such good order.' Across the 14½ hours of the two days 1,002 runs were scored off 311 overs.

The following Monday they started at Old Trafford, where it fell to the young Neville Cardus, surprised to be asked to report on cricket, to capture the moment for the *Manchester Guardian*:

> It was indeed easy to feel the sentimental aspect of the occasion. One came into the enclosure from the dusty town, and there were for many an old cricket lover strong tugs on the heart as they again saw the soft green splashed with the spring sun and the red pavilion and the county flag streaming in the wind.

Yet it was not as it had been before the war. Of the Lancashire eleven there were only three who had been in the side that left the field on the last day of August 1914 – and, when Gloucestershire got started later in the week, they would have only two. Yes, there were opportunities for newcomers, but where were they to be found?

Sussex arrived in Taunton on the Wednesday with four survivors from their last pre-war match. When they first announced their team, it only had nine men, and two of these withdrew. So there was an unfamiliar look about the assembled eleven. Two were newcomers, four had appeared in a bare handful of pre-war matches, and the 23-year-old Maurice Tate, who had had some games in 1914, had come close to joining Middlesex when his first approach to Sussex after being demobbed had received the reply, "We can't promise you anything."

Among this hastily gathered group was the 34-year-old Harold Heygate who had played five games as a 20-year-old in 1905 and who was recovering from a wartime leg injury. His brother Reginald had withdrawn ahead of the game, but Harold played – though, when his injury flared up in the field, it was soon apparent that he should not have done. He limped badly and, though an opening batsman, went in at number eleven and was bowled for a duck. The next day he watched the match from the pavilion, with a Taunton club cricketer fielding in his place.

Needing 105 runs for victory, his Sussex team were on course at 103 for six. Then three wickets fell for only one run, and he was persuaded by the former Somerset captain Sammy Woods to step out to bat. Some say he was wearing his blue serge suit, though Maurice Tate wrote that he had taken it off 'and came out in his waistcoat, watch-chain and all.' It was some while before he appeared out of the pavilion and, with the pronounced limp of his wartime injury, he made slow progress to the middle.

"He's taking an awfully long time, isn't he?" the Somerset bowler Len Braund grumbled and – perhaps mindful of Lord Hawke's pre-season exhortation to waste less time at the fall of wickets – the umpire pulled up the stumps and declared the match over. It all caused a great to-do, with some newspapers presenting it as a story of a war hero denied the right to bat by a petty-minded umpire.

A wounded soldier who received more sympathetic treatment was Arthur Denton of Northamptonshire. A lieutenant in the Royal West Kent Regiment, he had had a leg amputated during the war but reckoned that, with his artificial leg made of leather and cork, he could still play if he fielded close to the wicket and was allowed a runner when he batted. The county secretary wrote to his opposite number at Lancashire to ask if they had any objections to this. Back came the reply:

> I read your letter to our captain today, and his reply was: "If any fellow has been to the war and has had his leg off and wants to play he's good enough for me, and he can have twenty runners."
> And so say I. Does that answer your question?

Arthur Denton
between his
twin brothers

Denton was not available for the Lancashire game, but he played the next two matches, getting a great cheer when he stepped out to bat against Leicestershire. He had twin brothers six years older than him, both playing in that game, and in a delightful twist one acted as his runner while the other was his batting partner. His footwork was limited, but reporters complimented the 'pretty strokes' and 'magnificent defence' in his unbeaten 29. Later in the week at Derby, he made 27, 'his delightful driving stirring the admiration of the 3,000 spectators'.

For all the joy of returning to cricket, it was not long into the summer before the grumbles about the two-day games became widespread. As early as 1 June *The Observer* reported:

> The long hours are detested by the players and find no favour with the public. They are making cricket a toil instead of a pleasure to the players. With play going on so long, bowlers are afraid to let themselves go. They feel sure that, if they exert themselves to the same extent that they used to, they will be used up before the season is half over.

'The long hours were too much for me,' Pelham Warner wrote. 'After the middle of July I was "a dead dog".' His team-mate Harry Lee went further:

> Long hours of play, and night travel in difficult conditions, made cricketers more and more tired and bad-tempered as the season progressed, and some reputations were tarnished which never quite recovered their lustre.

Amateurs complained that it was ruining the social life of their evenings while professionals found themselves going to bed as soon as they had eaten. "Cricket is all bed and work," one complained. It was also clear, as Sydney Pardon had predicted, that most spectators did not stay till the close. When Surrey played Essex at The Oval on Monday 26 May there were 9,000 in the ground but, according to *The Times*, 'some time before the end arrived, the company had dwindled to about a thousand.'

There were some exciting finishes, played in a generous spirit, such as Lancashire's victory over Sussex at Old Trafford when the visitors fielded in steady rain till after 7.20 as their hosts, with seven wickets down and an eighth man incapacitated, scrambled the winning runs.

The Sussex players were wet through when they returned to the pavilion, and they did not reach the hotel at their next destination, Harrogate, till the early hours of the morning. Their match there had been brought forward to a 10.30 start to allow them time to catch the train back to Brighton the next evening, and inevitably they lost the toss and found themselves in the field on a cold, windswept day. They had won none of their 11 matches, Yorkshire were riding high and were fresh from a five-day break, but in the upset of the summer Sussex won by five wickets.

For the most part the summer's weather was good but, despite that, the reduced playing hours led to 45% of the matches ending in a draw. The counties had gone back to the simplest of point systems – the championship awarded to the county with the highest percentage of victories – but, with so many draws and so much variation in the number of matches played, it was not an entirely satisfactory method.

The two front-runners were Kent and Yorkshire, the counties who had between them won 10 of the last 15 championships before the war. On the morning of Monday 18 August, as the season entered its final fortnight, Kent, with six wins out of 10, held the lead on 60%, with Yorkshire, 11 wins out of 21, on 52%. At Bradford the Northerners – greatly strengthened by the new pair at the top of their batting order, Percy Holmes and Herbert Sutcliffe – won by an innings against bottom-of-the-table Warwickshire, while Kent travelled to The Oval to play

Surrey. It was Jack Hobbs' benefit match, carried over from August 1914, and it was watched by the largest crowd of the season: 18,000 on Monday, 12,000 on Tuesday.

In the pavilion on the second afternoon the 15 counties gathered to agree the shape of cricket in 1920, and this time there was unanimity. There would be a return to three-day cricket, with Saturday starts and a scoring system much as in 1914: five points for a win, two for first innings lead in a draw. Worcestershire returned to the fold, and the championship programme increased from 124 two-day to 186 three-day matches.

Meanwhile on the field Kent, 90 runs behind on first innings, were battling to avoid their first defeat of the summer. At 80 for six they looked beaten, but lower-order resistance ate into the remaining time and, when the last wicket fell, Surrey required an unlikely 95 runs in 42 minutes. The light was poor, a drizzle was thickening, but the Kent fielders stayed out. The great crowd – 'thousands in their places at an hour when in the ordinary way the ground would have been half empty' – cheered mightily as the free-scoring amateur Jack Crawford and the immensely popular Hobbs knocked off the runs with ten minutes to spare. When Hobbs cut the winning four, they surged onto the field and made for their hero.

'I was lifted up and carried along,' Hobbs recalled later, 'being finally deposited over the pavilion rails. My damp flannels were black where the enthusiasts had patted me. The thumb was all that was left of one of my batting gloves. I found a pound note in my hand; how it got there I have no idea. Altogether it was a wonderful finish to a benefit match; it panned out just as in a story for boys.'

The result left Kent, six wins out of 11, and Yorkshire, 12 out of 22, exactly level in the table. But, with rain about, the remaining games all ended in draws, and Yorkshire's 12 wins out of 26 produced a higher percentage than Kent's six out of 14. They might have shared the title if rain had not denied them both victories in the final round of matches. In fact, Kent might have won outright if they had not dropped an easy catch at deep square leg at the end of their final game at Lord's. The fortunate batsman was Frank Mann who, despite being wounded three times during the war, 'twice very severely', had played the full season with enthusiasm. His defensive batting on a spiteful pitch, denying Kent the championship, prompted 'stupid ironical applause' from some of the crowd, with the correspondent from *The Times* especially appalled: 'A better example of bad manners allied to appalling ignorance has seldom been seen anywhere at any time.'

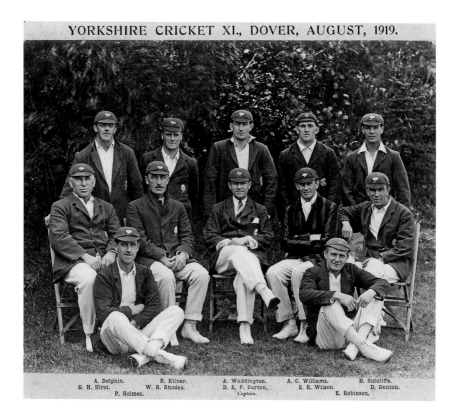

YORKSHIRE CRICKET XI., DOVER, AUGUST, 1919.

A. Dolphin.   R. Kilner.   A. Waddington.   A. C. Williams.   H. Sutcliffe.
G. H. Hirst.   W. R. Rhodes.   D. E. F. Burton,   E. R. Wilson.   D. Denton.
P. Holmes.   *Captain.*   E. Robinson.

Meanwhile, four miles away at Highbury, 60,000 spectators watched The Arsenal play Newcastle United on the opening day of the first full season of league football for five years. Unlike cricket, the structure of the game was exactly as it had been before the war – with the one exception that it had crept for the first time into the end of August and the beginning of May.

In September cricket wound down with a handful of festival matches and a four-day match at The Oval between the champion county Yorkshire and The Rest. There were as many as 6,000 on the ground on some of the days, and they were treated to centuries by Jack Hobbs and Frank Woolley. The 36-year-old Hobbs, batting with a damaged left wrist, took his summer's run tally to 2,594, more than 700 ahead of all others, causing *The Times* to write that 'the loss of four seasons had in no way affected his splendid powers.'

Hobbs himself believed that he was never the batsman after the war that he had been before. 'Cricket has lost much ground during the war,' he told *The Observer*. 'It is very poor today compared with what it was in 1914. We are particularly weak in bowling, especially fast bowling.' *The Times* agreed: 'The bowling of many of the county elevens was deplorably weak.'

21

In the first-class averages, eight of the top ten bowlers were spinners, the only exceptions being Warwickshire's 44-year-old veteran Frank Field, who appeared only occasionally, and Jack Gregory of the Australian Imperial Forces. 'I hope the Australians will not imagine that our present teams are really representative of our best form,' Hobbs said.

Yet, for all that, the pessimism of the previous winter had been dispelled. The crowds were back, and the calls for reform had died away, at least for the time being. In the words of the *Wisden* editor Sydney Pardon:

> The faint-hearts who had jumped to the conclusion that cricket would never again be its old self were utterly confuted. Even the hopeful spirits, among whom I include myself, were agreeably surprised, things turning out much better than they had expected. Such being the pleasant state of affairs in the first year of peace, I trust we shall hear no more about the need for drastic alterations to the game.

Two-day matches had been hard going for the players, but the Surrey keeper Herbert Strudwick, who had spent the previous four years working seven-day weeks in a munitions factory, was not inclined to complain: 'It was much easier than I had been having it during the war, and that was what mattered most.'

Amid the revival new heroes would emerge: the dependable opener who had enjoyed such a fine first summer for Yorkshire, the genial all-rounder who was starting to make his mark in a struggling Sussex side, and, further into the future, a 16-year-old soldier's son who had just broken into the Cirencester Grammar School first eleven, and a 14-year-old pit-pony boy from Nottinghamshire, learning to bowl fast in the Nuncargate second eleven. Sutcliffe, Tate, Hammond, Larwood: soon enough they would become household names as English cricket, so weakened by war, regained its glory.

HERBERT SUTCLIFFE'S 161

England v Australia, The Oval, 14-18 August 1926

This appeared in 'Masterly Batting – 100 Great Test Centuries',
compiled and edited by Patrick Ferriday and Dave Wilson.

Using complicated statistical measures, they ranked Test hundreds
and invited various writers to describe the leading ones.
This innings by Sutcliffe was in tenth place.

It was half past five on Monday afternoon when Herbert Sutcliffe's innings began. England had spent a hot and sultry day in the field, their energy sapped as the Australian lower order recovered from 122 for six to 302 all out and a first innings lead of 22 runs. Such was England's frustration that, according to Neville Cardus, their fielding declined visibly during a ninth-wicket stand of 67: 'The returns to the keeper were often inaccurate. I got a sense that we were falling a little out of humour.'

Invigorated by this change of fortune the Australians came down the steps of the Oval pavilion with a purposeful bounce, to be followed by England's opening pair: Jack Hobbs, 43 years old now, playing on his beloved home patch, and his trusty 31-year-old partner from Pudsey in West Yorkshire, the unflappable Herbert Sutcliffe. If they could only reach close of play without setback, the disappointments of the day could be put aside. The teams would start the morrow on level terms.

The Ashes were at stake. In the aftermath of the Great War of 1914-18, in three five-match series, Australia had beaten England 5-0, 3-0 and 4-1. Yet now the two teams were playing the final Test of 1926 with the series still locked at 0-0. Test matches in England were three-day affairs and, though the bowlers completed their overs at a brisker rate than now (411 in the three days at Lord's), a mixture of rain and good batting meant that not one of the first four games came close to a conclusion. So it was resolved that this Oval Test would be played to its conclusion, however long that took. One or other team would win the Ashes here in South London, and every spectator knew it.

There were 32,000 of them that Monday, standing several deep around the ground, many of them barely able to glimpse the action. Several times the ambulance men fetched fainting girls out of the packed throng while on the grass the boundary rope had inched forward in places. By close of play they were all exhausted – by the heat, by the discomfort and by the sheer tension of the play.

Herbie Collins, the Australian captain, used four bowlers that evening: paceman Jack Gregory and three slower men: leg-spinners Arthur Mailey and Clarrie Grimmett and the brisk off-spinner Arthur Richardson. Gregory was past his best, carrying a leg injury, so mostly that evening Collins attacked the batsmen with his two leg-spinners, Mailey cheerfully flighting it high and tempting the false shot, Grimmett miserly with his almost round-arm style. Mailey's deadliest weapon was his googly, Grimmett's the top-spinner that scuttled on. Hobbs and Sutcliffe played the two of them judiciously, picking the deliveries to hit and never once lofting the ball into the air. By stumps they had reached 49 for no wicket: Hobbs 28, Sutcliffe 20.

Hobbs and Sutcliffe. Nineteen times before this day they had walked out together at the start of an England innings, and the average of those partnerships stood at a reassuring 100. All England went to bed praying that they would continue serenely in the morning, laying the foundations of a winning total.

Hobbs and Sutcliffe. More than any other players in those years they raised the status of the professional cricketer – though in different ways. Hobbs, the master craftsman, had the most placid of temperaments, and he carried himself at all times with a modest decency that was inspiring. The son of a Cambridge college servant, he remained deferential to those born into a higher social station.

Sutcliffe, by contrast, was a self-made man, ambitious and confident, acquiring the vowels of the amateurs and calling them by their Christian names. An orphan brought up by strict Congregationalist aunts, he had started his working life at 13 as an apprentice boot-maker and was rising through cricket – and through a sports outfitting business – to a social status unknown to previous generations of paid cricketers. Indeed, it was his mission to raise the standing of his profession. When he became a senior player in the Yorkshire side he would advise the younger men: "Make sure your manners and bearing are better than those of the amateurs. Remember that you are representing Yorkshire, not just yourself."

"Everything had to be done to the highest standard," his daughter Barbara recalled. "He dressed immaculately, and he didn't like anything out of place. He bred pedigree boxer dogs, and he often sat with them in the evening in his office, doing his books for the shop, all in his beautiful handwriting."

As a batsman he had three great shots: an off-drive, a back-foot push behind point and a fearless hook. 'There was method in everything he did,' his Yorkshire team-mate Bill Bowes wrote, describing how if there were two men back for the hook he would only take it on when he had 40 on the board. "By that time," he reckoned, "I've so much confidence I think I can miss them both." On such days he could be an electrifying sight. At Scarborough in 1932 he took on the Essex fast men, Farnes and Nichols, and he raced from 100 to 182 in 20 minutes.

He was the master of the quick single. He opened with Derbyshire's Denis Smith against the Indians in a Festival match. "If he was my regular partner," Smith said, "I'd average another 15 runs an innings."

He was also a batsman with a magnificent defence. In accordance with the lbw laws of the time he would – if the situation required – happily ignore or kick away balls pitched outside his off stump, and he would lean forward with elegance to present a calm and unflinching bat to anything straight.

If ever there was a cricketer for a big occasion, it was Herbert Sutcliffe. In a career that spanned the 21 years between the wars, he scored 50,138 runs at an average of 51.95. But in Tests he averaged 60.73, higher than any other Englishman, and in Ashes Tests his 66.85 is second only to Bradman among the major batsmen. Len Hutton thought he had a higher level of concentration than any other player he knew, while to Bradman 'he had the best temperament of any cricketer I ever played with or against.'

When he was out, he would return to the dressing room with not a hair out of place. 'The sort of man who would rather miss a train than run for it,' Robertson-Glasgow called him. After a wash and rub down, Bowes wrote, 'he would dress methodically, then produce a writing case and sit down to ten or fifteen letters.' Always a good team man, he would look up from time to time: "How are we doing?"

He was, in the words of the cricket writer A.A. Thomson, 'a personality as dependable as fallible human nature will allow.'

'He was not born to greatness,' Cardus wrote. 'He achieved greatness. His wasn't a triumph of skill only, it was a finer triumph, a triumph of character, application, will-power.'

Character, application, will-power. Never did he need those qualities more than on Tuesday 17 August 1926 – with the Ashes at stake and all England wiling him to succeed. The country was still healing the wounds of the General Strike in May. What a boost to morale it would be if England's cricketers could win here at The Oval.

There was no overnight covering of the pitch, just two policemen on duty to prevent the interference of intruders. They were standing out on the square at two in the morning when the sticky air turned dramatically into a violent storm, tropical in its intensity. All across the South London sky there were flashes of lightning, claps of thunder and fierce rain lashing down. The pitch, so placid at close of play, quickly became sodden, lakes of water forming all across the field. Outside the walls of the ground the long queue dissolved in an instant, men running in desperation for whatever shelter they could find.

By the morning, when the players arrived, the puddles had drained away. There were birds on the outfield, feeding on the worms which had come to the surface, and in the air was a misty steam as the water on the field and on the surrounding seats evaporated in the warmth of the day. Against all expectations play began, as scheduled, at eleven o'clock. Percy Chapman the England captain ordered the heavy roller, hoping that, by bringing the moisture to the surface, the pitch would be dead for a time while his openers grew used to the new conditions.

Before play began, the umpire Frank Chester looked into the England dressing room. He had expected an anxious atmosphere, but instead he found Hobbs puffing at his pipe as if he were about to step out for a festival match while Sutcliffe was calmly brushing down his sleek, black hair. "The wicket's a bad 'un," Chester said, but the two batsmen seemed to show no flicker of concern.

Hobbs turned to Sutcliffe as they patted down the pitch at the end of the first over. "Jolly bad luck, that rain," he said. "It's cooked our chances." He repeated the remark to the umpire 'Sailor' Young, who offered no words of comfort. "Yes, it's hard luck," he replied.

With sawdust all around them and the ball biting into the surface, leaving indentations that needed regular flattening down, the two batsmen concentrated solely on survival. Sutcliffe's first run of the morning came after forty minutes while at one point Hobbs was content to play out eight successive maidens from the medium pace of the off-spinner Arthur Richardson, bowling round the wicket with a cluster of fielders in the leg trap. Frank Chester recalled an early delivery from Mailey to Hobbs that pitched on leg, spat and spun viciously, missing the off stump by a whisker. "We'll not get 70 on this," Sutcliffe whispered to him, and Chester agreed.

It was a timeless Test, and the knowing South London crowd showed their grasp of the game, loving every minute of it. "Steady, now, Jack boy," one man called out when Hobbs broke loose with two boundaries. Then, when Sutcliffe let yet another delivery go past him and an impatient spectator called out "Don't 'urt the ball, mate", his neighbours were quick to tell him to "put a sock in it." The *Manchester Guardian* had a correspondent nestled among the masses. 'We did not want runs,' he reported. 'We longed to see

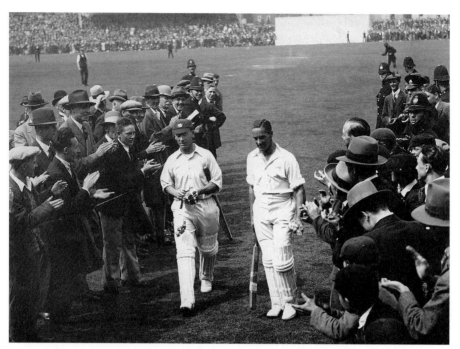

Hobbs and Sutcliffe leaving the field at lunchtime

the bowlers worn down: such was the grim spirit of the day.' Meanwhile, in the trees that overlooked the ground opposite the gasworks, a swarm of boys hung like monkeys to the branches. 'They regarded it as a huge spree and roared the changing score to their friends below and to passers-by in the street with happy-go-lucky cheerfulness.'

By twelve o'clock the sun was out, and the effect of the heavy roller had worn off. Now, in the 90 minutes till lunch, the pitch was at its most spiteful. 'The Australians were on tiptoe,' Hobbs wrote later, 'and undoubtedly should have got many of us out.' Indeed, the next England batsmen – Woolley, Hendren, Chapman – were all stroke-makers, much less well-suited to battling it out on such a devilish pitch. One false shot from Hobbs or Sutcliffe, and the game would swing decisively towards the visitors.

Perhaps the Australian attack was not at its supreme best – Grimmett still to reach his peak, Mailey too slow and flighty for the surface and the left-armer Macartney, now primarily a batsman, past his most potent. The real danger lay with Richardson, and some say he was at fault in bowling always a leg-stump line. Yet, in the words of *The Times*, 'the pitch was horrid', and the Australians 'bowled on it each of them as well as he knows how. Nearly every ball cut out a little fid of turf when it pitched.' Through it all Hobbs and Sutcliffe 'remained masters of their fate. Their artistry in manipulation of the bat was consummate, their judgment infallible, their patience inexhaustible.'

The two men gave not a chance, and they were still there at lunch. In two and a half hours, on the stickiest pitch umpire Chester ever saw, they had lifted the total from 49 to 161. Hobbs, the freer of the two, had moved from 28 to 97; Sutcliffe, with his immense self-control, from 20 to just 53.

The players and umpires made their way towards the pavilion, but the two batsmen remained for a minute in the middle, meticulously clearing the little divots of earth and patting down the pitch with their bats. "Well played, Jack," said Sutcliffe. "Well played Herbert," said Hobbs. Three words each, but in that very English way they acknowledged the ordeal of what they had been through. Back in the dressing room, they were still unbuckling their pads when they were summoned to the office to meet the Prince of Wales.

'What Hobbs and Sutcliffe achieved that day,' Pelham Warner wrote, 'will be talked of as long as cricket is played. They have made their names immortal in cricket history.' Len Hutton, then a boy of ten, was still writing about it sixty years later: 'If I could be granted one wish, I would be tempted to ask for a rerun of their famous stand. Wilfred Rhodes, who played in the match at the age of 48, used to talk about it with a faraway look in his eyes.'

Yet the job was not done. By the time play resumed the pitch had eased, and the bowlers' run-ups had dried sufficiently to allow Gregory to take the ball. Hobbs soon completed his hundred, and pandemonium broke out. Cheer after cheer – "Hip, hip, hooray" – rent the London air. Then the joyous crowd burst into a rendition of "For he's a jolly good fellow". Within minutes, though, they were clapping again, this time with a heavier heart, as Hobbs made his way back to the pavilion, bowled by Gregory for exactly 100.

The England lead was only 150. It fell to Sutcliffe to ensure that the hard work of the morning would not be in vain. The next batsmen all made contributions but, even with the pitch growing more benign, each in turn departed without reaching 30. Yet Sutcliffe himself, growing more expansive as the day wore on, though never weakening in his powers of mental application, continued remorselessly. By tea he had made a faultless 125 not out. Then in the day's closing over from Mailey, he misread a googly and was bowled for 161. The England total was now a formidable 375 for six, and many a lesser mortal would have strode off, head held high, proud of his innings. Not Herbert Sutcliffe. Aghast at his momentary lapse, he thumped his bat on the ground in self-disgust.

In the two sessions since lunch he had scored 108 runs, but it was not his scoring strokes that the *Times* correspondent chose to describe in detail. Not the calculated shots to leg, nor the many gentle pushes into off-side gaps. 'What every one who saw it will remember to his dying day was the graceful solidity of his defence, his subordination of self to side, and his almost uncanny wisdom.'

When he came out of the pavilion, he was besieged by well-wishers and autograph hunters. Patiently he stood and talked to them all. Then outside the gates he was mobbed by an even greater crowd. It took four mounted police and a whole posse of constables to clear a path to a waiting car. Then, as the vehicle drove away, it was followed by hundreds of running, cheering admirers. Several of them had to be removed from the car's footboard.

Next morning England took their total to 436. Then, in front of Prime Minister Stanley Baldwin and the King of Iraq, they bowled out Australia for 125, with the 48-year-old Wilfred Rhodes – recalled after a five-year absence – taking four wickets.

The vast crowd in front of the pavilion cheered themselves hoarse. "We want Hobbs," they chanted. "We want Sutcliffe." Pelham Warner in *The Cricketer* was full of the significance of the moment: 'Had we been beaten, despondency would have crept over the land. As it is, our cricket will be fortified and refreshed.'

Given the importance of the match, and the difficulty of the pitch, the batting of Hobbs and Sutcliffe in that second innings ranks still as one of the greatest achievements in all Test history. Some regard the innings of Jack Hobbs, always the most popular of cricketers, to be the greater, because he scored more runs in that crucial morning session when almost every ball was full of venom. Men still argue whether it was he or Wally Hammond who is the greatest English batsman ever.

But what of Herbert Sutcliffe, less elegant, less powerful, but with an inner steel that was at its very best when the going was toughest? As he said to the editor of *The Cricketer*, "Yes, Mr Warner, I love a dog fight." And that day at The Oval, when all England held its breath, he was the supreme master, batting with calm determination for almost four more hours after his partner's dismissal.

It was indeed a triumph of character, application and will-power.

WALLY HAMMOND

This was my contribution to a series called 'My Favourite Cricketer' which appeared in the Wisden Cricketer.

If I could sit on a magic carpet and fly back in time, I would love to see Barry Richards at the crease again, in a match which mattered to him, or Garry Sobers, bringing his bat flashing down once more from that high backlift, or David Gower on a sunny day, languidly easing the ball to the cover boundary. They all stay with me, reminders of golden days.

But if the carpet is waiting for me, let it take me all the way: to sights I have never seen – to the wristy, nimble-footed Ranjitsinhji glancing to leg, to the fluid, graceful Victor Trumper dancing down the pitch, and, most of all, to see for myself that greatest of English cricketers, Walter Hammond.

Put me down at the Nursery End at Lord's at ten minutes past twelve on Friday 24 June 1938, the house full for the Second Test against the Australians, and let me watch him walk down those pavilion steps. A princely figure stepping out, exuding calm assurance. It was 20 for two on that sunny morning, soon to be 31 for three, and the ball was rearing up awkwardly. 'In this sulphurous moment of crisis,' Cardus wrote, 'he walked down the steps like the Queen Mary gliding down the stocks to a flowing sea.' No Sky Television in those days, darting off for a quick advert. The crowd sat in awe; it was worth the admission charge just to see his entrance.

Or stand me outside a beer tent at Cheltenham, on a Saturday in August, with the Cotswold farmworkers celebrating their harvest with pints of Flowers Bitter. They had come to see Wally, the boy from Cirencester Grammar School; he rarely let them down.

In the 1928 Festival he hit a century in each innings against Surrey and, agile and sharp-eyed at wide first slip, set a still unbroken record of ten catches in the match. The next day, Saturday, opening the bowling against Worcestershire, he took nine for 23, caught the tenth and scored 80. To those weather-beaten Cotswolders outside the beer tent, he was a god playing with mortals. Then on the Monday, bowling a brisk medium pace unchanged for 34 overs, he took another six wickets. He was, in the words of Robertson-Glasgow, 'the sort of cricketer any schoolboy might wish to be.'

At Lord's that day in 1938 he was at his imperious best. That summer, a professional who had turned amateur, he had become England's captain, a mighty responsibility in those class-conscious days. He saw off the early threat of the fast bowlers, then played with such controlled purpose that the crowd were clapping his century soon after three o'clock, his double soon after six.

It was the force of his driving, between square cover and mid-off, off front foot and back, which was so remarkable. There was a grandeur about it, a power that was allied with apparent ease, and it was thrilling to see. 'I can't think that human agency could do more to a ball,' Robertson-Glasgow wrote. 'To field to him at cover-point was a sort of ordeal by fire.'

His double century that day was his fourth against the Australians, another record he still holds. 'I can recall no instance,' Bradman wrote, 'when his superb artistry shone so brilliantly.'

He was the leading English batsman in the national averages in each of the last five summers before the war and again, at the age of 43, in 1946. Indeed, if he had not played after the war, when his back was bad, he would have ended his Test career with an average above 61, second only to Bradman.

Second only to Bradman. That was the cross he bore through his career. He scored a record 905 runs in five Tests in Australia in 1928/29, then Bradman overtook him with 974 in England in 1930. He hit 36 double centuries in first-class cricket, Bradman 37.

Yet take me on that magic carpet, and it is Hammond I want to see. Not just because he was the greatest all-round cricketer of them all – batting, bowling and fielding – but because, in everything he did, he thrilled the crowd. He was not a utilitarian, a remorseless accumulator like Bradman; he was a man who gave lifelong memories to those who saw him.

He was not the most popular cricketer among his peers. He could be a difficult man, aloof, moody, harsh at times, and his conversion to amateur status was not universally welcomed. After his playing days he moved to South Africa and to relative obscurity. As a result his star has fallen below that of Jack Hobbs, a much gentler, more deferential character.

Yet it is Hammond I most wish I had seen.

Perhaps we have come to view our sportsmen too close up. Perhaps it all works better if we watch them from the boundary. For all his inner demons Hammond became a free man with a bat in his hand. A true artist. A great entertainer. A cricketer who lifted the spirits of every spectator: the grandee at Lord's *and* the farm labourer at Cheltenham. His glory transcended social class.

At Lord's he was bowled for 240, coming off to one of the greatest receptions in the history of the ground. I wish I had been there.

WE WERE PRISONERS NO LONGER

How English Cricket Survived the Second World War

This appeared in the 2010 edition of the Wisden Cricketers' Almanack.

The news on Thursday 24 August 1939 was ominous: German threats against the Polish city of Danzig, a treaty between Hitler and Stalin, an Emergency Powers Act passing through parliament. Yet county cricket was playing on: in the words of Neville Cardus, 'a haven of peace in an unruly world'.

"We didn't know a great deal about what was happening," Northamptonshire's Dennis Brookes recalled, years later. "We read what Chamberlain was saying, but even then we didn't think there was going to be a war." That afternoon at Northampton the Lancashire captain Lionel Lister was waiting to bat. He received a message from his Territorial Army unit, unbuckled his pads and departed. "It was then we realised there was something afoot."

Wednesday 30 August was the last day of sunshine. At Lord's, as the members in the Long Room clapped a Bill Edrich century, a man was removing the bust of WG Grace to safety.

By Friday, with children being evacuated from the cities, county cricket was confined to one venue: Hove, where Yorkshire agreed to play out the last day of Jim Parks' benefit match. In an eerie atmosphere they dismissed Sussex for 33, won by nine wickets and set off in a hired char-a-banc through blacked-out towns and villages. 'The farther we got from Brighton,' Len Hutton wrote, 'the deeper was our conviction that we would be lucky if we ever played cricket again.'

The summer was over: for Hutton, only 23 years old and already holding the world record Test score; for Hedley Verity, the great slow-left-armer, seven wickets for nine runs on that last day; for Sussex's Jack Holmes, no longer to captain England in that winter's Tests in India; the in-form Edrich of Middlesex; and Northamptonshire's gentle skipper Robert Nelson, who on Thursday evening had slipped away from Taunton ahead of his team. All went their separate ways.

On Sunday morning, 21 years after the Armistice that concluded 'the war to end all wars', Prime Minister Chamberlain announced that the country was once more at war with Germany.

In the First War little cricket had been played. Lord Hawke, President of MCC and Yorkshire, set the tone, striking from future consideration any Yorkshire cricketer who did not volunteer. At The Oval the Surrey Secretary, asked about the nets, replied: "They'll be up, but I don't expect our fellows will use them much. They'll be afraid of being jeered at by the men in the tram cars."

The Bradford League caused controversy by not disbanding, but by 1917 the mood had changed. 'The nation had by then re-adjusted its life to the state of war,' *Wisden* recorded, 'and no objection was felt to an attempt to stage some exhibition matches in the cause of charity.' In a one-day game at Lord's, 7,000 spectators saw an England Army XI, led by Captain PF Warner, defeat an Australian Army XI.

By 1939 Warner, now Sir Pelham, was 65 years old. When the MCC Secretary and Assistant Secretary volunteered for service, he became Deputy Assistant Secretary, determined they would continue to fly the flag at Lord's.

Some saw cricket as a distraction – Surrey's Errol Holmes said it felt 'rather like going on a picnic when your home was on fire' – but many recognised its potential to raise morale. As *The Cricketer* put it, 'It takes people out of themselves, and if we are a fortress let us have some fun inside the fortress so long as it does not conflict with military exigencies.'

There was no question of the counties staging more than occasional one- or two-day matches. The players were dispersed about the country, and several of the county grounds found themselves put to other uses. For the Whit Bank Holiday of 1940 Nottinghamshire played a two-day game against Derbyshire, both teams near full strength, but it was not the serious affair it had been twelve months earlier. When Derbyshire's Copson failed to arrive, one of the umpires batted in his place.

At Lord's a programme of charity matches emerged as the summer progressed. The first, in early May, was between the City of London Police and the London Fire Service. The police brought a band, the fire service displayed 48 of its engines, and in bright sunshine a crowd of 1,600 gathered.

Warner planned a great two-day match for the Whit holiday, Over-30s versus Under-30s, featuring 22 of England's best cricketers. Then Germany invaded Holland and Belgium, and the serving cricketers were summoned. The match was cancelled.

Hundreds of thousands of British troops escaped from the beaches of Dunkirk, Paris fell and Britain stood alone, awaiting attack.

The former England captain Gubby Allen was at the Air Component base in Folkestone, where the Dunkirk evacuation was co-ordinated. His brief diary reveals how his life then went on:

4 June	Air Component disbanded
7 June	Saw 'Gone with the Wind'
8 June	Eton Ramblers v XL Club at Lord's – took nine for 23
10 June	Italy declares war
14 June	Paris captured
15 June	Sandhurst v MCC, stay Percy Chapman at Worplesdon
17 June	France asks for Armistice

The leagues in the Midlands and North continued, though as in the First War the Bradford League stood out, the only one still to pay its professionals. With each team allowed four professionals, and with military duties causing much coming and going, more than 100 first-class cricketers appeared in Bradford during the war, 36 of them Test cricketers. The most popular was Learie Constantine, the electrifying West Indian all-rounder.

In the South two new clubs were formed in 1940: London Counties and the British Empire XI. The former emerged from a meeting in Andrew Sandham's cricket school in South London. Its primary purpose was 'to augment the depleted income' of professional cricketers; they played clubs around outer London, and Jack Hobbs was their president. The club's philosophy, never to let up against weaker opposition, led to some one-sided contests, but much money was raised, some of it passed on to local charities. Travel was difficult, some players came from night duties in the police or fire service, but – as Somerset's Frank Lee put it – 'it augmented our meagre salaries and prevented us from going rusty.'

The British Empire XI began in early May with a hastily arranged match, played for a barrel of beer, against Rosslyn Park. It was a great success, and by the end of the summer they had played 37 games. The brainchild of the 19-year-old Desmond Donnelly, it was a more idealistic venture than London Counties. They played as amateurs, aimed to entertain, raised money for the Red Cross and St John Ambulance, and hoped to create international fellowship by picking sides that drew from all the cricket-playing countries. Donnelly, fresh from public school on the Isle of Wight, was a tea-planter's son, and he listed himself as DL Donnelly (Assam). Other regulars included Bertie Clarke, the West Indian leg-spinner and medical student, Ray Smith, the Essex all-rounder and farmer, and Robert Nelson, the Northamptonshire captain, an officer in the Royal Marines. Pelham Warner became president, and four times that summer they played at Lord's.

Donnelly enlisted in the RAF the following year. After the war he took his idealism into politics: standing in the 1945 election for the Common Wealth party, then serving for 20 years from 1950 as an independently-minded Labour MP. But arguably the British Empire XI was his greatest achievement. In the six years of war it played 243 matches, raising £15,000 for charity.

Trevor Bailey, the leading schoolboy cricketer of the early war years, played occasionally, and he recalls "the sessions in the bar after matches, the girls who liked cricketers and the autograph hunters. I can't remember any of the games, just the fun." The person who made the biggest impression on Bailey was Bertie Clarke: "the first black West Indian whom I got to know really well. I was fascinated by his enthusiasm, ability and unfailing cheerfulness."

In August, while the Battle of Britain raged in the skies over south-east England, cricket continued at Lord's. Playing for Sir Pelham Warner's XI, Essex's Reg Taylor, freshly decorated with the Distinguished Flying Cross, was cheered all the way to the wicket, bowled for nought and cheered all the way back again. 'It is hard,' Warner wrote, 'to remember any cricketer receiving a greater reception.'

On Saturday 7 September, with the German blitzkrieg intensifying, air-raid sirens seemed to have ended the day's play at Lord's. Then an All-Clear brought the players back, and the last four wickets fell in seven balls. In the evening Warner stood at the top of the pavilion, watching the fires blazing in the London docks. Sirens, gunfire, shell-splinters, smoke: there would be no more cricket that summer.

Wisden called it 'a strange and dramatic end', though – with its offices suffering extensive damage – the almanack did not appear till December 1941, fifteen months later. Less than half the size of its predecessor, it nevertheless followed tradition and listed the fixtures for 1941.

The county cricket clubs encouraged members to pay their subscriptions and, with little expenditure, most of them reported small annual profits. Yet no maintenance work was undertaken, and the scars of war were becoming ever more visible. At Edgbaston several hundred seats were taken to local air raid shelters, the scorebox was damaged, and the 'Shed', where players took lunch, destroyed. At Old Trafford there was extensive damage to pavilion and stands, as well as a bomb crater in the middle of the ground.

The Oval spent the war first as a barrage balloon site, then an assault course; then a prisoner-of-war cage was erected. There was damage to the Tavern and to the terrace in front of the Long Room. The Surrey Secretary worked from his home in Wimbledon, organising teams to play around the county, but it was hard to keep track of the players. He would have wanted the young Bedser twins, but at the start of June 1940 they were on the Belgian border. "We got issued with a Colt revolver and six rounds of ammunition," Sir Alec recalls. "That was all we had when the Germans came." They ran across a cornfield as the planes approached, dived for cover and felt the spray of shots between them. "It was all over in seconds. You thought, 'Thank God for that' and just got on with it."

In the rush to the coast, they were stranded on a roadside when a van pulled up. The driver was a Surrey member from Wimbledon. "We can't leave you two behind," he called out.

Others were not lucky. Robert Nelson died that October in an air raid on his Marine unit in Kent. Ken Farnes, the England fast bowler, was killed in a plane crash in Oxfordshire; Gerry Chalk, the Kent captain, was shot down over France; and Maurice Turnbull, Glamorgan's Secretary and captain, was killed while trying to halt advancing tanks in Normandy.

In July 1943 Hedley Verity, a professional cricketer who had risen to the rank of Captain in the Green Howards, was shot while leading his men against German fire in Sicily. At Lord's, on the Saturday following the announcement of his death, his Yorkshire captain Brian Sellers stepped out to toss for the Army against the National Police. In his blazer pocket he found a note from 1939, from the scorer at Hove. '6-1-9-7,' it read. Verity's last bowling figures.

Others survived, some after gruelling years in prisoner-of-war camps, some after great heroism. Bill Edrich was a bomber pilot, flying low-level missions into Germany and winning the DFC. One Saturday his squadron, stationed in Norfolk, was due to play at Massingham Hall, but they were called away in the morning to attack German ships near the Dutch coast. Two of their planes were shot down and, before taking the field, replacement cricketers had to be found.

'It was a hard and exciting game,' he wrote. 'But every now and then one's mind would flicker off to the briefing, and to joking with a pal whose broken body was now washing in the long, cold tides, and one saw again his machine cartwheeling down, flaming from nose to tail. Then a ball would roll fast along the green English turf, and in the distance the village clock would strike and the mellow echoes would ring through the lazy air of that perfect summer afternoon.'

His younger brother Geoff spent three years as a prisoner of the Japanese. Even in the Far East his battalion had sports equipment, and in Singapore, on their occasional rest days, they staged cricket matches, complete with typed scorecards. Edrich scored centuries in three such games, then at Changi he played in the famous 'Tests', beating Ben Barnett's Australians two-one.

"We were prisoners no longer," he said. "It was a Test match between England and Australia. We forgot everything else."

They were moved to Thailand, and there was no more cricket: only long days of work, meagre rations, dysentery and cholera. "We were in tents on bamboo slats. I looked out one morning, and I saw this boy from the 5th Norfolks. He was a skeleton. I thought, 'How's he walking?' You had to have a bit of luck, and will power. A lot of the boys died of a broken heart. They couldn't see the end. There was one march, when we moved camp, maybe twenty miles, when some of us were ready to pack in. And if you dropped out, that was it – you got a bayonet through you from the guards. But 'Keep going,' my friend said. You had to have one or two decent chaps with you to get through."

As the war continued, more troops found themselves overseas. Cricket was played in the relative luxury of the Gezira club in Egypt, where a young Jim Laker learnt to bowl off-spin on the matting and Wally Hammond, passing through, hit two centuries. It was played in the Pentagular tournament in India, where by 1944 the Europeans included Denis Compton, Joe Hardstaff and the young Reg Simpson. The Bedsers played twice on a hastily created ground in Italy, where they persuaded their Surrey team-mate Arthur McIntyre to become a wicket-keeper. Also in Italy, in a prisoner-of-war camp, Bill Bowes and Freddie Brown played with improvised balls till the Red Cross sent supplies.

Spitfire pilots enjoying some cricket between bombing raids, 1941

Cricket was played in Afghanistan and Uganda, in Iraq and Sierra Leone, in the moat of a Polish castle, on the lava-strewn rock-like ground of Reykjavik and on the beach at Salerno. One officer in the Middle East described how his men carried everywhere a rolled-up cricket mat: 'On several occasions we've played an innings during an evening, then finished the match on the following day on the same mat – perhaps 200 miles away.' Wherever there were British servicemen, it seemed, there was some sort of cricket.

In the spring of 1941 Double British Summer Time was introduced, and Lord's often extended play till 7.30. For servicemen in uniform, entry was free: 'The gates of the temple,' declared the *Manchester Guardian*, 'are open nowadays to all who serve their country.' Civilians, meanwhile, could 'forget the war for sixpence'.

Father Time was dislodged by a barrage balloon cable, the pavilion bell was only rung for air-raid warnings, and the scorecard carried information about local shelters: 'Spectators are advised not to loiter in the streets.' The RAF based an Air Crew Reception Centre at the ground, forcing the two teams to change out of the same dressing room, and on Saturdays the members' lunch room became a makeshift replacement for the shattered local synagogue.

No bomb ever landed on the field of play at Lord's – unlike Folkestone where in 1942 a fielding soldier was killed – but in July 1944 a flying-bomb cut out overhead, causing the players to throw themselves on the ground. It landed in Regent's Park and, when two balls later Jack Robertson hit Bob Wyatt for six, the large crowd burst into song:

> *There'll always be an England, and England shall be free,*
> *If England means as much to you, as England means to me.*

Most fixtures were one-day contests, though no one considered limited overs. One team would bat, then declare; if the second team overtook them, their innings would continue till close of play. If both teams were out before close, a second innings would be started. Captains, on winning the toss, tended to field first.

In June 1941, in front of 15,000 spectators, the Army and RAF played a 6¼-hour match in which 98 eight-ball overs were bowled and 523 runs scored. Kent's Les Ames, in his first game of the summer, hit a century that included three sixes into the pavilion. It was, according to Raymond Robertson-Glasgow, 'not first-class cricket, but it was first-class fun.'

A new audience was gathering. At the Varsity match the spectators around the Tavern jeered the Cambridge team's brand new caps, considering the expense 'a failure to take the war seriously'. Then in July, when Frank Lee opened for London Counties, *The Times* reported that 'he was not considered by a section of the crowd to be sufficiently exuberant; apparently it is considered that only the "hit or miss" technique is suitable to one-day cricket.'

Such cricket continued through 1942 and 1943. Edgbaston shook off its wounds sufficiently to stage a cricket week in 1942. The Minister of Labour, Ernest Bevin, thought it would lift the spirits of local munitions workers, and in six frantic weeks the ground was restored from its desolation. For August Bank Holiday 1943, Lord's staged a two-day match between England and the Dominions. Admission was now a shilling for all, and more than 38,000 paid. They were treated to 940 runs and a thrilling England victory minutes from time.

Two new teams were created in 1944: a Royal Australian Air Force XI, featuring a young Keith Miller, and a West of England XI, formed by the Gloucester club cricketer George Elliott. The latter side consisted mainly of county cricketers stationed in the west though, in that summer of D-Day and the liberation of Paris, Elliott's task of raising teams was never ending: 'Either a bowler was posted overseas or a batsman to the North of Scotland. More phone calls, taxis, crowded trains, and one more player, hot and sometimes bad tempered, was propelled onto the field almost too tired and bewildered to hold up his bat.'

When after the war Leicestershire advertised for a new Secretary, one to sort out the loss of their home ground in Aylestone Road, Elliott's skills in crisis management won him the job.

The war in Europe ended in May 1945, and five three-day Victory Tests between England and Australia were staged. They were not official Tests – too many cricketers were still elsewhere – but the cricket was dynamic, and a total of 367,000 people watched the 15 days. It was the first first-class cricket in England since 1939.

Three of the Tests were played at Lord's, the others at the war-ravaged grounds of Bramall Lane and Old Trafford. For the latter game Lancashire employed German prisoners-of-war at three farthings an hour to repair and paint the ground.

The Fifth Test at Old Trafford took place the week after Victory in Japan. The sight of packed Manchester omnibuses labelled 'Cricket Ground' and gates closed at mid-day added to the general euphoria. When Bill Edrich hit the winning runs, levelling the series two-all, *The Times* declared it 'as good a game of cricket as the heart of man could throb for'.

Bill's brother Geoff, down to six stone, was now in Japan, and he woke one morning to find his guards all gone. The war was over at last, and he arrived back in England in November, gradually rebuilding his strength with pints of ale. In the years of county cricket that followed, he was a great team man, he never lacked courage – and he walked when he was out. He was haunted at times, but the lessons of his war never left him.

Many cricketers had had easy wars as physical training instructors, but others – like Trevor Bailey driving past lines of emaciated prisoners at Belsen – had seen sights that would never leave them. They had lost important cricket years but, as Alec Bedser says, "The war made men of us. It toughened us up. After that I was never nervous when I played cricket."

Home Gordon in *The Cricketer* noticed a greater acceptance of umpire's decisions: 'I have seen a few shocking verdicts, but none of the pre-war disgruntlement on returning to the pavilion.' He attributed this to 'the widespread inoculation of obedience and discipline.' "You had a better attitude," Bedser says. "You learnt just to get on with things. You didn't ask questions."

The war did raise questions, however, not least in social attitudes. In 1943 Learie Constantine booked into the Imperial Hotel, Russell Square, but on arrival he was called "a nigger" and told that his presence would be unacceptable to their American guests. He took the hotel to the High Court and won his case. Then in August 1945, the only black man in the side, he captained the Dominions against England at Lord's. It could not have happened in 1939.

Wisden questioned the sustainability of the amateur-professional divide. By the late 1930s, it argued, few of the county captains were genuine amateurs, and those few were 'survivors of an almost lost society'. The war accelerated the demise of that society, and by 1952 England had a professional captain, Len Hutton. 'If someone who had risen from the ranks was good enough to lead an army regiment in the field of battle,' he wrote, 'professional cricketers could be good enough to lead England in the field of sport.'

Questions were raised about the shape post-war cricket should take, with MCC setting up a special committee in late 1942. Rival entertainments, such as cinemas and ice-rinks, were growing in popularity, and there was a view that the county game would need an injection of cricket's wartime spirit. There were calls for a one-day knockout cup, for Sunday play, for 'natural pitches', for a two-day, one-innings county championship. The committee voted in favour of the one-day cup but, with the problem of the drawn game unresolved, the idea was shelved. The 1939 experiment with eight-ball overs was dropped; otherwise the first-class summer of 1946 differed in only minor respects from that of 1939.

There were few new players when the counties once more took the field. Somerset and Glamorgan had an average age of 38, Surrey and Yorkshire 36. 'Once the initial freshness had worn off,' Frank Lee wrote, 'we found it all far more strenuous than we anticipated.' 'I was always hungry,' Bill

Soldiers removing the prisoner-of-war cages at The Oval, 1945

Edrich said. 'I had to renew a lot of cricket gear so the coupon situation soon grew difficult.'

Lancashire appealed for £100,000, to create a modern Old Trafford with a capacity of 40,000, but donations fell well short of even half that sum. Surrey relaid its entire field with 80,000 turfs brought from Gravesend Marshes, employing shilling-an-hour volunteers from the local flats. There was little money even to heat the pavilion, but the county could not bring itself to accept a proposal to host greyhound racing.

The next summer, 1947, was a golden one, the hottest since 1911, and the crowds that flocked to the grounds, crowds who lived with bomb sites and ration books, were uplifted by the devil-may-care batting of Denis Compton and Bill Edrich.

Brian Castor was Secretary of Surrey. A prisoner of war under the Japanese, he wanted nothing more than to return to the England of the 1930s. Yet in his heart, when he surveyed the packed Oval that summer, he knew the reality: "It won't always be like this," he said.

English cricket would soon need to adapt. For now it was proud to have survived the war.

PARTNERS IN TIME

This piece, about the Essex opening pair Dickie Dodds and Sonny Avery, appeared in the Autumn 1998 issue of the Cricket Society Journal.

Hard now to imagine what it must have been like in the Spring of 1946. Six summers of cricket lost to the war, and at the end of it many of the counties left with only half a team. "We lost the nucleus of the Essex side," Sonny Avery told me when I met him last year. Farnes, Eastman and Ashton dead, O'Connor and Nichols too old to return. "We had to start from scratch."

Captain TC Dodds, fresh from war service in India and Burma, arrived for a trial as a leg-break bowler. "You're just the man we need to open the batting," he was told, and the day after his demob he received a telegram, telling him to report to Ilford the next day to play Sussex. His dreams had been of Middlesex and the grandeur of Lord's, not the flat farm lands and East End streets of Essex. "I didn't even know where Ilford was."

63 in his second innings, but the runs dried up in the next five games, and by the time he boarded the train home from Brighton, one and six in his two knocks there, he was wondering if he would be playing in the next game. "They didn't have a team sheet. It was all very casual. I didn't know what the drill was. You just tag along automatically. My recollection is, I asked Tom Pearce at Victoria, 'Am I wanted in the next match?' And he said, 'Oh, yes, you're very much wanted.'"

These were times of great change for Dickie Dodds. Back to civilian life after nearly seven years in the Army. Living every day with this travelling band of cricketers. And inwardly working through the implications of his spring-time conversion to Moral Re-Armament. Tom Wade, the wicket-keeper, had probed his secret out of him in the Ship Hotel, Brighton. "He noticed that I didn't drink," Dickie remembered. "He was the straightest person I ever met, and he got it out of me." Some of his team mates were not impressed. "You can't play cricket unless you drink beer," they said. And off they all went to Brentwood, where he was to team up for the first time with Sonny Avery, back after six weeks out with a finger injury. Sonny, too, had been in India during the war, working with Toc-H.

In the world of literature, George Orwell launched an allegorical assault on Stalin's Communism in 'Animal Farm', Evelyn Waugh wistfully recalled a pre-war country house world in 'Brideshead Revisited' and TS Eliot completed his 'Four Quartets', reflections on time with a chamber music structure.

In my beginning is my end. Now the light falls
Across the field, leaving the deep lane
Shuttered with branches, dark in the afternoon.

"Brentwood was a very pretty little ground," Sonny told me. "A little on the small side, but all round the boundary the trees were covered with blossom. I've got very good memories of Brentwood."

Memories of 1934. The first county game there for many years, and a nineteen-year-old Sonny at work on the pulleys of the old scoreboard. Hard at work as Kent score 623 for two in the day, Bill Ashdown a triple century. "One year he was the Essex coach at the beginning of the season," Sonny remembered. Essex, without headquarters, gathered for pre-season training at Colchester, and that was the extent of the coach's involvement. "Just one week. That's all."

Memories of 1946. "I had a very good week there. I think I got a hundred against Northampton and, following up, eighty or ninety against Gloucestershire." At the end of the week he was selected for the Test trial at Canterbury. England were having to start again, too. Seven years on, they were sifting through the county players to find the post-war Test batsmen. Brookes and Crapp, Ikin and Robertson. Now Avery of Essex to be put in the spotlight. He scored 102, 83* and 44 at Brentwood, and Dickie managed just 5, 6 and 13.

Would Dickie make it as a cricketer? And did his God want him to be one, anyway? It was a summer of inner struggle, and as they left Brentwood his frame of mind was very different from Sonny's. He didn't drink, he didn't smoke, he didn't swear. But would he admit to any envy of his opening partner? Like Geoff Boycott, out lbw first thing and sitting all day with a towel over his head as the next two batsmen piled on the runs: "Those are my runs they're scoring." "Geoff Boycott is dead honest," Dickie reflected. "That's what people like about him. I could be as jealous as hell. But you have to stop fear, jealousy, ambition blocking you."

Dickie was still in the team when they arrived at The Oval for the next match. A glorious summer day in late June, the crowds filling the ground. "Cricket was far bigger than it is now," Dickie reflected. "You didn't have television or anything." At Wimbledon, Tony Mottram lost in straight sets, the last Englishman knocked out on the first Saturday. At the Lyric Theatre, Angela Baddeley and Emlyn Williams were appearing in a matinee performance of Terence Rattigan's 'The Winslow Boy'. And all round London queues were forming outside shops, as people stockpiled flour before the arrival of bread rationing.

The Oval in 1946. There in the heart of London the ground had lived the pain of those past seven years like no other. Even before the 1939 season was out, it was requisitioned by the military, and Surrey's last match was re-routed to Old Trafford. After two days the match was abandoned, and the players arrived back at a Euston station full of evacuating children. Then the ground had prisoner-of-war cages built on it. It became a searchlight base, even an assault course. In the winter of 1945/6 the groundsman Bert Lock had 80,000 grass turves brought back from Gravesend Marshes, and among the Saturday crowd to watch Essex were some of the shilling-an-hour volunteers who helped to lay them.

Essex might have been a wandering side, happy to travel together around the country, but Surrey were one of the great counties, keen to restore the glory of their pre-war world. Sonny was a boy from East Beckton in the heart of the East End, and he took lunch with his fellow professionals. The rations were less severe in the committee room where Dickie sat with the two captains, Tom Pearce and Surrey's Nigel Bennett. Major Nigel Bennett. So desperate were Surrey to find an amateur to captain their 1946 side that they undertook a search for a Major Bennett who played occasionally for the seconds before the war. Only Nigel was not the right Major Bennett. He had called at The Oval to renew his membership and, in the confusion of that post-war reconstruction, he had come out with the county captaincy. A non-bowler, he was on the scorecard for this Essex game at number ten, and he contributed scores of 0 and 0.

By mid-afternoon Surrey were all out for 162, and it was time for Dodds and Avery to try once more. Sonny, selected for the Test trial, was in the best form of his life. Dickie, tagging along, was not sure if he had found his calling. Dickie asked Sonny to take first strike. "If he did this," Dickie remembered thinking, "at least I'd be in no danger of returning first ball to the pavilion." Such was the state of his confidence. Alongside him Sonny was giving a first outing to a bat an Essex member had just given him. "It had belonged to this chap's son," Dickie remembered. "I think perhaps he'd been killed in the war, and the father wanted Sonny to use it. That appealed to Sonny. He had that streak of sentiment."

> *Home is where one starts from. As we grow older*
> *The world becomes stranger, the pattern more complicated*
> *Of dead and living.*

Twenty years earlier, at The Oval, Hobbs and Sutcliffe brought back the Ashes for the first time since the Great War. And, while they were scoring their centuries on a damp and difficult wicket, an eleven-year-old Sonny was playing in the streets of East Beckton, up against the lamp post or with a wicket chalked on the wall. "I never went to watch, but I used to read about it, imagine the players. Hobbs, Sutcliffe, Hendren. I loved reading about the games." It was Patsy Hendren who scored 222 at Leyton in 1933 when Sonny, an eighteen-year-old office boy, sat at his window and looked down the wicket at every shot. "When I should be working, I was watching – and that's where I learned a lot, by watching. Patsy Hendren, he never lifted the ball from the ground."

The summer of 1926, and a seven-year-old Dickie was in the back garden of his father's Bedfordshire vicarage, a net rigged up as he faced up to Wilfred Gell, village fast bowler and vicarage gardener. It was another world from Sonny's, but "when you saw Sonny," Dickie explained, "you wouldn't say he was an East Ender. He was a universal type of man."

"I made my debut at The Oval," Sonny told me. "In 1935. I was with Tom Wade at Chelmsford. The idea was to help the groundsman in the morning and to practise in the afternoon. But how could we practise? Tom went off to be a wicket-keeper, and I was a batsman. This girl called me. 'Come along,' she said. 'You're playing at The Oval tomorrow.' I thought she was pulling my leg." He scored 28 not out in the first innings, batting at number nine. But somehow his memory was sharper when he recalled his second innings. "I didn't last very long. Alf Gover got me out for a duck, caught at the wicket. The following season I was promised I would play in every game. In actual fact I played none."

At The Oval in 1946 the scoreboard was soon moving. "I can remember in that game," Dickie said, "discovering how, if I dropped my left elbow when I played straight, the ball would go like a bullet to the mid-wicket boundary. I think it was Bedser, he was furious. If you drop your elbow at the point of impact, it'll turn the ball. I found myself observing it. 'Well, fancy that.' It kept happening."

Dickie liked to play his shots. He put bat to ball, and in time he became one of county cricket's most adventurous openers, driving and hooking from the very first ball. "What a beautiful stroke player he was," Sonny remembered. "A very fine batsman."

By contrast Sonny let the ball come onto the bat. "I wasn't a fast scorer. I was mostly an on-side player. Had I had coaching, I could have improved my off-side play." "He was very much a professional," Dickie remembered, "and a thinking player. He thought far more about technique. He was an artist, a craftsman. In another age he would have been a great leather-worker – or a sculptor, carving beautiful things on churches. He took pleasure in his craft. If you take pleasure in it, you give pleasure to other people."

There was plenty of pleasure for those who liked to sit in the sun and watch the runs flowing. 235 for no wicket at close of play. "I bet you wish you could bat on this every day," a tired Alf Gover quipped to them as they left the field. "Well, you all managed to get out on it," Dickie retorted. How Alf would enjoy telling that story in the years that followed! And till 1994 his audiences could turn to the page of record Essex partnerships and find Dodds and Avery, The Oval 1946, written there.

On Monday morning the partnership ended at 270, and Tom Pearce was waiting in the pavilion to award Dickie his county cap. At the start of the innings he had declined first strike, aware only of the potential humiliation of returning first ball. Now he was off to Foster's in Bruton Street to order himself an Essex blazer. And Sonny went on to his first double century.

A week later it was the Test trial at Canterbury, the famous lime tree inside the boundary, and Sonny made 79 out of a total of 175. Robertson 0, Compton 5, Watson 13. 'Avery played the bowling on its merits,' *The Times* reported, 'and made some of the other batting look rather poor stuff.' He must have been so close to an England cap. "Oh no," he told me. "I knew I wasn't good enough. I was out of my class really." In 1947 he was missing half the season with injuries. "It's such a long time ago to remember the detail," Sonny told me. "Here I am, 83 years, not out, stricken with illness."

"Running through his life," Dickie reflected, "there was a sort of sadness that repeated itself over and over." The Test trial that did not see him picked, the finger injuries, his mother's sudden death, then later the murder of his daughter in a terrible raid on the jewellers where she worked. "She only went in that week out of the goodness of her heart," Dickie told. "It made him wonder why, if there was a loving God, He allowed these things to happen."

Dickie scored his thousand runs in 1946, two thousand in 1947. There was a tour of the West Indies coming up, several England regulars were having the winter off, and Dickie had hoped that he would be selected. "But it was not what God wanted for me," he explained, and Lancashire's Winston Place was preferred. Like Sonny in 1946, Dickie would never come so close again. But they would both spread pleasure around Essex's nine grounds and, though Sonny was never converted to Moral Re-Armament, he joined Dickie from time to time: they went to the Assembly Shop at Ford's Dagenham plant, to the home of the East End revolutionary with the hand grenade on his mantelshelf, to the meetings they addressed inside East Ham Town Hall. "Look at the long mackintoshes," Dickie laughed as he inspected the old black-and-white photograph. "Of course, there was no central heating in those days."

Dickie Dodds and Sonny Avery

There is a time for the evening under starlight
A time for the evening under lamplight
(The evening with the photograph album).

Communism and Christianity. They were the two faiths available in that post-war search for a better world, and there in the East End Sonny's mother distributed Communist leaflets with her lodger. Then she visited 'The Forgotten Factor', Moral Re-Armament's play, and "I remember how radiant she was," Dickie said. Only weeks later she died during a routine operation, and Essex gave Dickie the match off to go to the funeral. "It's very unusual to get three days off to go to a fellow professional's mother's

47

funeral," Dickie reflected. "I don't suppose they'd ever do it these days." And, when Dickie's first wife died, Sonny gave Dickie's son a lift to the burial. "He was a great soul. He could take on my son at fifteen, who'd just lost his mother, for two or three hours on that journey, and at the end of it they were radiant. Because he had a soul that could communicate."

Dickie had given his later life to his religion while Sonny gave his to cricket coaching. First as captain of Gloucestershire Seconds, then at Monmouth School. "He loved seeing the craft, the skill, coming alive in a boy. I'm sure he was a wonderful coach. Sport was in him. He was impelled towards it. I really believe that almost everybody's got a destiny of one sort or another."

A month after my visit, Sonny lay dying in a hospital ward, and Dickie and he met for one last time. "He was so ill I hardly recognised him," Dickie recalled. "Gradually he focused me as I sat by his bed, and he became more animated as we talked of old days in the sun. We began to laugh, as Essex players always seem to do, at the fun we had."

"I could ring him up, and it was just the same as if we saw each other every day. That's what Marjorie and Kathleen found so odd. You go through so much together, the ups and downs. Sonny used to say, he'd go up the back lane when he got nought – so he didn't have to meet the people in the street."

What was it Robertson-Glasgow wrote in the 1947 Essex handbook? 'The keynote of Essex at its cricket is its intimacy, its sense of companionship. It is Community Cricket, a share-out of hopes and disappointments, of triumph and reverse. All of which makes for the best kind of entertainment. For entertainment is the healthy child of skill and laughter.'

"Then I told Sonny to remember that we all get a second innings. He looked at me and smiled. 'I only hope my next one is better than my last.'"

> *In my beginning is my end. Now the light falls*
> *Across the field, leaving the deep lane*
> *Shuttered with branches, dark in the afternoon.*

The blossoms around the Brentwood boundary, the newly laid turves at The Oval, the lime tree at Canterbury. "As I drove away from Monmouth, I saw a small tree in a garden centre there. The thought came to plant it in memory of Sonny." A weeping cotoneaster in the middle of a rose bed in Dickie's front lawn. "There are white flowers in the Spring, followed by year-long red berries." A constant reminder of a friend.

Dickie was 78 years old when I met him – not out and in good health.

> *In my end is my beginning.*

A BREAK IN THE CLOUDS

with Eric Hill

Middlesex v Somerset, Lord's, 10-13 May 1947

*After my first two books, in which I reconstructed county matches of
the 1950s and 1960s from players' memories, I started work on a third
volume, set in the 1940s. Unfortunately it was too long ago, there were too
few cricketers with the right degree of recall, and I abandoned the project.*

*But I did write up this one game with Somerset's Eric Hill, and it
appeared in a now-defunct magazine called Cricket Lore in 2000.*

"As a kid," Eric recalls, "I had assumed my first appearance at Lord's would
be opening the innings for England. With Len Hutton. That was how I
would first appear at Lord's."

Eric Hill, born July 1923. The son of a Taunton shopkeeper, who sells
cigarettes and sweets. He attends Taunton School, and in his spare time he
hangs around the County Ground with his friends, always on the look-out
for autographs. "We got it pretty well sussed out: which ones would sign,
which ones were better asked after they'd been in, how to avoid the blokes
who used to chase us away. I even got WR Hammond, and he would never
sign anything. I was on the ground early, on my own, and I saw him in the
pavilion, still in his civvies, smoking. So I went up to him. I said, 'Excuse
me, Mr Hammond' – they always reacted better if you asked them by name
– 'may I have your autograph?' And he signed. And his ash dropped into the
book. I kept the page very carefully after that."

Wally Hammond. The King. Top of the English batting averages each
year from 1935 to '39. Seven years on, in that first summer after the War,
he is 43 years old and struggling with a bad back, but the averages tell the
same story. First, WR Hammond, 84.90. Normal service has been resumed.

But where are the fast bowlers in 1946? Voce, Bowes and Gover, they
are all near forty when they take the new ball for England. They succeed
against the Indians, but in Australia there is humbling defeat at the hands
of Lindwall and Miller. The Spring of 1947 arrives with all England looking
for young fast bowlers.

The Spring of 1947. Winter has been the worst in living memory, fuel
supplies are low, and Harold Wilson, the Overseas Trade Secretary, arranges
timber imports from Russia. The government abandons its house-building
targets, and rationing is as severe as ever, even the sweets and tobacco in

Eric's father's shop. "But he always found things to buy and sell. I think he was the only one in Somerset selling those cartridge cigarette lighters, he had phony cough sweets that were off ration, and of course a lot of dodgy fags. Then he struck up a friendship with a lady who counted the coupons in the Food Office. She and her boyfriend ended up living above the shop."

Saturday the 10th of May 1947. The start of a new season. On the scorecard at Lord's there are two new names in the Somerset team: Tremlett and E Hill. Eric, a tall and correct batsman, playing as an amateur, and Maurice Tremlett, contracted as a professional, a bowler whose debut is eagerly anticipated. "I was surrounded by members, officials, newshounds," RJO Meyer, Somerset's new captain, writes. "And all they wanted to know was whether it was true that Maurice was the fastest English bowler since Larwood, whether he had already been booked for the West Indies winter tour, whether I had been told by the selectors not to over-bowl him."

Eric is 23 years old – "There was a sort of understanding that I would be given five matches, but I don't think anything was actually said. People didn't talk about these things so much in those days." Maurice is four days his senior and another Taunton youngster. "His mother was a customer in the shop. She loved the horses, but she'd only bet on the Classics and then only when the odds were over a hundred to one." And Maurice's father, 'EC', a post office clerk, "he was a proper stick-in-the-mud." Fred Endacott, another Taunton boy, remembers EC's monocle and his regular boast, 'M-My M-M-Maurice is going to p-play for England.'

There is an early morning shower, but the day is warm and the turnstiles are soon clicking with eager spectators. How did Neville Cardus describe them? *'Pale-faced, dowdy, worn crowds, existing on rations, the rocket bombs still in their ears.'* Can they imagine what runs they will see in the next four months, what carefree stroke-play? The county championship is here again. It is a time for fresh hope.

The Spring of 1947. The Chelsea Flower Show is open for the first time since 1939, building society mortgages are at record levels, and the Daily Herald Modern Homes Exhibition displays an interior designed to use the second-hand and improvised. *'Among the features of the bedroom are curtains made out of grey cotton dusters and decorated with unrationed woollen braid.'*

At Drury Lane the American musical 'Oklahoma' is the West End's most successful show.

> *Oh what a beautiful morning,*
> *Oh what a beautiful day,*
> *I've got a beautiful feeling,*
> *Everything's going my way.*

Eric Hill

Middlesex win the toss and bat. And Eric takes the field for the first time for Somerset. With Arthur Wellard and Wally Luckes, Horace Hazell and Bertie Buse, Frank Lee and Harold Gimblett. All the autographs that he collected so proudly as a boy.

"One year my father gave me this posh album for Christmas. I was waiting outside the pavilion, and Frank Lee came out and signed it. 'That's a nice book, isn't it?' he said. 'I'll keep it for you and get all the others to sign it.' So he kept it the whole bloomin' season and got all the counties to sign. What a disaster! They didn't count, you see. I hadn't collected them myself. None of them counted."

Now Eric is a man, and it is his turn to sign. "Tremmy and I were besieged by autograph-hunters."

Arthur – *'the ever youthful Wellard'* in the Times report – traps Brown lbw for 7, Maurice – *'a shade faster than medium pace and bringing the ball back sharply'* – bowls Robertson for 38, and Bertie Buse – *'so accurate'* – has Compton caught at deep square leg for 6. It is 99 for three, and Bill Edrich is joined by another debutant, Jim Eaglestone.

Eric's memory returns to the previous afternoon. A team talk in the old Taunton pavilion. The new skipper is RJO Meyer, founder and headmaster of Millfield School, and he is full of theories that have the old pros raising their eyebrows in disbelief. "RJO had a piece of paper, and we were instructed to go into our positions as if we were in the field. We were in the amateur dressing room; there was more room in there. 'Bertie's on at this end, making 'em boom a bit … Right. That's the end of Bertie, now it's Arthur.' And we all had to swap round for Arthur at the other end. 'Good. Now it's Tremmy.'"

RJO Meyer: an inspiring innovator or an eccentric amateur?

Eric completes the tale. "We got to Lord's, and Eaglestone came out to bat. Well, we didn't know him and, when he took guard, he was left-handed. And the pros, they all just stood there. 'Where do we go now, skip?' Dear old Jack Meyer. It took him ages to sort it out. It was total chaos."

Eaglestone is soon bowled by Bertie Buse, and the players return to normal for the right-handed George Mann. Or do they? According to The Times, *'Somerset challenged with a close and attacking field, which intimidated neither Edrich nor Mann.'* "RJO did that from time to time. There was one game at Taunton against Gloucestershire, when Charlie Barnett thrashed us everywhere. It must have been 150 for two when Jack Crapp came in, and RJO stuck us all round the bat, all the lot of us. Nobody on the boundary. No mid-on, no mid-off. Of course the ball went flying through a few times, and we all spread out again."

Attack is always full-scale with RJO, and he subjects Essex's Tom Pearce to the same treatment at Ilford. "Tom looked round at us all in the great slip cordon. 'I bet you buggers are nervous,' he said. And he hit us all over the place." The Times confirms the story: *'Nobly Pearce did his work, driving the ball away through gaps which could not be filled, so many fieldsmen being apparently needed in the slips and at short leg.'*

Here at Lord's runs soon come in the open spaces, and Middlesex reach 156 before Bertie Buse dismisses George Mann. Maurice Tremlett takes his second and third wickets, Bill Edrich in *'a faultless display'* completes his hundred before falling to *'a magnificent catch on the leg side by Luckes'*, and *'the rest of the batsmen persevered long enough to return the non-discreditable total of 231.'* Buse, 33 overs, six for 52.

The Somerset twelve a month later at Chesterfield : (back) M Coope, H Gimblett, WHH Andrews, MF Tremlett, H Hazell, HTF Buse, J Lawrence; (front) FS Lee, WT Luckes, RJO Meyer, GWL Courtenay, AW Wellard. The eleven at Lord's had E Hill and GES Woodhouse in place of Coope, Andrews and Courtenay

Bertie Buse. With his little moustache and his hop-and-jig run-up he is, according to Robertson-Glasgow, *'like a butler anxious not to awake echoes upon a stone floor'.* He is not fast or even fast-medium. "But he wobbled the ball so much," Eric recalls. "We played Yorkshire at Sheffield one year, and he had a field day. I was up at short leg, and he bowled Hutton, I remember." Wisden fills in the details: May 1951, Yorkshire all out 77, Buse six for 33. "That night we went to a stage show. We had our own box. A conjuror in orange tights with beautiful blondes and god knows what. We'd all had a few, celebrating Bertie's success – not at Bertie's expense, I should add – and all of a sudden he stood up unsteadily, looked at the audience, then at us, and he made this great announcement. I can still see him. 'Just like my fucking bowling.'"

Buse, six for 52. Tremlett, three for 47. "Frank Gillard from the radio interviewed Maurice after the first innings," Eric remembers. "A curiously starchy sort of interview. 'Is there anything especially you remember about your first bowl in county cricket?' he asked, and Maurice replied, 'Well, after my first over, I found I was unable to speak.' He never talked like that normally, but he was being interviewed with one of those big microphones. He wasn't a great talker. He was just a natural bowler. Ran in and bowled."

It is May 1947. At Hampden Park in Glasgow a Great Britain football team beats the Rest of Europe by six goals to one. 'The match of the century,' it is called, the British forward line is Matthews, Mannion, Lawton, Steele and Liddell, and there are 134,000 spectators in the ground. Racketeers outside are selling three shilling tickets for a pound.

Here at Lord's *the pale-faced, dowdy crowd'* watches the Somerset openers walk out to the middle. Harold Gimblett and Frank Lee. Harold's debut was in 1935, the most romantic of all cricket tales. How the farming boy from Bicknoller, rejected after a trial at the County Ground, was told to make up numbers the next day at Frome. How he missed his bus, hitched a lift in a lorry, then came out to bat at a dismal 107 for six. "I had to lend him my spare bat," Arthur Wellard likes to tell. "You should have seen the lump of wood he brought. Tape and string all round it." Harold scored the fastest century of the English summer, and for the rest of his life he carried the inner demons of such premature stardom. Till he died by his own hand in 1978.

"He was a funny light-and-darkness sort of bloke," Eric reflects. "He could be full of fun one minute. Then something would work on his mind. There'd be a lot of people saying, 'Bad luck, Harold, you ought to be in the England team,' and his wife Rita always felt she was a cut above us cricket crowd. And these two things reacted on Harold." Great debuts, it seems, make for great stories – but not always for happy endings.

Beside him is the quieter Frank Lee, the greengrocer's son from nearby in St John's Wood, whose debut here as an MCC Young Professional in 1923 was less distinguished. "The atmosphere was apparent as soon as I left the pavilion," he writes. "Absolute fright must have overcome me, for it appeared to me that I was watching my ghost walking to the middle, a feeling which rapidly dispersed when I heard the clatter of my falling wicket, when deep shame replaced it."

Gimblett and Lee. They are happier in the quiet backwaters of Somerset, but here they add 56 for the first wicket when *'suddenly Lee was caught at short leg and just before the close of play Buse was leg before wicket.'* 59 for two, and The Times reckons the day's play to have been *'interesting from the first ball to the last'.*

Maurice has three wickets to show for his debut at Lord's, but Eric must wait till Monday for his chance. "In actual fact, I made my first appearance at Lord's on February the 16th, 1942. With a slight sleet falling and snow on the ground. Signing on for the RAF. The Swearing Officer kept saying 'King

George the Sixth, his Hairs and Successors,' and none of us could stop giggling. The most solemn moment of our lives. We did the signing in the Long Room."

The boy Eric has dreamt of stepping out with Hutton, but he is a man now and those years of War have given his cricket a different perspective.

On Monday morning it is 68 for five when his turn arrives, and Bill Edrich waits to test him out. Bill Edrich, with his Distinguished Flying Cross for low-level, daytime bombing raids in a Blenheim. Empty of ammunition, he has seen a Messerschmitt close down on him and aim for the kill, only to discover that the German too has no firepower.

Eric has a Distinguished Flying Cross, too, and he recalls the headline in the Bristol Evening World: 'MOSQUITO ACE IN SOMERSET ELEVEN'.

Eric has navigated 53 Mosquito reconnaissance missions, none more dramatic than the sortie beyond the Lofoten Islands off Northern Norway in July 1944. The Norwegian resistance has lost track of the German battleship Tirpitz, sister ship of the Bismarck, and it is threatening vital convoys that are heading for the Russians. North Norway is at the extremity of the Mosquito's range, the fuel tanks only just adequate. Three days earlier, they had set out in search but had found no sign of the Tirpitz; the following day another crew hit bad weather and were killed as they crashed into Scottish mountains. Eric and his pilot, Frank Dodd, do not need to be told that their mission is a perilous one.

They refuel on Shetland, and after a long flight they locate the Tirpitz, descending for close-up photographs. Then the German fire begins. "Frank did a quick turn, and the perspex bubble top of the cabin blew off, with all the maps, the navigation bags, the telegraph equipment." Open to the wind and not far from the Arctic Circle, they return for more pictures, then away they go. Cloud everywhere. They are desperate for navigational help – but their answering code is lost in the sea. "I sent them our names, ranks, service numbers, but they just used the code challenge."

For over four hours they fly above the clouds. Not wanting to go down and use up precious fuel. Not knowing if they are still on track. "Frank wasn't much of a talker, and I suppose I wasn't either. We were both trying to disguise our fear. I remember it being very tense."

A brief break in the clouds reveals an unusually still sea, and that is good news for their fuel consumption. "We were both thinking what we would have to do if we ditched, but neither of us said a word about it. The hardest thing was trying to think of something to do to divert our attention."

It is over nine hours since they left Shetland, and for four hours they have flown with no top on the plane, the fuel gauge slowly approaching empty. Gradually the sky is growing dark.

Mosquito

"We decided to go on until it was absolutely critical or until we could see something. Then I saw this gap in the cloud, and I said, 'Frank, there's land.' We went straight down onto an airfield near Wick."

A lucky escape. Batting at Lord's holds no such dangers, and Eric prepares for his first delivery. "I was probably a good deal more blasé than I ought to have been," he reflects.

At Portsmouth Harbour a crowd of half a million gathers to welcome home the King and Queen after their 14-week tour of South Africa. "Come what may," King George declares, "nothing will ever shake my belief that this old country is, at heart, as young and vigorous as she has ever been."

"Clench your teeth when you first go in," is Frank Lee's advice for nervous debutants. But Eric needs more than clenched teeth to cope with what comes next. "Bill Edrich was bowling. He was a round-arm slinger. About three times as fast as anybody I'd ever faced before. And he was swinging it. I missed the first ball completely." The ball misses the stumps, and his charmed life continues.

> Oh what a beautiful morning,
> Oh what a beautiful day.

Back in the 1930s Eric's father, a Somerset member, sent him to the ground for coaching. And Arthur Wellard, perhaps spotting some talent in the lad, stayed late each evening to give him extra help. Arthur Wellard, the publican's son from South London. With his smart suits and his "Watcher, cock" worldliness, he cuts an impressive figure in this gentle rural community. "He used to lodge across the road from the ground," Eric recalls. "In St Augustine

Street, or Disgustin' Street as we called it. At first I didn't like the idea of Arthur – he used to drink and smoke so much – but then I realised all the others did as well. Well, all except Wally Luckes. 'I reckon I've bought that bugger twenty thousand orange juices,' Bill Andrews used to say."

Arthur Wellard is waiting to bat. On the balcony of the dressing room he watches closely these first efforts of his young protégé.

> *I've got a beautiful feeling,*
> *Everything's going my way.*

Bill Edrich sends down his second delivery, and this time there is no luck. Hill, bowled Edrich, 0. "As I walked off, I heard Jim Sims saying, 'Well bowled, William.'" The words echo down the years, and the scoreboard reads 68 for six.

"Dear Arthur," Eric sighs. "I fancy my failure to become a better cricketer was one of his real disappointments."

Johnny Lawrence top-scores with 30, Maurice Tremlett at number ten adds five, and Middlesex are batting again, 97 runs ahead. According to The Times, *'the lead seemed more than Somerset could battle against.'*

Middlesex versus Somerset. The London County, runners-up each championship season since 1936, and the West Countrymen, startling themselves with their fourth place last summer. Not since 1924 has a Somerset side travelled here and won, though such history is of little concern after a world war. "There was the odd time when Arthur would say, 'Oh blimey, we're going to play at so-and-so, I never get any wickets there.' But that was all."

Next year at Lord's Compton and Edrich will put on 424 in four hours against them, and that will become one of Arthur's favourite stories. "We got rid of Robertson, we got rid of Brown, and then these two buggers came together and they must have made about a thousand. I'd been bowling all bloody day, and the skipper says, 'Go on, Arthur, have one more go.' 'One more go?' I said. 'I haven't got any legs left.' 'One more go,' says the skip. 'Go on, Arthur, just one more go.' Well, I had one more go and then I dropped dead."

Wellard, 39 overs, nought for 158.

"When we came off," Eric remembers, "people said, 'Cor, that must have been tiring.' But it wasn't tiring at all. We were just thanking people for throwing back the ball."

Ever after, when Robertson and Brown open the Middlesex innings, Horace Hazell will counsel the new-ball bowlers. 'Don't get those other buggers in too early.'

Old and young: Arthur Wellard and Maurice Tremlett

Today Arthur bowls Brown for 0 and has Edrich caught for 3, *'a truly magnificent catch by Lawrence at fine short-leg.'* It is 18 for two, with Robertson and Compton to be removed next.

"I thought Jack Robertson was perfect," Eric says. "He was the sort of batsman I'd have liked to have been. He scored 200 against us at Taunton one year, and we'd stopped for a drink after the game. Some bloke came up. 'Cor, that Robertson, I've never been so bored in my life.' It was the most perfect batting I'd ever seen. I only saw him beaten twice."

Jack Robertson. The only batsman to score 2,000 runs in each of the first seven summers after the War. His Test average is over 46, but he plays just eleven times for England – and nine of those are on tours when leading players are missing. "When you think of some of the people who've opened for England in recent …" Eric lets the sentence die away.

1947 will be the summer of Compton and Edrich, 30 centuries and over seven thousand runs between them. But who ever mentions the third man in that summer's list of run-scorers? Their team-mate Jack Robertson, with 12 centuries of his own. This afternoon, according to EW Swanton, *'Robertson batted beautifully for 30, then made a horrible-looking hook with his head to the skies.'* Another wicket for Bertie Buse's wobbling medium-pace, and Middlesex are 63 for three. A lead of 160, and Denis Compton – *'no longer the slim youth one knew before the war'* – takes his score effortlessly into the twenties.

The summer of 1947. At Epsom a new camera records the finish of horse races. In Blackpool Stanley Matthews signs a transfer from Stoke City for £11,500. And on Lake Coniston Sir Malcolm Campbell prepares to raise his water speed record, his motor boat revolutionised by a jet engine.

Middlesex are comfortable at 63 for three – but not for long. RJO turns to Maurice Tremlett, and *'an immediate change came over the game.' 'Compton,'* The Times tells, *'was out to a beautiful ball, which came off the pitch very much faster than he expected. … For the rest there was a clatter of timber when one after another had taken guard to as good bowling as one could hope to see this summer.'* Tremlett, five for eight in five overs. Middlesex, all out for 78.

"The story went round that he hit Leslie Compton on the thigh, and Leslie had to go to the doctor to get blood moving through the vein. We thought this was highly dramatic. Even the old 'uns did. It suggested that Maurice was a tremendously fast bowler. He was quick, but he wasn't that quick." He searches the modern Somerset players for a comparison. "About Neil Mallender's pace, I should think."

"A wonderful bit of bowling," EW Swanton enthuses to Jack Meyer at close of play. "Certain to be England's first choice fast bowler for the West Indies tour."

But Jack cautions against such excess. "He's going to be a batsman, not a bowler. Please don't overdo the superlatives."

"OK," Jim Swanton agrees. "I'll keep it all toned down." And he goes off to write his column: *'Tremlett's possibilities stand out for all to see … If he can discriminate between all the advice he will receive and choose the wisest he may become a truly fine bowler.'*

'YOUNG BOWLER'S AMAZING SPELL AT LORD'S', the headline writer adds, and Maurice is condemned to the same blaze of publicity that greeted Harold Gimblett twelve years before.

Jack Meyer recalls the rest of that summer. "The new ball would only be four overs old, and the shouting would start. 'Put Tremlett on! Put Tremlett on! Tremlett! Tremlett!' Then when I invited Maurice to have a go, he would refuse point blank. He took a few wickets here and there, but he suffered agonies in the process."

When he goes to the West Indies, they change his action, and his ten tour wickets cost him 70 runs each. "Gubby Allen tried to get him swinging the ball," Eric says. "He was very different when he came back. Said he'd got a lot to learn about bowling."

By 1950 he will be just an occasional bowler, enduring the boos and catcalls as he runs up and sprays the ball everywhere. But, as Jack Meyer has forecast, he will be a front-line batsman. "I think he realised," Eric reflects, "that batting was a damn sight easier work than bowling." In 1956 he will become Somerset's first professional captain, and their third place in 1958 still remains the highest position in the county's history.

'With the reasonable proposition of making 176 runs to win', Somerset set off resolutely. Harold Gimblett is bowled by a ball that cuts down the slope, Johnny Lawrence – *'the stocky little Yorkshireman'* – survives till the total is 47, and Frank Lee – *'as of old, playing the yeoman's part'* – makes a *'gallant'* 38 before touching a rising ball into the slips. Arthur Wellard is sent in for some late fireworks, but *'in the gathering gloom'* both he and George Woodhouse are bowled by Bill Edrich's *'final burst of energy'*. It is 101 for five, 75 to win, and all to play for in the morning.

The teams retire to the bar, and Eric and Maurice settle themselves next to Arthur.

"Then a couple of the opposition would come and talk to him, and he'd have quite an audience. We used to get him telling yarns. He was a wonderful yarn-teller. I don't think he realised just how good he was. ''Ere,' he'd say. 'I've told you this before, I'm sure I have.' But we'd always find somebody who hadn't heard it and make him go on."

Their favourite is the tiger shoot from his tour of India with Lord Tennyson. "The Maharajah of Baroda," Arthur tells. "Nice kiddy. Had a place upcountry. About the size of Buckin'am Palace. Well, he had this goat tied up in his hunting hide, ready – see – for the tiger." The story is told, every word the same as the last time, though perhaps a gesture is different when night falls and the tiger appears, perhaps the gun blazes with a slightly sharper bang, or there is an extra inflection as he describes the petrified look on Alf Gover's face as he peers over the edge. "Blimey, me Lord, you've shot the bleeding goat."

"I learnt a lot listening to Arthur."

Life is a yarn, and maybe in time this match will make a good yarn, too.

While Arthur downs his pint, Johnny Lawrence sits with an orange juice. "A hell of a nice bloke," Eric says, "but he was strictly tee-total. On religious grounds. In fact, when he had his benefit, he refused to play the Sunday matches. And they were the main source of income." In the end it turns out to be a shrewd move. There is a leader in the Church Times, and the resulting donations provide a healthy sum.

Bertie Buse is another with a chequered benefit. Choosing Lancashire's visit to his home town of Bath in 1953, he is horrified to discover the turves on the newly-laid square have not knitted together. Lancashire's Roy Tattersall takes 13 cheap wickets, and the match is all over by six o'clock on the first day. "But he did all right in the end. In those days you had to pay the expenses of the away match, and the county let him off. And of course lots of people said 'Poor old Bertie' and made extra donations."

"No, the one who did worst was Nutty Hazell. The year he had his benefit the Lord's Day Observance Society started going to court to stop events. He had one very big match planned at Glastonbury – a lot of big names, a funfair and all sorts – and it got cancelled."

It is May 1947. The post-war divorce rate reaches a new peak, and the Bishop of St Albans calls for a ban on re-marriage when the former partner is still alive. Meanwhile the government launches a campaign to persuade more housewives to return to industry.

On Tuesday morning they return to complete the match. With Double British Summer Time, their 11.30 start is 9.30 by the sun, and *'in a misty humid atmosphere Meyer, after one lofty drive, lost his off-stump in attempting to repeat the stroke.'* Bertie Buse follows, and at 113 for seven there are still 63 runs to win. And all that is left is Eric and the keeper Wally Luckes, followed by Maurice and their tubby number eleven, Horace Hazell. In the words of The Times, *'This is when the match began all over again.'*

The new ball is taken, and this time Eric faces Lawrie Gray. "I was hopeless," he recalls. "I kept playing and missing, over after over, and Wally at the other end kept making these 'keep your elbow up' motions. Well, my bat was straight enough. It just wasn't in the right place." *'Hill faced a nightmare of a situation,'* EW Swanton reports, *'with 0 in the first innings and Middlesex round his bat like vultures.'* "Eventually I got a run, I don't remember how." *'Luckes is a stubborn batsman,'* The Times reports. *'He refused to be intimidated by the velocity of Gray and Edrich, and he found a sympathetic partner in E. Hill.'*

Now at the other end Eric faces Bill Edrich. "I straight drove him, and the ball hit one of the block-holes and bounced up over his hand. We ran three, and I began to feel it wasn't impossible to score runs."

In seventy minutes he and Wally add 38 of them, *'mostly painful singles'*. The target is down to 25 to win before the game turns once more. Wally is out for 26, caught at the wicket, and Eric follows immediately, *'out to a grand catch in the slips by Edrich'*. Seventeen runs to add to his first innings duck. He will play just four more times this summer, his place in the side not established till he returns here next summer and makes his first fifty.

'Hill was a tall, upright batsman,' the history books record, 'of undisputed correctness and style, but little luck.'

After four summers in the team, he becomes a journalist and for 45 years he watches with a keen eye his beloved Somerset. Watches the end of cricket at Glastonbury and Weston, the arrival of the one-day game and coloured clothing, a county championship played in empty grounds with the England players contracted to rest the last vital matches. "In my worst moments," he says, "I wish county cricket would finish."

But Taunton has had its share of great cricketers. The powerful Harold Gimblett and the wristy Peter Wight. The old roustabout Bill Alley and the ever-combative Brian Close. Botham and Richards at their best, and now the promise of Trescothick. "Let's not get down-hearted," he says, and his mind returns to Lord's in 1947.

Nine wickets down, and 25 runs still to win. Only Maurice Tremlett and Horace 'Nutty' Hazell stand between Middlesex and another victory over Somerset.

"We went back to Taunton to play Warwickshire in the next match," Eric remembers. "I made a few runs, then Charlie Grove got a hat-trick and I was stuck at the non-striker's end. And Horace came in and took guard. Claud Woolley was umpiring. 'What do you want, Horace?' he asked, and Horace looked up. 'Oh, I don't know, Claud, what have you got?'

Wisden completes the story: Hazell, bowled Grove, 0. Hill, not out, 32. "Peter Cranmer was the Warwickshire captain, and I remember, at the end of the game, as we all went out of the ground, he said, 'Well, I reckon that was a bloody fine game of cricket.'"

A fine game – but not as fine as this one at Lord's. In the words of The Times, *'it was as noble a game of cricket as man could ever hope to play in or any spectator be privileged to watch.'*

"Horace didn't have much of a record as a batsman, but he could bat. It's just that he didn't usually bother. 'I'm a bowler,' he'd say. He hit Hedley Verity for 28 in an over at Bath once, you know."

The ball misses Horace's leg stump *'by a whisker'*, then he gives a low chance to second slip. Maurice is lucky not to get an edge when he makes *'one terrific swish'*, and *'at half past one, after many alarms, the batsmen were still there.'* According to Jack Meyer, "they came in to lunch with not a hair out of place." 16 to win – *'and everyone had 40 minutes for nervous speculation.'*

"We were all smoking like chimneys," Eric recalls. "And I was twittering like an old fool."

The temperature in London is up to 82 degrees, the warmest May day for two years. "It's a nice day today," the weather man in the Air Ministry says, "but summer … By tonight, for the time being, you'll have had it."

Horace Hazell begins the afternoon with *'a splendid four through the covers'*, but Maurice Tremlett soon betters him when, *'with the coolest air, he struck Young for a superb six among the members' friends at long-off.'*

"By this stage," Eric recalls, "I was treating it like an ordinary cricket match, not thinking about the importance of it. 'It's here to be won,' that's all."

How else should one ever think of a cricket match? When you've flown four hours not knowing if your fuel will get you back to land, there is no other way to play the game. "I think we all felt, 'Thank God we got away with the War, and we're able to do this.'"

Four to win. Four runs for Somerset to record their first victory at Lord's since 1924, when Eric and Maurice were barely toddlers. Maurice drives another three, and the scores are level.

One to win. Horace survives the rest of the over and watches Maurice face Jack Young once more. 'M-my M-Maurice will p-play for England,' his monocled father has been boasting, and all Lord's is now saying it, too. Yesterday afternoon his five-wicket spell turned the match. Now he can finish the job with the bat. Not since the arrival of Harold Gimblett at Frome has English cricket known a more dramatic debut. His teammates watch on the balcony, their cigarettes all alight, and he drives the second ball of the over *'firmly past mid-on'*. One to win but, with the Middlesex players making for the pavilion, *'the batsmen gaily ran three just to ensure the scorers had not made any mistake.'* That's what Maurice has learned to do playing for Rowbarton Brewery down in Taunton, and why should he play any differently here at Lord's? "I was so used to the country stuff," he will tell John Arlott years later, "that I made poor Horace run three – just to make sure, as you do in village matches." *'What fun it all was.'*

176 to win. Even in Wisden the score is recorded as 178 for nine.

For EW Swanton, it is *'a piece of cricket to live long in the memories of those lucky enough to see it.'* For John Arlott, Maurice's performance is *'an experience to warm a cricketer's lifetime.'* The Middlesex players line up in front of the pavilion, and they clap in the two batsmen.

The sun is out. For the rest of this glorious summer the clapping will be for Middlesex, as their batsmen pile up totals at speeds now unimaginable: 310 in one afternoon session at Leicester. In the words of Neville Cardus, *'the strain of long years of anxiety and affliction passed from all our hearts and shoulders at the sight of Compton in full flow.'*

England is an old country 'as young and vigorous as she has ever been,' King George declares, but the youth and vigour of Maurice Tremlett's bowling is but a brief shaft of sunshine. He will play another 388 first-class matches, including three for England, but there will be just three more occasions when he will take eight wickets in a match. Great debuts make for great stories – but not always for great careers.

In the Somerset dressing room, the singing starts. "Whenever we won, Nutty Hazell used to lead us in a rendition of 'The Three Black Crows'."

> *I'll go away and get my gun*
> *An' shoot those buggers one by one.*
> *The more I sows, the more I grows*
> *The more it's eaten by those bloody crows.*

"It was a ridiculous thing, but we all used to bawl it out."

Jack Meyer's cheerful Somerset side will follow this triumph at Lord's with nine successive defeats. Not till the Bath Festival at the end of June will the crows be back on their tree.

"We all went home on the train," Eric remembers. One by one they disembark: Bertie Buse in Bath, Horace Hazell in Bristol, Jack Meyer for Street, Wally Luckes in Bridgwater. More than forty years have passed, and only Eric remains from that journey. He sits at home, only a few fields from where Harold Gimblett set out for Frome in 1935, and his mind focuses once more on that 1947 railway journey.

"It was just Arthur, Maurice and me by the time we got to Taunton. We were met at the station, and we all repaired to the Crown and Sceptre."

The regulars gather round to hear the story of the day. Let's imagine how Arthur might have told them. "And this lad 'ere, 'e 'it this ball right into where the members were sitting. Cool as a cucumber, 'e was."

Tomorrow they will rise early for the visit of Warwickshire. No second triumph for Maurice – 0 for 33 in seven overs and a pair – and Eric's hopes of glory, as he carefully advances to 32, are snuffed out by a hat-trick at the other end. Only Arthur receives any praise from Wisden, his 33 overs on the first day showing *'fine stamina'*. This evening he downs his last pint and heads home to Disgustin' Street. "It was 254 paces from the public bar to his front door."

'SOMERSET WIN BY ONE WICKET,' will read the headline in tomorrow's Daily Telegraph. 'LONG SUSPENSE AT LORD'S.'

> *Oh what a beautiful day.*

The clouds clear, and once more we can see our county cricket in all its glory. *'Test matches may come and go,'* the Times correspondent writes, *'but a county match with a finish so tense and yet so friendly can in enjoyment never be excelled.'*

BERNIE CONSTABLE OF SURREY

This piece, written anew for this book, has been developed from an article I wrote in 1997 for a now-defunct magazine Cricket Lore.

Has any county had a bowling attack to rival Surrey's in the 1950s?

There was Alec Bedser, the supreme medium-quick bowler with his deadly leg-cutter; Jim Laker, as good an off-spinner as the game has seen; slow-left-armer Tony Lock, who twice in the decade took 200 wickets in a season; and paceman Peter Loader, taker of a Test match hat-trick. Even Len Hutton, talking to Bob Appleyard on the boat to Australia in 1954, had reluctantly to concede that the great Yorkshire side of the 1930s were not their equal. Surrey had four top-class bowlers and, in those years of uncovered and often treacherous pitches, each posed a different challenge.

But what of the men whose job it was to score the runs? There was Peter May, the outstanding English batsman of the decade, and in the later years of their success the emerging talents of Ken Barrington and Micky Stewart.

Who else was in that side? The ever-ebullient Stuart Surridge, captain for the first five years; Arthur McIntyre, the dependable keeper; Alec's brother Eric, an off-spinning all-rounder, and three batsmen whose names have been largely forgotten: Tom Clark, David Fletcher and Bernie Constable.

Even at the height of their success Bernie Constable knew that it would be like this. "In years to come," he would complain in his high-pitched, chirpy voice, "when they recall this Surrey side, they'll talk about the bowlers and they'll talk about Peter May. But there won't be one mention of we poor batsmen who've had to score our runs on these bloody pitches."

How right he was! Yet, with Peter May often away on Test match duty, it was Bernie – the unsung, long-forgotten Bernie Constable – who scored most runs for Surrey in their golden decade, the only one of the batsmen to top 10,000 championship runs in the 1950s.

In April 1997 I met him at the Marquess of Granby pub, near the Sandown Park racecourse. He and his wife had moved to Sawtry in Cambridgeshire, to be near their daughter, and he was back in Surrey for a few days.

"Wednesday, twelve o'clock," I said to him on the telephone. "I'll be carrying a couple of Wisdens."

"And I'll be a doddery old git," he replied with a high-pitched laugh.

He was doddery, too. 'He moved so lightly as to suggest a dancer,' one history of Surrey said of his running between the wickets and his fielding in the covers, but there was no sign of that now. At the age of 76 he had put on weight, and he was adjusting to life with a newly replaced hip.

Bernie Constable

We found a table, perhaps too close to the juke box, but it did not matter. His voice was strong enough to be heard above Oasis and the Spice Girls, strong enough to turn heads on the next table when he talked of Laker and Lock, Bedser and Barrington and May. I doubt if their heads would have turned if he had mentioned Constable.

"My debut match was against the West Indies of all people. Constantine and Martindale – and George Headley, the Black Bradman as they called him."

The Oval, 26 July 1939. The eighteen-year-old Bernie, a leg-break-and-googly bowler, was in his second summer on the Surrey staff. The amateur captains in those two years, Errol Holmes and Monty Garland-Wells, both believed in cricket being fun. "ERT Holmes loved to see people bowling leg-spinners. Whether they got hit all over the place, it didn't make any difference."

"Did you get hit all over the place?"

"No, I got a couple of wickets. I had George Headley dropped when he had about 20. A little dolly went up at mid-on to a chap called Eddie Watts." 'Headley,' *The Times* reported, 'gave a simple catch to mid-on off Constable, a slow leg-break bowler who needs to be more accurate in his command of length.'

At lunch the teams were presented to King George VI. Then Headley batted on, 'the innings of a man who was working out a thesis of his own and who was not to be troubled by mere bowlers.' Bernie settled for Vic Stollmeyer and Manny Martindale as his first victims in first-class cricket.

It was the end of August before he played again for Surrey: against Lancashire at The Oval – or it would have been at The Oval if the ground had not been requisitioned by the military. The players travelled to Old Trafford, arriving at four in the morning, with several of them sleeping in the pavilion. Bernie took nought for 22 in three eight-ball overs in the first innings, and Lancashire were set to score 352 to win on the final day.

It was the young Bernie's chance, the match set up for his leg-breaks, but it was not to be. German troops had gathered at the border with Poland, and the game was abandoned. "Kids were being evacuated on the station when we got back to London."

Bernie became a despatch messenger in the RAF, finishing up in Holland. "The four-and-a-half years I was in the RAF, I hardly played any cricket at all."

"Did it sit in your mind during those years that you'd just got into the Surrey side?"

"It certainly did. More so when I came out and I found I'd missed seven years of my cricketing life. Bowling these things," he said, his wrist turning across the top of our drinks, "you have to bowl them every day. And coming out, I'd lost it. I couldn't bowl them. I had to be a batsman."

In 1946 he had a last hurrah with the ball, taking five for 131 for the RAF against Worcestershire, but it was his century at The Oval for the Combined Services against Surrey that provided the first real glimpse of his future.

Clearly not valuing the game in the great scheme of cricket, he referred to it as a "so-called hundred", though he hit it, going in at number eight, off a Surrey attack that included Alf Gover, Jim Laker and Eddie Watts.

His "first real hundred" came three years later in August 1949 against Middlesex. Ten years on from his debut, he was now 28, his bowling rarely used and his batting yielding only an occasional fifty – but Surrey, in those makeshift post-war summers, persisted with him, and he repaid their confidence in 1950 when he scored 1,389 runs and became a regular member of the Surrey side, a side that was challenging for its first title since 1914. Most importantly he was awarded his county cap.

"You came onto the same rate of pay as everybody else, but it wasn't a lot in those days. We didn't play for money. We played for glory, there's no doubt about that. The only time you started thinking about money was when you married and the children started coming along."

The pub's fruit machine spilled out its winnings, and Bernie stopped to laugh.

31 August 1950. It was eleven years exactly since that last day's play before the War, and for the championship decider at The Oval only Laurie Fishlock and Bernie had survived from the ill-fated trip to Old Trafford. Showers scudded across the sky while they compiled a century partnership, a stand that set up victory over Leicestershire and a share with Lancashire of the title. 'Surrey were a patchy batting side,' *The Times* recorded in its end-of-season review, adding that 'Constable several times popped up to supply what was required.'

The spectators swarmed onto the outfield at the match's conclusion, but none of them could guess how, in the years that followed, such triumph would come to seem routine.

"We had a great team spirit. Of course, we had a good side, but we all blended well. We all matured at the same time."

Arthur McIntyre, Stuart Surridge, the Bedser twins and Bernie, they came up together through the Young Players of Surrey. "I scored 150 not out against Ham and Petersham as a fifteen-year old," he said proudly. "The twins were playing, and Stuart Surridge was captain. That must have been 1936."

Alec and Eric Bedser were working in an office, Arthur McIntyre was on the Oval ground staff, and the young Bernie worked behind the bar and did odd jobs at Kingston Indoor Cricket School, next to Bentalls department store.

"Billy Graburn got me the job." – WT Graburn, one game for Surrey in 1894, then for many years the county's cricket instructor – "He was well seventy-odd, an old man, but he got me this job. I'd only just left school, and I said, 'Well, it's a job, I suppose.' I used to sweep out the nets and make the tea. After a while they got me a game for the Young Players of Surrey, and I suppose that's how it all started."

Little did they realise, but the backbone of county cricket's greatest side was forming. "Most of us came from ordinary families, you know. I rang Alec up the other day, when he got his knighthood, and I said, 'Little did I know in 1936 I'd be calling you Sir.' He said, 'Well, you won't now, will you?' They've never changed. They've always kept as Alec and Eric. That's what I like about them. Just played their cricket, and that was it. Still the same today as they were then."

For years Bernie travelled to and from games with the Bedsers. "I only got a car myself when I had to get around the county for my benefit in '59. A Ford Popular, cost me five hundred quid, and I had to borrow that from the bank."

David Fletcher, Tony Lock and Peter Loader joined them after the war, working their way up from Surrey club cricket. With Jim Laker, Peter May and Tom Clark, then Micky Stewart and Ken Barrington, they would win eight titles in nine years, seven in a row from 1952.

"What you've got to remember is that Tony Lock, Jim Laker and Alec Bedser were bloody good bowlers. We didn't have time to get a lot of runs, but we got enough for them to bowl at."

There was no time for a century against Warwickshire in May 1953. The Midlanders were all out for 45 and 52, losing in a single day's play, with Bernie's 37 the highest score of the match.

There was no time for a century against Worcestershire in August 1954. The visitors were skittled out for 26, Bernie grafted a patient 29, and at 92 for three Stuart Surridge declared, sealing Surrey's third successive title when Worcestershire were all out for 40.

"When you come down to thinking of our careers as batsmen at The Oval, we never got our full quota of innings. When we did bat, we had to get on with it so our records were nothing. We didn't mind so much all the while we were winning but, when people look at averages, they're very false, aren't they? Only the greedy people want to get averages. When you get too many people playing for themselves, you're not successful."

He witnessed the change in Ken Barrington's approach from a free-scoring youngster to a batsman who came to avoid risk. "He worried more about failure than success, which is wrong in my opinion. When people worry about failure, that's when they start becoming selfish. He was on 98 in a Test match, and it took him 40 minutes to get to 100. Well, you can't tell me you need 40 minutes to get two runs. Sometimes, when people went off to play for England, they changed – from being one of the boys, one of the team, to thinking more about themselves. Not Locky, he was too raw to worry about things like that. He just bowled. But Jim Laker was more of an educated man; he used to think about things. If Jim didn't feel as though he could bowl on a wicket, he didn't want to. The funny thing is, he was a good enough bowler to bowl on any wicket."

There was a refreshing simplicity to the way he saw it all. "I think you can try too hard at any game, can't you? And if you try too hard, you get worse."

There were aspects of the modern game he did not like. "Somebody gets caught on the boundary, and they've all got to run over to kiss him. Because he's caught a ball. If we'd have had to kiss every time we took a wicket, we'd have got sore lips ... They get more injuries by so-called training than they do by playing. I never got any pulled muscles or anything, and no one was faster between the wickets than me ... They say they play too much cricket. How can you play too much cricket?" But then he stopped. "Let's face it. When you get old, you think they're not as good as you were. I don't thnk the game's changed that much."

In his autobiography Peter May called Bernie 'one of those important but unspectacular players on whom sides rely more than is usually recognised.'

"I used to bat a lot with Peter. You had to keep your eyes open. He used to drive it back so fiercely, you had to be ducking out of the way. They used to come back like rockets."

Short and dapper in a side of big men, Bernie worked his runs off the back foot. "I could always play the turners. It was the quickies I had difficult scoring off. I couldn't stand up and hit them off the back foot like Peter May. He had the height."

His father was a boat builder from Hampton-on-Thames: "I'm a fourth generation of boat builders, never rowed a boat in my life." He learned carpentry and joinery, and he spent his winters as a shop-fitter at Job's Dairies in Sunbury-on-Thames. "I could have been worse off, couldn't I? All my brothers finished up working in factories. I've met a lot of people playing cricket, from the dustman to the Queen. You can't do better than that, can you?"

In May 1956 Surrey played the Australians at The Oval. In the visitors' first innings, on a pitch that took turn from early on, Jim Laker took all ten wickets, not for the only time that summer. Then the Australian captain Ian Johnson pitted his own off-spin against the Surrey batsmen, bowling 61 of the 67 overs from the pavilion end, while Bernie scored a patient 109 that set up the first victory by a county over a touring Australian side since 1912. 'Constable batted with thoroughgoing professional efficiency,' recorded *The Times*, 'playing always within his limitations, using his feet neatly and cutting, driving and sweeping whenever he felt that no risk was entailed.'

Part of Bernie wanted to underplay his triumph – "Johnson just bowled all day; I think they were saving the fast bowlers for the Tests" – but another part wanted to thump his chest. "I think good pitches make mediocre batsmen look good. A batsman to me is a chap who can stay there on a dodgy wicket and get runs. People used to go on that Ted Dexter was a good player, but you couldn't ask him to play out an hour and a half on a dodgy wicket when the ball was turning. This fellow Gower is the same."

Though Bernie was always neat and tidy, he never caught the eye as a stylist, but he made the most of his talent. "I worked the game out myself. My batting, I knew very well what I could do and what I couldn't. Cricket is a game you've got to work out in your own mind, and I was good enough to do that. On a bad wicket I reckon I was a better player than Peter May."

By 1960 Surrey's dominance was over. No Peter May or Jim Laker, they sank to seventh in the table, and Bernie was out all summer, having his kneecap removed. He returned the following year with a career best 1,799 runs, but the Oval wickets were easier and his old friend Alec Bedser had retired. The great team was breaking up fast.

2 September 1964. The Oval. At the age of 44 he stepped out to bat for the last time for his county, the last survivor of the Surrey side of the early 1950s, let alone the pre-war days of the Young Players of Surrey. But, as he said, "We had to keep playing to keep ourselves in a living."

War had come and gone, rationing was over, now Britain was in the grip of Beatlemania. In front of the familiar gasometers Bernie hit a 'delightful' 61 not out and led the team off after an innings victory. Behind him, clapping, was Graham Roope, an 18-year-old debutant who would still be playing in 1982 when the country was at war in the Falklands.

After retirement Bernie worked full-time for Job's Dairies, and for four more summers his batting graced their Wednesday afternoon works team. "I could get a hundred every time I walked out there." There was a change of management, the team was disbanded, and he put away his pads for the last time.

In a great age of English county cricket Bernie Constable played for the most successful side of them all. He rarely missed a game, and his chirpy humour and cricketing brain gave much to the spirit of the team. His 30s and 40s on awkward tracks set up totals for the more famous bowlers, and his cover fielding, anticipating the batsmen's shots, added to the great physical presence of that Surrey side in the field.

"I learned more from Bernie than from anybody else in cricket," Micky Stewart said to me once.

We stood in the car park, and Bernie told me of his disappointment that he and his wife had not been drawn to go to the Palace to share their fiftieth wedding anniversary with the Queen. He also told me of his hope that, with his new hip, he would soon be back on the golf course. Alas, it was not to be. A fortnight later he died of a heart attack.

"I'm just an ordinary bloke," he said as we parted. "I've always gone through life saying that no man is better than me, and I'm no better than anybody else. I had respect for myself, and I had respect for other people."

71

RUPERT WEBB – A FULL LIFE

This appeared in a little booklet published by Roger Packham and Nicholas Sharp, to raise funds for the Sussex Cricket Museum, on the occasion of Rupert Webb's 90th birthday in July 2012. Rupert died at the age of 96 in August 2018.

The main challenge in writing the piece was to stay off the subject of his long feud with his former captain Robin Marlar.

"You know Rupert, don't you?" came the voice down the telephone. "We're wondering if you could write something about him for his 90th birthday."

My brain, if it had had any sense, would have told me, "You haven't got time. You're much too busy at the moment." But no. "Wonderful," I found myself thinking. "I can drive across to Rottingdean and listen to some more of Rupert's stories."

It was two in the afternoon when I settled down in his front room, and at seven he was still going strong, the tales of his life tumbling out of him with a vigour that many a man half his age would envy. He's had so many careers, all successful – photography, cricket, business, modelling, acting – and, if he so wanted, I'm sure he could start another, even at the age of ninety, entertaining audiences with his stories. He's a natural.

I asked him about his birth, and he was away. Before the First World War his father had had a gent's outfitter's shop in Harrow, but he had been called up at the age of 45 in 1917 and the shop was lost. There followed years of unemployment and, with three children, "they weren't far off starving." Then, in the autumn of 1921, came a lucky break. Despite no experience of printing, he was taken on as a compositor by the HM Stationery Office. It was a cause for celebration, and celebrate they did. "He and Mother went out for the night and got pissed, and nine months later I came along."

There were brains in the family. A cousin went to Cambridge University. But Rupert had to leave school at 14. So he took work at the local Kodak laboratory where his brother had become a manager. 15 shillings for a 44-hour week. They liked his handwriting and had him filling in forms for their Air Ministry weather station.

Then came the cricket, which he had played at school. He was given a game in the Kodak third eleven, and within weeks, as a little 15-year-old, he was replacing the long-serving first-team wicket-keeper. It was Business House cricket, against teams such as Harrods and Selfridges. At the Kodak ground there was a huge complex: tennis courts, bowling greens, rugby and football pitches, all beautifully kept.

In the summer of 1940, not yet 18, he found himself picked for a Harrow XI, captained by the sports master at his old school, to play in a Red Cross charity match against an eleven raised by the great Middlesex and England batsman Patsy Hendren. Then at the last minute he was transferred to Hendren's side. He kept to the Middlesex leg-spinner Jim Sims, and he had a good game.

Hendren approached him in the bar: "Were you born in Middlesex, lad? … Would you like to play for the county? … Well, if we both survive the war and you still want to play, come and see me."

His call-up papers arrived. He had passed City and Guilds exams at Kodak, and he applied to follow his brother into the RAF as a photographer. But he found himself reporting to Berwick-upon-Tweed to join the King's Own Scottish Borderers. "Sixty of us in a room with forty beds. I spent the first night sleeping on the floor. Then at 5.30 in the morning they blew the bagpipes for breakfast. 'Hold your hands out.' I got a sausage in one hand and a piece of bread in the other. That was breakfast. We had 20-mile route marches, then Saturday afternoon half marathons."

Cricket came to the rescue, though the standard was not what it had been in Harrow. He travelled to Inverness for a game where he made a century – "They were bowling the ball half way down the wicket" – and the Colonel was delighted: "I don't think they'd ever won a match before." Several more hundreds followed that summer, but their time in Scotland was drawing to a close. The word on the grapevine was that they were to be sent to Burma.

He had made one unsuccessful attempt to get himself transferred to photographic duties: "Get out of here … I'll have you sent down to the army gaol in Preston." Yet, at the last minute, he was called up to the Navy as a photographer. At Edinburgh he watched his comrades march out of the gate, on their way to the Far East, and he was left standing on his own. "Instead of going to Burma, I finished up at a training camp at Butlins in Skegness."

There followed two years at sea, when he became a Leading Photographer, a semi-detached role that suited his independent spirit. There were dangerous moments, dodging U-boats off Greenland and Norway, but there were also quieter times when he was able to make some money. On one occasion he was lowered into one of the small boats, where he rowed some distance away and took pictures of the vessel that he developed in the dark room and offered to the crew. "I sold about 2,000, at a shilling each. The chap who ran the canteen came to see me. 'You've got every bit of silver on the ship,' he said. 'They're all coming in for sixpenny ginger beers and offering me ten shilling notes.'"

In March 1946, now 23 years old, he returned to Kodak – "The war turned me from a silly, skinny lad into a man" – and he began playing cricket for them again.

"Are you going to see Patsy Hendren?" his team-mates asked.

"I don't know. I've got a secure job with a pension here."

"I'd go if I were you,' one said. "If you don't, you'll never know how good you are."

So he set off for Hendren's house, where the great man himself answered the door. "I can't remember your name," Hendren said, "but you're a wicket-keeper, aren't you?"

He was granted leave from Kodak for the summer of 1947, and he played for various MCC and Middlesex sides. It was the golden summer of Denis Compton and Bill Edrich, and the keeper's gloves at Middlesex had just passed from the veteran Fred Price to Compton's brother Leslie. Price took Rupert aside one day. "I'm sorry to have to tell you this," he said. "You're a better keeper than Leslie Compton will ever be, but he'll be in the team as long as Denis is playing."

Then came a message that Patsy Hendren, now coach at Sussex, wanted to see him. In late July Rupert played a two-day, second-eleven match for Sussex against Kent at Aylesford Paper Mills, and at the end of the first day he was offered a three-year contract. Billy Griffith, wicket-keeper and Sussex Secretary, was not planning to play much longer.

The following May Rupert made his first-class debut on the low, slow pitch at Bristol. "Your first match?" his opposite number Andy Wilson asked him kindly. "Well, keep down. We always call this a knees-and-ankles wicket. Whatever you do, keep down."

His first victim, stumped off Alan Oakman, was a ruddy-faced 20-year-old who had just left a career in the Army and, struggling for runs, was wondering if he had done the right thing: Tom Graveney. It was a different story two years later: "We played on a dreadful wicket at Worthing, and he got 200 against us."

For thirteen years Rupert spent his summers behind the stumps for Sussex and his winters as a salesman, later a manager, for Powell Duffryn, a national company that had started in mining in South Wales and, following the nationalisation of coal, was diversifying into such fields as heating oil, engineering, haulage and shipping.

Rupert can still recall a journey back from Stourbridge after one of his first games, when the captain was Hugh Bartlett. "I was always a tiny bit scared of skippers," he admits. "He walked down the coach to speak to me. 'Rupert,' he said, 'I'd like you to know how well you kept on such a difficult wicket.'"

The captaincy never seemed an easy matter at Sussex. In mysterious circumstances Bartlett stood down in the winter of 1949/50, to be replaced by the duo of the occasional amateur Robert Hunt of Horsham and the

Cambridge undergraduate Hubert Doggart. Rupert was at the ill-tempered meeting in the Grand Hotel, Brighton, when the committee, led by the Duke of Norfolk, was outvoted and walked out.

Peace was restored with the appointment as captain of the professional Jim Langridge. As the team set off for Cambridge for the first game, they were greeted by the Duke who, by way of apology for all the recent problems, tipped one of his horses for a race the next day. "Put as much on it as you can afford," he told them. Rupert took his advice. "It won at 20 to one. I got three or four months' salary out of it."

Rupert's favourite captain was David Sheppard, who led the county for that one summer of 1953 when they came so close to pipping Surrey to the championship title. In Rupert's eyes Sheppard was as good a batsman as Peter May, and he was inspirational as a leader of men: a hard competitor on the field and the kindest of men off it: "David always had time for everybody. If you had anything on your mind, he'd walk round the ground and listen to you."

In those years the professionals had to know their rank, even to the point where Rupert was required to give up his place in the side (and his match fee) to an inferior amateur who fancied a game. It happened several times. "I'm ever so sorry, Rupert," Jim Langridge told him on one occasion. "I argued last night till I was blue in the face."

Towards the end of Rupert's career Jim Parks was turned into a keeper, and Rupert ceased to be a regular member of the side. He retired at the end of 1960, at the age of 38, with a final tally of 449 victims. Only four Sussex keepers have taken more.

Never one to accept meekly the lot of the professional cricketer, Rupert got himself elected onto the Sussex committee for a three-year term. He was hoping to use the position to secure a pay rise for the playing staff, but he soon realised the impossibility of his mission. He was sidelined onto the Ground sub-committee and, when he raised the question of earnings in full committee, he found the Secretary prepared for him, with figures showing that several counties were paying their players even less than Sussex. "I should never have bothered," he says now. "They didn't want a professional on the committee. I just about survived the three years."

Life moved on, away from cricket. He rose through the ranks at Powell Duffryn. His son, after nine years in the RAF, went into the repair of aeroplanes. Then, after retirement and the death of his wife, he undertook the renovation of a Victorian house in Worthing. Around this time he bumped into an attractive lady at a filling station, took her telephone number and nine months later got round to ringing her up. She was an actress, Barbara Whatley, and she became his second wife. At their wedding there was a large home-made card from her co-star for three years in the West End. The card had seven words scrawled on it: 'love love love love love love Spike.'

From his marriage flowed a new career in modelling, in which his good looks and his understanding of photography brought him a steady stream of work. One assignment for Nestlés, involving a three-hour shoot in London, went Europe-wide and earned him £3,000 – which, as he points out, is not far off half of the £7,500 he received in 13 summers as a Sussex cricketer.

He has been seen in every tube train in London advertising the *Independent* newspaper. He has been an angry farmer on a tractor in a Conservative Party manifesto, an American art dealer in a French and Saunders show, and a customer in the background of a *Specsavers* advert, for which Michael Parkinson took 15 takes to get his entrance and his line right.

Then, of course, he was Duckface's father in the final wedding of *Four Weddings and a Funeral*. At one stage it was a speaking part, with Rupert in the midst of the brawl telling his daughter to calm down, but alas his lines were left on the cutting room floor. An old friend, watching the film in an American cinema, was so stunned to see the close-up of him coming down the aisle that he jumped out of his seat, shouting "Rupert."

A slight stoop has caused him to retire from the work, but he retains his vigour for life. That child created in the autumn of 1921, in the joy of his father's return to employment, has lived life to the full. He's never been short of work, and there's no sign that he's running out of steam.

At seven o'clock, when I had to leave, he was still going strong, telling tales of Alec Bedser and Bill Alley, of the game at Old Trafford that was over in a day and the time Ted James was run out, leaving him on 49 not out. He also told me of the fund-raising event with Ted Dexter which he organised recently at his local church.

Dexter was the last of Rupert's captains at Sussex – after Hugh Bartlett, Jim Langridge, David Sheppard and Hubert Doggart. There was one other, I think. I seem to have forgotten his name.

JIM LAKER'S 9/37

England v Australia, Old Trafford, 26-31 July 1956

*This appeared in 'Supreme Bowling – 100 Great Test Performances',
compiled and edited by Patrick Ferriday and Dave Wilson.*

A sequel to 'Masterly Batting', the book ranked Test bowling performances.

*This nine-wicket haul came in at number 21. Quite why Laker's
10/53 in the second innings was down at number 50, I never grasped.*

The Ashes were at stake. The series, level at one-all, was in its fourth match, and there was a band of heavy rain heading towards Manchester. On every one of the nine Australian tours since 1905 the Old Trafford Test had ended in a draw, most of them spoilt by the weather, one abandoned without a ball bowled. If the forecast was right, there was every possibility that this would be a tenth successive game without a result.

'Que sera sera,' sang Doris Day on the latest hit record. *'Whatever will be, will be.'*

Friday 27 July 1956. England's innings closed on 459, and at four o'clock a crowd of more than 30,000 spectators sat attentively in rows, watching the Australian openers as they proceeded cautiously and without alarm. Twenty-eight overs had been bowled – 10 of pace from Statham and Bailey, 18 of spin from Lock and Laker – and the scoreboard showed a total of 48 for no wicket.

'The future's not ours to see.'

The newspaper headlines were all of Colonel Nasser, the Egyptian President, and his sudden decision to nationalise the Anglo-French Suez Canal Company. If the imperialist powers do not like it, he told a cheering crowd of supporters in Alexandria, they can choke to death on their fury. Eleven years on from winning the war, Britain was in no mood to accept such a threat. A strongly worded note of protest was sent to the Egyptian government, warning them that they must face the consequences of their actions.

'Que sera sera. What will be, will be.'

Peter May was the England captain. He was no great tactician – had never led a team other than England – but, in his own words, "I was always a great believer in variety if one was not getting anywhere. So I switched the two bowlers round." Left-arm Tony Lock would now come in from the Warwick Road end, Jim Laker from the Stretford end.

Laker trotted in for the first ball of his tenth over. It pitched on middle-and-leg, spun in a little and the right-handed Colin McDonald failed to reach the pitch of it. The ball caught the edge of McDonald's bat and finished in the ever-safe hands of Tony Lock at backward short leg. Laker had drawn first blood. Australia were 48 for one.

'There have been off-spinners – though few – who spun the ball as much as Jim Laker,' wrote John Arlott. 'Some of them had comparable control. But no one has ever matched him in those two departments and had, also, such a quality of intelligence.'

"He had everything you look for in an off-spinner," Glamorgan's Don Shepherd reckons. "He was a big lad. He had a lovely action. He spun it, he had flight, he had change of pace and he could bowl round the wicket, too. If you're going to be an off-spinner, you'd want to be like Jim Laker."

"To me Jim was an absolute artist," his Surrey team-mate Micky Stewart says. "His control was immaculate, and the spin he imparted on the ball was incredible. I fielded at short leg, either at bat/pad or forward close in, and I could hear the snap of his fingers, followed by the zzzzzz of the ball coming down the pitch. My forward position was real 'Bomb Alley', but such was Jim's accuracy that I never felt in any danger. He was the number one finger-spinner that I've ever seen."

"Jim was in a class of his own," was Trevor Bailey's opinion. "He was surely the finest off-spinner in the history of the game."

The best ever, that is now the common wisdom, but it was not what people thought at the start of the summer of 1956. The 34-year-old Laker, in and out of the England team throughout his career, had played only two of the last 16 Tests before that year. Indeed, he might not have been at Old Trafford if Yorkshire's Bob Appleyard, so magnificent in Australia in 1954/55, had stayed fully fit.

Australia had gone one-up at Lord's, but England had levelled the series at Headingley with an innings victory on a pitch that started to crumble on the second day. Surrey's Tony Lock had been recalled in place of Yorkshire's Johnny Wardle, and he and Laker took 18 of the 20 wickets as the Australians, unhappy to find themselves batting on such a surface, were all out for 143 and 140. 'The loss of the toss cost us the match,' the Australian skipper Ian Johnson wrote. 'The pitch was so much out of character in the way it collapsed after the first day. Normally it plays beautifully for three days at least. Still, we reasoned, those things are part and parcel of the game, and we could make amends on a true surface at Manchester.'

And why not? The Old Trafford Test the previous year had been a five-day classic of high run-scoring, won by three wickets by South Africa with three minutes to spare. 'Here at Manchester,' Jim Swanton wrote in his eve-of-match report for the Australian game, 'the various factors – the weather, the absence of recent cricket on the ground and the availability of covers to keep off more moisture than is welcome – have all combined favourably, and there can be no excuse for anything but a true wicket that lasts.'

Some time before the toss on Thursday morning Jim Laker was drinking a cup of tea in the Old Trafford pavilion when Don Bradman, now an Australian selector, returned from the middle. "What do you think of the track?" Laker asked him, and the Don replied cheerfully: "It's nice and flat, isn't it? It's just what our fellows have been waiting for. They'll get a packet of runs out there."

Laker had already formed a different opinion. The pitch had an unusual reddish-brown colour, the result of the plentiful marl the groundsman Bert Flack had been using that summer, and it was dry. "I knew the ball would turn," Laker wrote. "There was no grass to bind the wicket. It *looked* good, but it was not solid enough."

Had England instructed the preparation of such a pitch? Or was it part of a general malaise in which counties were preparing result wickets? Or just an accident, the result of over-marling?

Geoffrey Howard, the Lancashire Secretary, was in Blackpool on Tuesday afternoon where the county were playing Gloucestershire. He was busy chartering an aeroplane to fly the two county teams south when there was a phone call from Bert Flack, the groundsman at Old Trafford. "The wicket's a bit dry," he said. "I think I ought to give it a bit of water."

Minutes later, the telephone rang again, and Peter May came through. "What's the wicket like?" he asked, wanting to think through his final team selection.

"As far as I know, it's exactly the same as last year," the Lancashire Secretary replied. "Bert Flack's just been on the phone. He said he's going to put a bit of water on it."

"Oh, don't put water on it."

"I should have said, 'That's nothing to do with you'," Geoffrey Howard reflected years later. "But, when you're in the middle of doing something else, you don't think things through. So I rang back to Bert Flack. I didn't tell him not to water it, but I told him what Peter May had said."

The pitch needed another watering, but it never took place.

As at Headingley England left out a paceman in favour of a second spinner, won the toss and made first-day runs on a slow, easy-paced track. At 174, moments before the fall of the first wicket, the *Test Match Special* team welcomed the old Lancashire and England wicket-keeper George Duckworth into the commentary box. He knew Old Trafford well. What were his thoughts on the pitch? "I wouldn't like to be a pace bowler on there," he said, "but spin bowlers should get something out of it in a day or two."

The England top-order, with Hutton retired and Compton out of action, had been unsettled all summer, and for this Test they called up the Reverend David Sheppard, the former England captain who was now a curate in Islington. Three months into the season, he had found time to play just four first-class innings, and he strolled out to bat "in rather a light-headed mood". His first ball from Ray Lindwall was a bouncer, and it reminded him that, unlike his recent London Clergy fixtures, this was "a serious game". He buckled down and, shortly before lunch the next day, cheered on by a group of boys from his parish, he completed a fairy-tale century.

With hindsight there were signs that the pitch was already becoming more difficult. On the first evening May was caught at slip off a leg-break from Richie Benaud that turned sharply and lifted to catch the shoulder of his bat. Then between innings, when the groundsmen brushed the wicket, the clouds of reddish dust that blew up – "more akin to the Sahara than Manchester" – caused consternation among the Australians in the press box. Yet at four o'clock, with the score 48 for one, there was no sense of what was about to unfold.

The brushing of the pitch before the Australian innings

The Lancastrian crowd sat in rapt attention, all but a few boys who were busy collecting stray bottles that would fetch them threepence each in a new scheme at the ground. One enterprising lad is said to have made himself four pounds while others were rumoured to have brought empty bottles from home.

Number three in the Australian line-up was the left-hander Neil Harvey, the star batsman in the side. Eight years earlier, as a teenager, he had scored a century on Ashes debut in the famous match at Headingley in which they had hit a record-breaking 404 for victory. England's only front-line spinner that day was a young Jim Laker, whom they punished severely.

"In his early days Jim used to lose it a bit if someone got after him," Tom Graveney reckoned. "George Emmett used to say, 'Have a go at him. He won't bowl so well.' But he soon got over that."

Laker was a mature bowler by 1956, and his third delivery to Harvey pitched on the line of the left-hander's leg stump, spun past his outstretched bat and clipped the off stump. 'It was a ball that might have bowled anyone,' the journalist Bruce Harris wrote. Jim Laker went further: 'It was the ball that won the Test series.'

Harvey stared at the pitch before departing and, though Jimmy Burke and the young Ian Craig took Australia to 62 for two at tea, there was already a growing feeling of apprehension in the Australian camp, fanning the sense of grievance that they had carried across the Pennines from Headingley. At this point Laker had figures of two for 29 off 13 overs.

What a summer it was for slow bowlers! Of the 23 men who took 100 wickets, 17 were spinners, led by Don Shepherd, who had that year converted from bowling medium-pace and who took 177 wickets with his off-breaks. Laker took 132, though he missed several county games to rest his over-worked spinning finger. "It was twice the size of the one on his other hand," Micky Stewart recalls. "Also, from time to time, the seam of the ball would split the finger to the bone, which he treated with friar's balsam."

Back in May, playing for Surrey at The Oval, Laker, bowling round the wicket as he mostly did at Old Trafford, had exposed the weakness of the Australians against finger spin, taking all ten first-innings wickets in the tourists' first defeat at the hands of a county side since 1912. The pitch did not reward turn as it did at Headingley and Old Trafford, leading Laker to consider it "from a technical point of view" the best of his performances that summer. Indeed, such was his psychological hold over the tourists, even at that stage of the season, that five of his ten wickets came from deliveries that did not turn.

When play resumed after tea at Old Trafford, Burke fell to the first ball, caught at slip off the bowling of Tony Lock – a wicket that, in time, would achieve a significance nobody could have dreamt of. Then, off Laker's first ball at the other end, Craig played back – as the Australians were inclined to do – and was lbw to "a nasty one that fizzed off fast". It was enough to destroy any last calm that existed in the Australian camp, and the sight of Ken Mackay striding out only made matters worse. His approach to batting at Headingley, Neville Cardus wrote, 'probably spell-bound his younger colleagues into the delusion that the pitch was a pitfall … He defended with his pads as though not to one spinning ball only but to several, aimed at him simultaneously from all parts of the ground.'

Within the over Mackay had edged the ball into the hands of Alan Oakman at slip. "I am no fairy foot," he admitted later, "and my antics at pad play must have resembled an elephant on ice."

The tall, fair-haired Oakman was playing in his second and last Test for England – and what a pair of Tests they turned out to be! Dropped after an unsuccessful debut at Headingley, he had got a late call-up from the Chairman of Selectors when Tom Graveney withdrew with a bruised finger. "I was at home in Hastings on Tuesday evening when the doorbell rang. There was a policeman there, leaning on his bike. We weren't on the phone, and Gubby Allen had rung the station. 'Do you know where Alan Oakman lives? … Can you tell him to get to Old Trafford tomorrow?'" In the field David Sheppard asked not to field in the leg trap – "I haven't been playing much cricket; my reflexes aren't what they used to be" – and Oakman found himself in the firing line, where he held five catches in the match.

In two overs since tea 62 for two had become 62 for five, and nobody in the Australian camp had the calmness of mind to prevent the situation degenerating further. 'The fellows were angry,' Ian Johnson wrote. 'They succeeded in hiding their feelings from the public at large, but they "blew up" in their batting. As things worked out, if we had kept something of our first innings alive that evening, we could have saved the match and, with it, the rubber.'

In Australia 18 months earlier they had been undone by the pace of Tyson and Statham, and they had arrived in England expecting a fresh barrage of fast bowling, only to find themselves up against Laker and Lock and for the second match in a row "trapped on a stinker".

The veteran all-rounder Keith Miller brushed at the dusty pitch with his glove. "Fellows, I think we're going to have an early end to this match," he said, and he promptly hit Lock for a straight six. When Miller faced up to Laker, Oakman took up position at short leg, almost in touching distance of the batsman. "If you don't look out, I'll hit you in the bollocks," the Australian told him.

"I thought, 'He's kidding me.' I wasn't wearing a box or anything. Then I thought, 'Is he?' But he just stabbed at it, and that helped it on its way to me."

"He batted like a complete novice," was Laker's verdict.

Richie Benaud did no better, attempting a big hit that landed in the hands of Brian Statham at 'cow-shot corner', a position where, even on the stickiest wicket, Laker insisted on having a man. For the third time Laker had taken two wickets in an over, and off the first ball of his next Ron Archer charged down the pitch, swung recklessly at the ball and was stumped.

The counter-attack had failed spectacularly, but orthodox defence fared no better, with Maddocks and Johnson, both playing back, bowled in Laker's next over. In 22 balls since tea the Surrey off-spinner had taken seven wickets for eight runs.

'Batting bereft of all heart and skill,' Alan Ross called it, but the Australians in the press box reserved their fire for the wicket. 'Let's have it straight,' Bill O'Reilly wrote. 'This pitch is a complete disgrace. What lies in store for Test cricket if groundsmen are allowed to play the fool like this?'

What a controversy it was! Late in the match, when the groundsmen were working flat out to dry the ground, Bert Flack ran past the Australian captain. "Blimey," he said. "They won't even give me time to cut my throat. Thank God Nasser's taken the Canal. Otherwise I'd have been plastered over every front page like Marilyn Monroe."

The *Manchester Guardian*'s Denys Rowbotham even managed to turn the Australians' complaints into an attack on post-war social policy: 'In this Welfare State age of all things on a platter and made easy, is a turning wicket a dishonour and no longer a challenge to personal skill? If it is, it is the humbug of sentimental socialism.'

"The pitch was not that bad," Peter May thought. "Jim just dripped away at their nerves, realising that they had got a little obsessional about him and the wickets."

'Naturally I was proud of my return of nine wickets,' Laker wrote, 'but it would never have been as profitable if there had been much sanity in the Australian display.'

From four o'clock to 5.15, with 20 minutes for tea, Australia had collapsed from 48 for no wicket to 84 all out. On only one other occasion since 1900 – South Africa at Edgbaston in 1924 – has a Test team lost all its ten wickets inside an hour of playing time, and this one at Old Trafford was in a contest between the two best countries in the world at the crucial point of an Ashes series. There has never been another collapse as momentous, and it was executed almost single-handedly by one man.

The crowd stood to applaud as Laker, with an air of nonchalance, sauntered off the field with figures of 16.4 overs, nine wickets for 37 runs. To this day, after 341 matches spread across 140 years, they remain the second best bowling figures in an Ashes Test, one of only two instances of a bowler taking nine or more wickets in an innings.

The only better Ashes figures came in the second innings when, across four wet days, Laker took all ten wickets for 53 runs to give him the greatest match statistics of all time: 19 for 90 off 68 overs.

Bowling one more over than Laker, Tony Lock managed just one for 106. The discrepancy was extraordinary and, in the years that followed, Lock took plenty of ribbing. "We used to say to him," Don Shepherd recalls with a chuckle, "'Tell us about that match at Old Trafford when you and Jim shared all those wickets.'"

"I felt a bit sorry for Locky," Alan Oakman says. "He was a great trier, but he didn't even look like getting a wicket. He got quicker and quicker, and he finished up bowling at leg stump. At the start he'd been applauding Jim's wickets, but by the end you could see him just folding his arms."

"Tony tried too hard," Trevor Bailey reckoned. "He was closer in temperament to a fast bowler, and at the end the ball was coming down at fast-medium. If Johnny Wardle had been bowling at the other end, Jim would never have got 19 wickets."

If Lock was excitable on the field, Laker was quite the opposite, even by the unexpressive standards of the 1950s. His appeals were quiet, his reaction to wickets matter-of-fact, his bowling without hurry or fuss. 'He moved to his mark with a constabular stroll,' John Arlott wrote. 'In the moment before he turned, he looked up into the sky, often with half a smile.'

"If anybody hit him for four," Bailey said, "he would regard his finger and go back to his mark."

"He told me how he once talked to Bobby Locke the South African golfer," Micky Stewart recalls. "Locke trained himself never to do anything in a hurry. Everything was in the same slow way: walking on the fairway, addressing the ball. 'By nature I'm quite excitable,' he said. 'I've schooled myself so that I've got total control, so I've got repetitive rhythm.' And Jim did the same. He didn't rush about."

Colin Cowdrey, writing of Laker's performance at Old Trafford, called him 'the calm destroyer': 'He was in perfect rhythm. The batsmen played and missed so often, yet you couldn't tell from his expression.'

The England players leave the field victorious

Nor could you tell at the end of the match, as he strolled off the field, his sweater slung over his shoulder, that he had won the Ashes for England with the greatest bowling figures in cricket history.

19 for 90. Like Bradman's batting average of 99.94, it is off the scale of other Test match statistics. Yet, like that 99.94, it falls tantalisingly short of the perfection of 'all 20', as Laker himself – with his delightfully dry wit – acknowledged in the final Test at The Oval. He was standing in the gully when the first Australian wicket fell, a diving catch by Tony Lock off Frank Tyson, and he turned to David Sheppard. "I haven't really got anything to play for in this match now."

SUMMER'S CROWN

To accompany 'Summer's Crown', my book on the county championship, Christopher Saunders produced a set of 18 county-themed limited editions. Each county's book was specially bound in an appropriately coloured cloth, with the signature of a captain and an eight-page supplement with extra material on that county. The following pages feature four pieces plus some quirky morsels which I wrote for these supplements.

I have also included two articles written for the Wisden Cricketer on championship-winning counties – Warwickshire in 1911 and Surrey in 1971 – and one on the championship itself for the 2015 Wisden Cricketers' Almanack.

HAPHAZARD AND ILLOGICAL

This article was written for the 2015 Wisden Cricketers' Almanack, to celebrate the 125th anniversary of the 'official' formation of the County Championship.

As long ago as 1927 the *Manchester Guardian* compared the county championship to the British constitution – 'for it has grown up more or less by haphazard, it contains some things hardly to be defended by exact laws or logic, and its origins cannot be easily traced.'

The Football League has always been so much simpler. It was founded in 1888 with the teams playing home and away against each other, 90-minute games with two points for a win and one for a draw. It's three for a win now, but otherwise it remains largely unaltered – a competition that has always drawn big crowds and been easy to understand.

Not so the county championship. Cricket historians, a quarrelsome fraternity, can't even agree when it started, with *Wisden* at various times opting for 1864, 1873 and 1890. Twenty years ago the almanack stated that Gloucestershire had been champions three times; now it records that they have never won.

The games have been played over three days, four days, even in an unsuccessful experiment in 1919 over two days – and, for many years, the hours of play were left to the counties to agree, some games scheduled for 19 hours, others only 17.

In 1894 the nine counties all played each other home and away. But, when five new counties joined, that was abandoned and counties played whatever games they chose. Surrey and Yorkshire, with large professional staffs, arranged home-and-away fixtures against all the other counties, but Middlesex, relying on the availability of their many amateurs, did not bother with the lesser counties. It was a higgledy-piggledy system, with the championship decided by convoluted percentages that were forever being adjusted and which stretched the arithmetical skills of cricket followers.

The county game captured the public imagination in the last years of the 19th century, the crowds for the crucial matches much bigger than for the England-Australia Tests. The second-class counties yearned to be part of it, and the number of counties rose from eight in 1890 to 16 in 1905. Yet it was not long before people were saying that this was too many. There was too much cricket, too few spectators to watch the games, too little money to support the whole edifice. In 1914, on the eve of war, Gloucestershire and Worcestershire called meetings with a view to pulling out.

It was the same story in the 1930s when only three counties – Kent, Middlesex and Yorkshire – were said not to be reliant on appeals and borrowing. Leicestershire went into merger talks with Lincolnshire. Northamptonshire were on the brink of folding up.

Lucky football with its 90 minutes, come rain or shine, and its simple win, lose and draw. Cricket, by contrast, has struggled to find a satisfactory points system, one that encourages positive but not contrived cricket. How could it be right that, both playing 28 matches in 1930, Lancashire, with 10 wins, could be champions ahead of Gloucestershire with 15?

Then there were the match regulations. In the 1960s they were changing constantly – two summers when the follow-on was abolished, a summer when the first innings was limited to 65 overs in some matches, another when bowlers were not allowed to polish the ball. In 1964 a proposal for a three-year moratorium on further change was well supported, but within twelve months the counties had forgotten that. Nothing has ever seemed to be quite right.

Cricket has never wanted to be like football. For many years it was hard for a professional to move counties. Tom Graveney, an experienced Test batsman, had to spend a year playing second-eleven cricket when he moved from Gloucestershire to Worcestershire in 1961.

Further back, in the early 1900s, the regulations were tightened to end the growing practice of recruiting 'colonial' cricketers from Australia and South Africa. 'Under the present system,' wrote *The Times*, 'a millionaire with a hobby for cricket could make Rutland the champion county in about four years' time, and there need not be a Rutland man in the winning eleven.'

In 1975, though there was no millionaire benefactor, Leicestershire became the first county to win the championship without a home-grown player in their first-choice eleven. And *The Times* had been proved strangely prophetic. The previous year, under a reorganisation of local government, Rutland had been incorporated into Leicestershire.

The 1970s were years of greater democracy in the county game. With four trophies to be won each summer, and two overseas players allowed, the gulf between big and small counties narrowed, with all 17 winning something between 1969 and 1981. That is a trend that has been reversed in recent times – with two divisions, the easier transfer of players and the greater financial spoils going to those with Test match grounds. WG Grace had proposed promotion and relegation back in the 1890s, but would the smaller counties have voted for it in 1999 if they had seen where it would lead? It was sold as a way of creating some end-of-season excitement, with three-up, three-down giving every county a turn in the top flight.

The changes keep coming. Money is always a problem. Every failure of the England team brings a fresh appraisal of the structure. And now there is the seemingly unsolvable riddle of the schedule, how to fit T20, 50-over cricket and the four-day championship into the crowded English summer, along with all the international matches.

Yet, for all its faults, it is still the competition the players themselves most want to win. In a 2009 survey, 274 out of 301 county cricketers chose it as the most important domestic competition. And, if at least one England coach has had little respect for the county game, that is not the view of the Australians – as the 35-year-old Chris Rogers testifies: "Our chairman of selectors, John Inverarity, said to me that he wanted me to play in the county championship. If a young player wants to develop his long-form game, I would advise him to play county cricket and to expose himself to the great variety of conditions. I wouldn't have been the Test batsman I am without it."

"County championship cricket is our English breeding ground for Test matches," Geoffrey Boycott says. "It's not just about the techniques of the batsman and bowler. It breeds character, it breeds courage, all the things which you cannot get out of one-day cricket."

The championship is 125 years old in May, and it's weathered many a crisis. An anachronism handed down from Victorian times? Try telling that to the Yorkshire folk who cheered the victory of their team, their largely home-grown team, last September at Trent Bridge.

As that *Guardian* editorial of 1927 wrote, 'It must be a pretty sound thing after all since it has survived its own deficiencies and has provided some healthy excitement in its closing stages.'

THE WICKET-KEEPING GARDENER

Jack Board of Gloucestershire

Jack Board started his working life as a gardener, playing his cricket for the Highlands club on the Bristol Downs. It is not clear that he ever kept wicket for them but, when he had a trial for the county in 1890, WG Grace looked at his hardened hands and exclaimed, "They're made for keeping." So good an impression did Board make in the game that, at the end of it, the doctor was telling the press that at last he had found a successor to 'Frizzie' Bush, the county's 40-year-old gloveman.

What did people look for in a keeper at that time? Not the soft hands modern coaches want, it seems. Grace's brother, the Coroner, said he was "a capital man, with hands as hard as iron. He holds the ball and is content merely to stop it."

Board was taken onto the staff for the summer of 1891 and, before the county's first-class programme began, he kept wicket in some early-season games: for Grace's Thornbury club against St George and Lansdown and for the Gloucestershire eleven against Fifteen of Glamorgan.

Then, out of the blue, he got a telegram from WG, asking him to call on Mrs Grace. He went to the house, and she told him that he had to be at Lord's on Monday morning, to play for the South against the North. WG had asked her to give him two pounds for his travel expenses.

"I didn't know where Lord's was," Board said later. "I was only a poor gardener. Mrs Grace wrote out on a piece of paper all the instructions. I was to take a ticket to Paddington and then a cab to Lord's, and I was not to pay the cabman more than eighteenpence. At Lord's I was to ask for WG Grace."

South versus North was the first great match of the summer. Of the leading cricketers of the day, only two were missing: Arthur Shrewsbury, the Notts batsman who had cried off with a cold, and Harry Wood, the Surrey keeper whose withdrawal had brought in the 24-year-old Jack Board. It was a prestigious fixture, which attracted a large crowd, and some in the press, notably the *Birmingham Post*, questioned Grace's selection of the untried colt.

The match was being staged for the benefit of the professional Arnold Rylott, who had been on the ground staff at Lord's since 1872. The weather was warm and sunny, and more than 6,000 people came to watch each day.

"When I got there," Board said, "WG introduced me to the professionals' room. I remember him saying to a group of players, 'Look after him.'"

Jack Board

He was not overawed, it seems. He did not make runs – 'caught in the long field' for four and 'clean bowled' for one – but, keeping to bowling he had never seen the like of, including the great George Lohmann, he conceded only 11 byes, just one more than the North's Mordecai Sherwin (who was suffering from a bout of rheumatism).

On the last day, when the North were all out for 91, Board took two catches and a stumping. 'He acquitted himself with credit,' the *Western Daily Press* declared, 'considering the high test applied to his capabilities.' In their view he had more than answered the 'distressingly bilious' attack on his selection by the *Birmingham Post*.

"When the match was over," Board recalled, "WG took me in at the amateurs' gate and saw that I was paid. They wanted to deduct a sovereign from me for Rylott's benefit, and he said, 'No, take half-a-sovereign. He's a youngster who's never played in first-class before.' Then he drove me in his cab to Paddington, travelled with me, and I rode through the streets of Bristol with him to his home. WG was WG in those days. His name was a household word the world over. I felt somebody. There was a lot of pride in me. WG told the cabman to drive me home, and a week later I played my first county game."

Board loved Grace and was the happiest of men under his captaincy. He whistled and sang, he talked all the time, and he rarely let an injury stop him playing. Knocked unconscious before one match, he insisted on still playing, only obeying Doctor Grace's instruction to go home to bed when he was promised his full match fee.

Though notorious for his reckless running between the wickets, he turned himself into a decent bat. At Bristol in 1900, he hit a brilliant 214 against Somerset.

It was never dull with Board. Once, when he missed Woof's signal for an inswinger, the ball flew past him. "Stop 'im, Jack," cried WG, only to get the reply: "I couldn't stop 'e. 'E went t'other way that 'er did."

Later captains found him difficult. He was often in dispute with the committee on matters of pay and, in the words of a friend, "His incessant chatter made him rather unpopular in dressing rooms; his companionship did get a little tiring on long night journeys."

But the Bristol crowd loved him, and he kept for the county till 1913, his hands done up with yards of adhesive tape and his gammy thumb stiffened by a bevelled piece of steel that protruded a quarter of an inch beyond the nail. In all matches for the county, he claimed 1,017 victims.

LANCASHIRE v YORKSHIRE

Old Trafford, 7-8 August 1893

The morning of August Bank Holiday Monday saw bright sunshine and a blue sky. According to the *Guardian*, the people of Manchester were soon on the move: 'The great number – practically all but those who were enthusiastic for cricket – took advantage of the cheap fares and found their pleasures on the sands of Blackpool and Southport, or the hillsides of Derbyshire, in North Wales, or, it might be, by the waterfalls in the Ingleton district, which had been made the more delightful by recent rains.' Many made their way on steamboats to the Isle of Man, while Manchester's Belle Vue Gardens drew great crowds with a wide range of entertainments, including 'a magnificent spectacle of the American-Indian War and a splendid display of fireworks'.

The August Bank Holiday had only been created 22 years earlier, and for the men who worked 50 weeks a year it was a special day. The great crowd that gathered at Old Trafford reflected that – with 'an ugly rush for seats' when the gates opened an hour before the start. The *Yorkshire Post* reported that an electrical system at the turnstiles transmitted the numbers to the Secretary's office, and by 12.30 it had reached 15,186. Late in the afternoon, when the decision was made to close the gates, it was up to 22,554 which, with the addition of members, took the attendance close to 25,000, a full 5,000 more than the ground had ever housed before – and four times as many as turned up for the first day of the Test against Australia later in the month.

County cricket was capturing the popular imagination much more than the international matches, particularly in this summer when for the first time Yorkshire and Lancashire were the leading contenders for the championship title.

The cricket they witnessed was not on the face of it an ideal one for such a large crowd. The pitch was damp from rain the previous day, and the sun on it made batting devilishly difficult. At one o'clock a violent storm brought half an hour of torrential rain, soaking those without umbrellas, and it was 2.45 before the match resumed. In all, the great crowd saw only 4½ hours of cricket, during which twenty wickets fell for just 129 runs. 'Yet', wrote the *Guardian*, 'so keen was the bowling and fielding that the play never seemed slow.'

Lancashire 64 and 7 for no wicket, Yorkshire 58.

'It was a bowler's day with a vengeance,' wrote the *Yorkshire Post*, 'and what with cheering the hits and the fall of each wicket, the twenty-odd thousand lungs were pretty well employed throughout the day.'

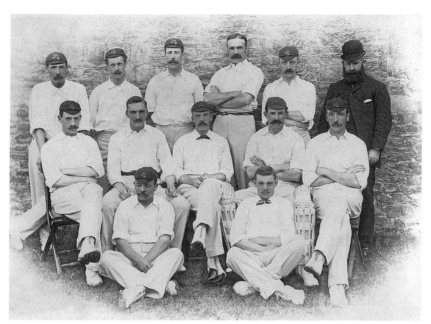

Lancashire at Bristol and Taunton 1893: (back) F Ward, A Tinsley, AP Smith, FH Sugg, W Oakley, Lunt (scorer); (middle) GR Baker, AC MacLaren, SM Crosfield, AM Kemble, A Ward; (front) J Briggs, CH Benton

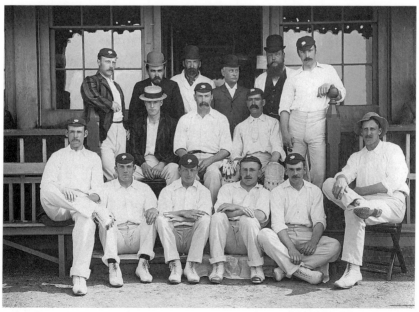

Yorkshire at Taunton 1893: (back) R Peel, unknown, A Rylott (umpire), Turner (scorer), H Draper (umpire), TA Wardall; (middle) A Sellers, G Ulyett, D Hunter; (front) E Wainwright, JT Brown, R Moorhouse, GH Hirst, JT Mounsey, J Tunnicliffe

The great cricketing rivalry between the white- and red-rose counties was in its infancy, with the annual fixtures not set in stone on the bank holidays. There was not yet that grim determination to avoid defeat at all costs that characterised many of their inter-war contests. But Yorkshire, after years of little success, were striving for the championship, and this Old Trafford game was spiced with strong feeling.

'It was the most sensational match I ever witnessed,' wrote the long-serving dressing-room attendant William Howard in 1928. 'From the start to the finish the game was full of thrills, a feeling of animation prevailed round the ground, every ball bowled was watched as if something extraordinary was going to happen.'

The Yorkshire cricket writer AA Thomson grew up with a vivid account of the match from his Uncle Walter, who watched both days, staying overnight in a Manchester hotel; 'It rained during the night – he heard it beating on his window – and when he got back to Old Trafford in the morning the pitch was steaming under a hot sun. The ground was once more packed, as though nobody had been home. From the first moment a devil of excitement, a kind of infectious madness, began to rise like mercury in an overheated thermometer. It rolled and swelled all round the spectators. It invaded the playing area, rattled the umpires and caused world-famous batsmen to do things they would not have done had they been calm and in their right mind.'

In this atmosphere with the batsmen 'groping and not coping' with Yorkshire's slow-left-armer Bobby Peel and with four catches for the tall Tunnicliffe – 'Uncle Walter said he seemed to have as many arms as a hat-rack' – Lancashire were dismissed for 50.

The only man to last long was the young amateur Archie MacLaren, whose dismissal – caught at the wicket off Peel – was the first of several moments of controversy during the day. "I was not within a foot of the ball," he claimed – or, in Uncle Walter's version, "never within an ensanguined mile."

Though it was a working day, 12,000 were in the ground when Yorkshire set out to score 57 runs for victory. The two amateurs Arthur Sellers and Stanley Jackson, the *Guardian* reported, 'started in the proper way. They hit out at everything and scored 24 in twenty minutes.'

Johnny Briggs was bowling, and he turned to Sellers. "I think it's all over now, sir, bar shouting." Then came the moment which turned the course of the game. Briggs struck Jackson on the pad and appealed for lbw. The ball ran away, and the batsmen started out on a leg-bye. Then the umpire made a motion, which seemed to suggest he had given the lbw, and the batsmen stopped. "Surely not," Jackson said, and at this point the umpire's signal turned into that for a leg-bye, though the batsmen had not yet run it.

Amid the confusion, with Jackson still stranded in mid-pitch, the ball was returned to the keeper and he was given run out.

So bewildered were the scorers that they sent a messenger to the middle to establish what had happened. Indeed, such was their muddle that right up to lunchtime the total on the board included the leg-bye that had been signalled but never run.

The umpire at the centre of the storm was Alfort Smith, a former Derbyshire wicket-keeper, and he was again in the thick of it when at 41 for four the schoolmaster Ernest Smith, 'the man most likely to win the match for the visitors' according to William Howard, hit a cover drive that barely left the ground. The Lancashire captain, the solicitor Sydney Crosfield, dived forward and claimed the catch, tossing the ball in the air, a gesture that at the time was not common practice and which one newspaper described as 'questionable conduct, apt to prejudice the umpire in the fielder's favour'.

The flustered umpire raised his finger, and the batsman was furious. 'There were some very bitter words spoken in the dressing room when he came in,' wrote Howard. 'The baying of the crowd had scarcely time to die down,' said Uncle Walter, as Peel came and went, showing his displeasure when he was given lbw. Lunch was taken at 42 for six.

The umpiring remained a topic for some days, especially when Yorkshire discovered that Alfort Smith was a Lancastrian.

After the interval the batsmen tried bold shots, a policy that soon reduced them in the feverish atmosphere to 46 for nine. 'One of our members,' wrote Howard, 'had been banging his tall hat to such an extent that it looked like a concertina.'

The keeper David Hunter, no batsman, joined the veteran 'Happy Jack' Ulyett, a man who in his day had opened for England. Ulyett was nearly lbw, nearly stumped, edged a lucky four and found himself on strike to Briggs with six wanted for victory. He was 'the coolest man on the ground', and he decided to settle the match as quickly as he could, driving the ball hard at Briggs who dropped it. Then he jumped out of his crease and hit the ball high towards the long boundary for what, in the laws of that time, would have been a four. There, in front of the rails, was Albert Ward. Even before the ball settled in his hands, 'there was a tremendous shout and a great stampede, such as has probably never been seen before at Old Trafford.'

Amid the pandemonium Ward held the catch, retaining the ball as a memento of the game. 'Hats were waved in a perfect frenzy of delight' as the fielders ran off and 'the two Yorkshire batsmen slowly and sadly followed.' Meanwhile in the pavilion the row about Crosfield's catch flared up again.

Roses cricket was fast developing its own special flavour.

A YEAR OF TRIUMPH – FRANK FOSTER IN 1911

This piece, based on a recently published book by Robert Brooke, appeared in the Wisden Cricketer in September 2009.

The summer of 1911. A large anti-cyclone sat over Denmark, and England enjoyed day after day of unbroken sunshine. Temperatures reached the high 90s, setting records that would stand till 1990. Indeed, it was so hot that *The Times* took to running a column listing Deaths by Heat. In London alone, it was estimated, 2,500 children died.

Cricket's county championship was in its 22nd year, settling into a familiar pattern. In early July, at the halfway stage, the Big Six – Yorkshire, Kent, Surrey, Middlesex, Notts and Lancashire – were yet again at the top of the table.

Then came Warwickshire, under their 22-year-old captain Frank Rowbotham Foster, an amateur of the wealthy family who owned Foster Brothers, the gents outfitters. The county, after several years of mediocrity, had looked to his youthful vigour, and he had almost let them down, announcing his retirement before the first match in May. He had fallen in love, planned to announce his engagement and to concentrate on his business. In his absence they lost to Surrey by an innings, and his father took him aside. "They want you, my boy," he said. "You had better go."

He led from the front – an attacking batsman who believed that the runs on the scoreboard should always run ahead of the minutes on the clock; a left-arm, round-the-wicket bowler who, despite a loping, eight-pace run-up, generated surprising pace off the pitch. He scored a three-hour 200 against Surrey, he hit a century and took 12 wickets against Yorkshire, and in late July, in his 17th match, he completed the double of 1,000 runs and 100 wickets. Only Grace and George Hirst have achieved it in fewer matches.

He was a natural cricketer, one who never bothered with a net. "He'd just stroll onto the pitch," wicket-keeper 'Tiger' Smith said, "and look a fine all-rounder and a good slip. His confidence was amazing." Off the pitch he was no different. Drink, women, horses, cards, billiards, he lived life to the full.

The professionals came to love him, though not the veteran Dick Lilley. At Harrogate, in full hearing of the crowd, Lilley took to resetting the field, and Foster reprimanded him. At lunch the 44-year-old, smarting from being rebuked by "a young kid of 22", tried to organise a strike among the professionals, but such was Foster's steely resolve that the long-serving Lilley was dropped, for ever, after the next match.

Through July and August the sun beat down. Warwickshire won game after game, and the leaders Kent and Middlesex began to falter. The championship was something of an ad hoc set-up, with counties free to create their own fixture lists. Middlesex had never agreed to play Warwickshire, viewing them as an unattractive minnow, while Kent had stopped playing the Midlanders after an acrimonious match in Catford in 1899. Such was the variation in the games counties played, from 16 to 30, that the champions had to be determined by a complicated percentage system.

Warwickshire, brimming with confidence, started their final game at Northampton on Saturday 26 August, with a percentage of 72.63. That morning Kent won their penultimate match and moved ahead of them on 72.80. But, because they had played more games, a last victory for Kent would only take them to 73.84 where Warwickshire could reach 74.00. The task was therefore straightforward for Foster's men – victory at Northampton would make them champions.

Rain, long overdue, was forecast for Sunday and Monday. Foster, desperate to bat first in the sunshine, lost the toss. 'I walked away,' he wrote later, in a colourful memoir, 'thinking the end of the world. To get so near, and yet so far. Is it fate or is it Providence? God must decide the issue, but then I do believe in God.'

By lunch Northants were all out for 73. Foster, five for 18; the lion-hearted Frank Field, four for 27. At close of play Warwickshire were 226 for six. Rain arrived on the Sunday rest day, and by the end of a shortened Monday there were three Northants wickets standing between Foster and glory. 'It was the longest night of my life,' Foster wrote. 'I could never have slept.' He stayed up – 'playing cards, singing songs, everything' – and, when the day broke sunny, he went to the ground and, like a true hero, he took the last three wickets himself.

As they left the field, his father, with a tear in his eye, came out of the crowd and embraced him. 'There can be no question,' *Wisden* wrote, 'that Warwickshire's triumph was mainly due to FR Foster. Not since WG Grace in the early days of the Gloucestershire eleven has so young a captain been such a match-winning force for a county side.' A hundred years on, Foster remains by three years the youngest captain ever to lead his county to the championship – and the only championship-winning captain to complete the double. In all matches that summer he scored 1,614 runs and took 141 wickets.

Within weeks he was on the boat to Australia where he and the great Sydney Barnes bowled England to a 4-1 victory. Barnes took 34 wickets, Foster 32, England's most successful new-ball pair in Ashes history. Foster – called by Pelham Warner 'the best bowler of his type I have ever seen' – also scored 226 runs, with three 50s. Has there ever been an English cricketer so young who has achieved so much in such a short time?

Alas, as Shakespeare wrote, 'summer's lease hath all too short a date.' In the wettest of years, Warwickshire slid back to mid-table in 1912, a motorbike accident in 1915 ended Foster's sporting prowess, and his life spiralled downwards – addicted to gambling, dismissed from the family business, declared a bankrupt. His marriage went wrong, he was banned as a nuisance from the Edgbaston pavilion; he was even briefly a suspect in the murder of a Soho prostitute.

The grim details are recorded in a biography of Foster by Robert Brooke, the former Edgbaston librarian. Brooke is an unsung hero of English cricket history, a brimming fount of knowledge about cricketers, and this is his magnum opus, the result of 40 years of research. He suspects that Foster contracted syphilis in Australia, and he sets down with a chilling matter-of-factness Foster's decline into a nether-world of debt and fantasy.

In 1934, at the age of 45, Foster wrote to the England captain, pressing his claim for selection for the forthcoming Ashes series. He knew how to bowl at the Australians, he said, ignoring his slight lameness and the fact that he had not played cricket of any standard for twenty years.

In 1950 he was in Southend, facing charges of larceny and intent to defraud. He failed to appear at the magistrates' court, explaining later that he had had to go to Lord's to tell them about a local bowler called Bumstead who, if taken to Australia that winter, would win England the series 5-0. Indeed, Foster added, there would be 'a hell of a row' if he was not chosen. Brooke's footnote says it all: 'There is no trace of a cricketer named Bumstead playing successfully, or at all, in Essex or Southend newspapers at around this time.'

In the cruellest of ironies, Foster was committed to mental hospital in Northampton, the town of his greatest joy forty years earlier. He spent his last years there, as a hundred years previously had the peasant poet John Clare, whose *Remembrances*, a melancholic poem about lost youth, provides the title for Brooke's work: *The fields were sudden bare.*

> *Summer's pleasures they are gone like to visions every one,*
> *And the cloudy days of autumn and of winter cometh on.*

On 29 August this year the Northamptonshire team will drive to Birmingham for a 40-over match, a hundred years to the day after Foster and his triumphant men made the same journey home by train. Outside New Street station thousands stood and cheered them. A golden afternoon at the end of a golden summer. And none glittered more brightly than Frank Rowbotham Foster. In the words of his *Wisden* obituary, he was 'a most attractive figure on the field … the personification of youthful energy'.

AFTER A LONG NIGHT AT THE STEELWORKS

Dai Davies of Glamorgan

Dai Davies would become a stalwart of the Glamorgan team for many years, the county's first home-grown professional, but at the start of June 1923 he was a 26-year-old club cricketer, with a hot and dusty job in the steel works at Llanelli.

At 10 p.m. on Friday 1 June he was ending his eight-hour shift when he learned that his replacement had not turned up. They had all been paid a production bonus that afternoon, and the man had spent so much of it in the White Horse that he was unfit to work. So Davies was persuaded to do the night shift, only returning home for breakfast and bed at 6 a.m.

At 11.30, after four hours' sleep, there was a knock on his bedroom door. "There's a car outside," his mother told him. "They want you to play for Glamorgan at Swansea." And, after a wash and a shave, off he went, arriving at the ground at about 12.45 where he tried to enter the gate next to the pavilion.

"Where do you think you're going?" the gateman asked.

"I'm playing," he replied.

"Oh no, you're not," the man said, all too used to people trying that stunt. "Get out of it."

'So I held my cricket bag in front of me,' Davies wrote, 'and charged past him, almost knocking him down in the process.'

Northants were batting – 50-odd for no wicket – and he hurriedly changed and went out. 'I'd never even seen a county match before, and there I was, playing in one. The end of the over came, and TAL Whittington, the captain, tossed me the ball. "You're bowling, Dai," he said and briefly discussed the field placing. With my fourth ball I knocked the opener Bellamy's middle stump clean out of the ground. I'd been on the field five minutes and got my first wicket.'

He got two more wickets during the afternoon, then after tea it was Glamorgan's turn to bat. 'I'd been bowling most of the afternoon following a 16-hour shift with only four hours' sleep, and I was more than thankful to sit on the dressing-room bench. Then TAL Whittington snapped out: "Get your pads on, Dai, you're next wicket down!" I couldn't believe it. Was the man trying to kill me?'

He was not needed that night, returning home to spend much of Sunday in bed, but on Monday he made 58. It was the top score, and a collection was held for him on the ground.

On Tuesday he shared in an important opening partnership of 51 as they won by four wickets, Glamorgan's fourth victory in 2½ years in the championship, and he returned home with £35 – £10 for his match fee, £25 from the collection. 'It was more money than I'd ever had in my life before. I wasn't really concerned about the money, though, because I also had a three-years agreement in my pocket. I was a county cricketer. I'd made the grade.'

Dai Davies

YORKSHIRE v WARWICKSHIRE

Scarborough, 18-20 July 1934

It was the final championship match played by Jack Parsons, the last to retire of the Warwickshire team that won the title in 1911. And it was the first match played by Tom Dollery, captain when Warwickshire would next win the title in 1951.

They travelled to Scarborough without their captain Bob Wyatt, who left for Headingley to lead England against Australia, and the 44-year-old Parsons, now a vicar in a village parish in Shropshire, stood in for him. It was his first game for seven weeks.

The 1911 side had beaten Yorkshire at Harrogate, but such was the strength of the Northern county that in 37 subsequent meetings Warwickshire had won only once, though that once at Hull in 1927 was a famous victory, one that ended Yorkshire's extraordinary run of 76 matches without defeat. It was Parsons himself, before his entry into the church, who had won the match with a magnificent innings of 136.

Parsons, the most popular of men, was the quintessential muscular Christian. The son of an Oxford college chef, he had started his working life in a Coventry car factory but in the war his repeated bravery in Palestine won him the Military Cross and he became a highly respected officer. A classless character, one of the few to have played for both the Gentlemen and the Players, he knew how to handle himself physically, and at Hull he did so, standing up for himself in a fiery encounter with the combative George Macaulay, a medium-pace bowler who was, in the words of Robertson-Glasgow, 'a glorious opponent who had a stomach for the fight second to none'.

At Scarborough Yorkshire were missing four of their regular eleven: Verity, Bowes and Leyland at the Test, Sutcliffe with a leg strain. They, too, gave a first championship game to a youngster: Herbert Hargreaves, a fast bowler from Hull.

Rain fell throughout the first morning, and play did not start till 2.40. The pitch, hard underneath, had a damp surface, making it ideal for bowling, and Parsons, winning the toss, asked Yorkshire to bat. Their top order batted with great caution but, with George Paine's off-breaks gripping and turning viciously, they were soon 26 for five. The young left-hander Cyril Turner alone batted with confidence, making 51, and by half past five they were all out for 101.

The pitch had eased a little, but Warwickshire batted abysmally. 'Had they been trying to get out,' wrote the *Yorkshire Post*, 'they could scarcely have gone more successfully about it.' The rot started when Croom changed his mind about a second run, and his partner Kilner was left stranded in mid-pitch. Bates holed out with an uncontrolled hit into the deep, and the newcomer Hargreaves, 'bowling all over the place', took three quick wickets, including the newcomer Dollery who hooked the ball into the hands of deep square-leg. Play was twice suspended, for bad light and rain, and Warwickshire finished the day on 25 for eight. 'Beside Warwickshire's paltry few runs, Yorkshire's miserable score looked majestic.'

Next morning, with the sun shining, Warwickshire were all out for 45, the lowest total of the summer, and Yorkshire set about building a commanding lead. It was dour fare, 'the sort of cricket through which none but the greatest of enthusiasts could sit without restlessness', and at lunch they were only 51 for three. It was certainly not an ideal offering for the large contingent of schoolboys – 'They would have more profitably spent the day on their own fields with their own bats and balls' – and, when the afternoon session began, the crowd had grown considerably smaller. 'Numbers of people decided that Scarborough had more attractive entertainments to offer.'

Only Kenneth Davidson, soon to leave cricket for a professional career in badminton, showed much initiative and, though Warwickshire dropped five catches, some of them easy, Yorkshire managed a score of only 159. It left Warwickshire 216 to win, and at the close they were 99 for four.

What a last morning it proved! Jack Parsons and Reg Santall, whose father Syd had played alongside Parsons in the 1911 side, played their shots from the start, adding 46 in quick time, but the game turned when the young Len Hutton, in his first summer in the Yorkshire team, came on to bowl his high-flighted leg-breaks. Santall watched him carefully for two overs; then, when 'he could stand his tantalising donkey-drops no longer', he hit him violently back over his head, only for Cyril Turner, 'sprinting like a deer for fully fifty yards', to cling to a breathtaking catch.

Dollery was caught behind off his second ball, ending a miserable debut in which he scored 1 and 0 and dropped a simple catch at point. Peter Cranmer, the England rugby international, did no better, pushing an easy catch back to Macaulay, and they were 147 for seven: 69 runs still wanted and down to a tail 'not conspicuous by its batting strength'.

Parsons decided to attack Hutton, hitting him for two sixes and two fours inside two overs, but Paine hit the ball in the air to extra cover and was caught for 2. It was now 42 to win, and Warwickshire were down to the rabbits, Danny Mayer and Eric Hollies.

'Parsons realised that victory now depended solely on him, and he hit Macaulay low over the sight screen at the north end, the ball pitching on the terrace, then late cut the next ball for four.'

At this point the game got rather out of hand. Macaulay was 'in one of his keenest moods – almost too keen, to judge by a few of his appeals', and the close fielders were all 'nattering'. Parsons asked them to be quiet, only to receive the reply, "Tak' no notice of t'bloody parson." They started up again as Macaulay ran in, and Parsons pulled away. He went across for 'a conference' with the Yorkshire captain Brian Sellers, only to receive from him the reply: "What can I do about it? You know what they are."

He and Mayer added 30 runs, all scored by Parsons himself, before Parsons had what he later called 'a bang': 'He lashed out at Hargreaves and was clean bowled.' He had made 94 in under two hours, out of 121 runs added while he was at the wicket, an innings of power and authority from a man who had played little that summer.

In came Eric Hollies, the young leg-spinner from Old Hill in the Black Country. The rabbit of all rabbits, he had brought up his 100 first-class runs earlier in the match – in his 43rd innings – and now he had to survive while he and Mayer, still on nought, scored 12.

There was a two and a single from Mayer, then after ten scoreless minutes Macaulay beat Hollies, only for the ball to run away for a bye. This sent Macaulay into an outburst of abuse that terrified Hollies.

"It worn't 'is bowling wot frit me," Hollies said later in the dressing room. "It were 'is language. It were fearful. It's all over now, but I shor forget this day if I live to be thousands. I cor repeat wor 'e said. 'E come out wi' words I'd never 'eard at Old 'Ill."

Sellers tried in vain to pacify Macaulay and defuse the row, a task not made easier by his inability to understand a word Hollies was saying. Then, in the heat of it all, with eight runs wanted, Mayer lashed out at Macaulay's next two balls. The first, off an inside edge, crossed the boundary at long leg; the second, off the middle, reached the long-on boundary.

Macaulay threw his cap on the ground and stamped on it, the angry crowd surged forward from the terraces, and amid the tumult Mayer grabbed Hollies' arm. "Come on, let's get out of here," he said. Halfway to the pavilion, they were met by Kilner and Santall, waving bats to clear a path to safety.

Warwickshire had beaten Yorkshire, and the victory lifted them to fourth in the end-of-season table, with Yorkshire down in fifth. Between their championships of 1911 and 1951, only that once did Warwickshire finish above Yorkshire.

SURREY – CHAMPIONS IN 1971

This appeared in a series in the Wisden Cricketer in which different writers looked back at winning teams in the county championship.

The 1960s were not kind to Surrey. The county had become accustomed to success in the previous decade, flying the championship pennant for seven successive summers, but their great team had grown old together, the Oval square had become lifelessly low and slow, and the ground, with its air of shabby decay, no longer attracted the changing local population. Attendances in 1970 were less than one-fifth of what they had been in 1955, creating a financial crisis so dire that a *Cricketer* article in spring 1971 speculated on closure – or 'the even worse fate of amalgamation with Middlesex'.

No one felt the decline more keenly than Micky Stewart, the only one of the 1971 side who had played in the years of glory. "Never be an also ran," his bookmaker father had drummed into him. "Whatever you do, make sure you're number one." As a young man back in the 1950s it was easy to put those words into practice. He fielded close to the wicket as Laker, Lock and the Bedsers held mastery, and in one summer he took 77 catches. Never did that Surrey side take the field expecting anything other than victory.

How long ago that all seemed in August 1971. Stewart was approaching 39 years old, coming to the end of the last summer of his nine-year reign as captain, and a bright start, a Junetime lead in the championship, had been followed by seven weeks without a win. So often tipped for honours, they languished in seventh place, and once more the members were grumbling. Seventh place might be acceptable at Chelmsford or Hove, even at Lord's, but not at The Oval, not after what they had known.

John Edrich, the ever-dependable opener, was in top form for Surrey that summer. The young Graham Roope was stylishly reaching new heights, and the enterprising Younis Ahmed so often came good when it mattered. With Stewart himself and the all-rounder Stewart Storey, runs were rarely a problem.

The bowling attack was led by Geoff Arnold. Swinging the ball at pace and with control, he was at his peak, topping the national averages – though only 19 of his 75 championship wickets came on the dead Oval square. At the other end Robin Jackman bowled his heart out, and for extra pace and bounce there was the young Bob Willis, back from an Ashes tour of Australia. "He was very inconsistent," Stewart says, "and at times he lacked confidence. But on his day he could frighten the life out of batsmen."

At the start of the summer the slow bowling was done by off-spinner Pat Pocock, deprived of his England place by Illingworth's return as captain, and left-armer Chris Waller. Then, when the Pakistani tour ended in July, Waller gave way to the ever-popular leg-spinner Intikhab Alam. "It was hard on Chris," Stewart says. "He'd bowled really well, but he didn't have the experience or quite the aggression that Inti had. If we were going to have a chance, we had to attack." With Roope and Storey at slip, Stewart and Mike Edwards at short leg and Arnold Long behind the stumps, they did not lack for safe hands around the wicket.

With such talent, even with the dead Oval pitches, it was a mystery that they were as low as seventh in the table. Yet all was not lost. The previous summer Kent had won after starting July in bottom place, and Stewart, a man who enjoyed working these things out, had not given up hope. "We've got seven games left," Pocock remembers him telling them. "If we can win five of them, I think we've got a chance."

Win they did. Five times in a row. At Lord's Pocock and Arnold bowled them to an unlikely victory. At Kettering, on a pitch made for seamers, Arnold, Jackman and Willis destroyed Northants, with Stewart battling it out for a crucial 81. "I remember Sarfraz whizzing a couple past my ear and following through. 'I want to see your blood, Micky,' he said." At Bristol Roope led the way with a century, and he followed it with a career-best 171 at The Oval against a demoralised, Boycott-led Yorkshire who collapsed twice against the spin of Pocock and Intikhab. The spinners were to the fore again against Derbyshire, winning with ten minutes to spare after Storey had rescued a crumbling innings with 164, another career-best. Each of them was playing his part.

Warwickshire, top of the table, had completed their programme. So the maths was now simple. Surrey had two games, and they needed 14 points. Suddenly the title was theirs to lose. And lose it, they nearly did.

Victory at The Oval in front of their own supporters would have been the ideal finish, but the pitch was once again slow, the crowd was thin and Glamorgan, with nine wickets down, held out for the draw. It was now deep into September, and they drove down to Southampton in search of six points.

A heavy shower brought a late start, but by afternoon the sun was shining on them. They were 190 for one, then 240 for three, 60 runs from glory. But they collapsed to 269 all out, and that left them needing to take four Hampshire wickets on the Monday. Would the weather hold? Was there any truth in the rumour that Hampshire were planning to declare before the vital wicket fell? Four and a half months of cricket had come down to such twists of fate.

Monday brought sunshine. A large crowd arrived on trains from Waterloo and in cars that filled the local streets, and they were soon cheering as Arnold and Willis sent back Barry Richards and Gordon Greenidge. In the hardest of decisions Stewart had left out the wholehearted Jackman in favour of Willis, and shortly before lunch the youngster rewarded his captain's faith by yorking the diminutive left-hander David Turner.

Then at ten to three Intikhab found the edge of Richard Gilliat's bat, Arnold Long held the catch and the celebrations began. On came Stuart Surridge, Chairman of Cricket, with a bottle of champagne. On came a beaming Jackman with a tray of glasses. And on came Sheila Stewart to give her husband a kiss – much to the disgust of EW Swanton in the *Daily Telegraph*. "Get on with it," the Hampshire members shouted.

Champagne celebrations at Southampton

When Hampshire finally declared, still only four wickets down, Surridge ushered Stewart to the far end to a round of television interviews. "I should have been stronger and said no," he says now. "We were halfway through the game, and I was supposed to be opening the batting. John Edrich was livid."

They sank ineptly to a six-wicket defeat, finishing the season level on points with Warwickshire and winning only on 'more matches won'. It rankled with the ever-competitive Stewart but, at least, in his last summer he had taken the county back to where it had been at the start of his 19-year career. As his father would have said, he had made sure that they were once more number one.

For all the narrowness of the victory Alan Gibson in *The Times* wrote that Surrey were 'the most convincing champions for several years'. There was even talk of a new era to rival the 1950s.

It was not to be. With three one-day tournaments and an influx of overseas players, the age of big-county domination was over. In the nine years from 1968 nine different counties won the championship.

In the autumn Surridge persuaded a reluctant Stewart to return for one more summer, and his fairy-tale ending was ruined. Willis left for Warwickshire, Arnold was plagued by injury, and all the batsmen scored fewer runs. The champions slumped to twelfth place.

Not till 1999 would they again be number one.

QUIRKY MOMENTS IN THE HISTORY
OF THE COUNTY CHAMPIONSHIP

Lancashire 1895
A new pavilion opens at Old Trafford, a job that has run into several problems, not least the objection of the ground manager Fred Reynolds to the demolition of his house. He resolutely refuses to leave till one day he comes back to find the workmen all drunk; in the process of stripping the roof, they have discovered his supply of whisky.

Essex 1895
On a 'fiery' pitch at Leyton, in front of a 7,000-strong Bank Holiday crowd, fast bowler Henry Pickett – with his philosophy of 'keep as good a length as possible and hope for the best' – takes all ten Leicestershire wickets for 32 runs. It is the first instance of an 'all ten' in the championship. Essex lose, however, giving Pickett a first-class record that he still holds: best bowling figures in a defeat.

Sussex 1896
Against the year's champions Yorkshire at Hove KS Ranjitsinhji, starting the final morning on 0*, hits a dazzling 100. It is not enough to save the follow-on, however, and in the afternoon he hits 125*, becoming the only batsman ever to hit two first-class centuries inside a day. If his story is to be believed, it is not his most prolific 24 hours, for at Cambridge, spreading his favours between three different games, he claims to have hit three hundreds in one day.

Worcestershire 1900
'Our Ladies' Enclosure,' Philip Foley, the Secretary, writes to the Dean, 'is becoming quite the Hyde Park of Worcester and tea there with the cathedral in front and the match in progress is "quite the thing".'

Essex 1904
At Chesterfield 'Peter' Perrin hits 343, the highest score in Essex history. Unfortunately, like Pickett in 1895, he too finishes on the losing side and holds a first-class record: highest score in a defeat.

Hampshire 1909
At The Oval, in CB Fry's first match as a Hampshire player, the county loses to Surrey by an innings and 468 runs, the largest margin of defeat ever in a championship match.

Leicestershire 1919
Leicestershire arrive at Huddersfield with eleven men, one of whom Aubrey Sharp has damaged a finger the previous day at Old Trafford. They wire for a replacement, taking the field with the Yorkshire twelfth man 'Billy' Williams who is put in the slips where he holds four catches before the eleventh man arrives. He also fields as substitute for a while in the Yorkshire second innings, catching his captain Geoffrey Wilson for the second time in the match.

Derbyshire 1920
With key men absenting themselves to play league cricket instead, Derbyshire have the worst season by a county in championship history, losing 17 of their 18 matches, the 18th being abandoned without a ball bowled.

Northamptonshire 1921
Against Essex at Northampton local schoolboy Wilfrid Timms hits a six-hour 154. He misses the next match to sit his Cambridge entrance examination, but in August at Dover, as the senior of two amateurs playing, he finds himself captaining the side. At 18 years 326 days he is thought to be the youngest captain in championship history.

Worcestershire 1925
Worcestershire give a first and only game to the Reverend Reginald Moss, who at the age of 57 years and three months is the oldest man ever to appear in the county championship. He scores 2 and 0 but, given three overs on the final day, he dismisses Gloucestershire's Michael Green, caught at slip for 54. Ninety years on, among 358 men who have bowled for Worcestershire, his average of five runs per wicket remains at the head of the list.

Gloucestershire 1927
The championship's leading run-scorer (Wally Hammond), wicket-taker (Charlie Parker), fielder (Hammond) and keeper (Harry Smith) are all from Gloucestershire, the only year in which players from the same county have topped all four lists. In the championship Gloucestershire finish twelfth.

Somerset 1928
Somerset give a trial to the 16-year-old Wyndham Thomas, but the match at Chesterfield is ruined by rain, he does not bat or bowl and he never gets a second call. It is a fate also suffered by Arthur Ricketts who in 1936, despite opening the batting for the Men O'Mendip, has still not gone in when, with Somerset on 38 for eight, the game is abandoned. Up to the end of 2014, Somerset have been represented in the championship by 558 men, the most of any county, of whom 76 have played only once, also the most.

Middlesex 1933

Playing against Somerset at Lord's, Jack Lee is caught at mid-on by his brother Frank off the bowling of his other brother Harry. Two years later Jack is a first-class umpire, giving both his brothers out lbw during the summer.

Leicestershire 1947

Against Glamorgan at Cardiff Leicestershire give a first game to the Leicester City footballer Jack Lee. Opening the bowling he takes a wicket with his first ball, one of only two Leicestershire bowlers to achieve this. The other, Eric Tilley in 1946, plays four games for the county, but Lee has only this one game, in which he bowls just four overs. In 1950 he scores a goal on debut for the England football team but, as with the cricket, he never gets a second call-up.

Hampshire 1948

In pre-season nets, worried by the lack of young fast bowlers, the Hampshire chairman instructs the entire playing staff to bowl as fast as they can. The find of the session is Derek Shackleton, a young recruit from Yorkshire, who has been signed as a batsman who bowls occasional leg-breaks. Promptly turned into a medium-pace bowler, he takes 100 wickets a season each year from 1949 to 1968 – a record 18 times in championship matches alone.

Sussex 1955

Against Somerset at Hove, in the last match of a Sussex career that stretches back to 1928, the 45-year-old John Langridge holds five catches at slip, setting an unsurpassed championship record of 66 in a season. In Langridge's first match in 1928, Jim Parks senior hit 148*; now in his last Jim Parks junior hits a career-best 205*.

Glamorgan 1955

In the last match of the season, against Warwickshire at Neath, the Glamorgan eleven – Wooller, Parkhouse, Pressdee, Jones (WE), Hedges, Watkins, Pleass, Lewis (AR), Ward, Davies (HG), Shepherd – are all Welsh-born, the last occasion on which this has occurred.

Sussex 1968

Persuaded out of retirement by the England selectors, Ted Dexter arrives at Hastings in late July for his first championship game for more than two years. On the first morning, going out to bat against a strong Kent attack at 6 for two, soon to be 27 for four, he passes his previous highest Sussex score of 167. Hitting 6,4,6,4,3 off successive balls, he completes his double century before holing out in the covers for 203. He was playing better, he said, than when he played regularly; at that time, when he was in form, he would become careless; when out of form, consumed by doubt and theory.

Middlesex 1981
Against Essex at Lord's Middlesex become the first county in championship history to field an eleven all of whom have played Test cricket: Brearley, Downton, Radley, Gatting, Butcher, Barlow, Emburey, Edmonds, Selvey, Thomson, Daniel. Their pedigree does them little good as only a ninth wicket stand of 70 by Thomson and Selvey gets their total to 153, and in the field Edmonds bowls a nightmare spell, losing all control of line and length.

Leicestershire 1986
In the midst of an injury crisis Ken Higgs, the county's 49-year-old coach, makes up numbers against Yorkshire at Grace Road. It is his first game for four years but, with an enthusiasm reinforced – in his own words – by 2,000 wickets a year in the nets, he lopes in off six paces and takes five wickets for 22 runs, none of his five victims having been born when he first played for Lancashire in 1958.

Hampshire 1989
South African-born Robin Smith becomes the first Hampshire player to represent England in a Test against Australia since 1921. During this time, in 159 Tests against Australia, Yorkshire have provided 26 England players, Middlesex 25.

Warwickshire 2004
Warwickshire's sixth championship title is the most extraordinary in the history of the competitition. With the bowlers taking wickets at over 40 runs each, the worst of the 18 counties, they win only five of their 16 matches, but they remain undefeated and their large total of batting points sees them home by a comfortable margin.

Nottinghamshire 2010
At the close of the second day at Chester-le-Street nightwatchman Nottinghamshire's Ryan Sidebottom is 5 not out. Called away by England, he is replaced at the wicket next morning by substitute Darren Pattinson. This demotes Luke Fletcher to number 12 in the batting order, from which position he scores 23*. In so doing, he adds his name to an illustrious list on the *Wisden* website: Highest Score at Each Batting Position in County Championship Matches.

THE WAY IT WAS

These ten pieces were written for my series The Way It Was in the Wisden Cricketer. The majority appeared in the paperback edition of the book of that name.

THE SAVING OF WISDEN

Ken Medlock

March 2009

It was the autumn of 1960. At the Co-operative Wholesale Society headquarters in Balloon Street, Manchester. A meeting of the Non-Food Sub-Committee. With Ken Medlock, newly elected board member, attending for the first time.

He had been the Society's Chief Engineer, pioneering refrigerated meat counters, but he had given that up, taking a pay cut, so that he could tackle as a director the in-built inefficiency of the Society's wholesale-retail structure. His election, however, was to fill a gap left by death, and he found himself not on the Finance and General Services Committee but on Non-Food, dealing with footwear, textiles and funeral parlours.

"The first thing you were told to do when you joined the Board was to enlarge your letter box, because the minutes of the main board would run to 150 or 200 pages."

There, in his first batch of papers, some way down the agenda of the Non-Food Committee, was a recommendation to liquidate one of the subsidiary companies, one the Co-op had owned for 16 years, *John Wisden & Company Limited*. He was a keen club cricketer, and it caught his eye.

"I can still remember my words at the meeting," he says, almost fifty years on. "'You must be out of your tiny minds. You're liquidating the best known name in the game of cricket!'" No one else around the table had any idea; for them, it was just a company losing money. If his predecessor had been alive, *John Wisden* would have been shut down then and there. "I don't know why it's losing money," the new board member continued. "I want to know much more about this."

So the meeting withdrew the proposal and appointed him Chairman. The fate of *Wisden* now lay in the hands of the 46-year-old captain of Birch Vale Cricket Club in the Derbyshire and Cheshire League.

"Chance is a great thing in this world," he reflects. "I've gone through my life, and I've been lucky. Chances have come my way."

His first visit to cricket had been to the Headingley Test of 1921 where, sitting on the grass, he had watched the elegant Charles Macartney hit a century. Then in the summer of 1924, when Birch Vale's calico printing factory was down to a three-day week and the men spent their spare days practising on the cricket field, he was among the army of young boys retrieving the balls and hoping for a chance to bat. "At the end of the day they'd let us have a go. They'd put a penny on each of the three pegs. If you could bat for so long, keep the pennies intact, they were yours. I was so determined, I had bruises all over, but I made sure I kept the pennies."

On the rough pitch, he learned from Tom Holt, 'The Stonewaller', to get on the front foot and in time he progressed to the first team. All boundaries were scored as four in the league, and he is proud that his 118 against Hazel Grove in 1941 is the club record for that pre-six era.

He had a spell in the North-East, playing for a while at Burnopfield where the captain Joe Milburn – "a miner with shoulders like an ox" – brought his little boy Colin with him. Then back at Birch Vale, with its old wooden pavilion, its nissen hut for teas and its magnificent view across to Kinder Scout, he captained the club to its first ever championship in 1958. Despite his demanding job as the Co-op's Chief Engineer, he never missed a game – nor, if he could help it, did his team. On one occasion two of them were on holiday in Barmouth with their families, and he set off at 6 a.m. in his Jaguar, driving a round trip of 300 miles on pre-motorway roads to bring them back.

John Wisden was in the hands of a true cricket lover.

He visited Penshurst in Kent where the company manufactured not just cricket bats and balls but tennis racquets and balls, hockey and lacrosse sticks, table tennis sets and bowls. "They were trying to be all things to all people, and they were trying to sell everything through Co-op departmental stores. People don't go into departmental stores to buy cricket bats."

Dukes cricket balls were hand-stitched in a barn. With the Australian Kookaburra eroding sales, the unions were preventing the recruitment of new craftsmen. "I asked the managing director what the average age of the ball-makers was, and he said 73."

The new chairman set to work. He replaced the managing director, he closed down several production lines, and he set up a joint ball-making venture with Surridges, Gray Nicholls and Ives. All four companies' balls were made at the factory – though "everybody insisted on having their own names printed on them. At Test matches they used to bring out a box of balls with all the different makes, and people would talk about the differences. But it was only the name on them that was different."

These were the years before every club player carried his own bat, before every match had a new ball. "In the Derbyshire and Cheshire League a ball might last three matches, then we'd pass it on to the second team. At one point a firm brought out a kit for reconditioning balls. One club, Chapel-en-le-Frith, only reconditioned one side; it created so much swing that the league outlawed it."

The *Wisden* bats had been promoted by Denis Compton, but they had not met his request for a pay rise and for years the bats had carried no name. They traded with Herbert Sutcliffe's sports shops, and he suggested two young Yorkshire batsmen, John Hampshire and Geoffrey Boycott. "Well, we couldn't afford two so we chose John Hampshire. How shall I put it? On temperament."

A new world had opened up for Ken Medlock. He struck up a friendship with Learie Constantine, who suggested that, for the centenary of the *Wisden Almanack* in 1963, the company should donate a Wisden Trophy, on the same lines as the Ashes, for England-West Indies Tests. There were no sponsors or perimeter advertising yet in cricket, and MCC turned down the proposal. But, after the West Indies Board intervened, they relented – and at The Oval in August Lord Nugent, MCC President, presented the trophy to Frank Worrell. "We were going to make the presentation on the ground but, when the winning run was scored, all the West Indian spectators rushed on, somebody stole Conrad Hunte's bat, and we finished up in the West Indies dressing room."

Ken Medlock had 19 miniatures of the trophy to hand out but, in the mêlée, "I took 24 in with me, and there were none left when I finished."

By 1969 *Wisden* was economically sound, and the decision was taken to sell it. But there was another twist to the tale when Ken Medlock oversaw the clearance of the factory. Boxes of old bats, from the long-closed *Wisden* shop in London, had been lying in storage and were waiting to be burnt: curved bats from the mid-18th century, the first bat to have a splice, bats that had belonged to Grace and Ranji, Trumper and Jessop, bats signed by touring teams before the First World War.

"Nobody thought they were an asset. In those days cricket memorabilia wasn't a popular interest. But I couldn't see the purpose in destroying them. I had the feeling that posterity would appreciate them; they were the history of cricket bat making."

"Right, you can have them," he was told.

Just as he had become the accidental saviour of *Wisden*, so he now became the owner of cricket's greatest bat collection. Some he has put into the museum at Old Trafford, others have been displayed at Lord's, and he flew to Australia three years ago to donate the Trumper bat to the Bradman Museum. He was 91 years old, carrying a century-old bat, but the security staff at Christchurch Airport said it was an offensive weapon and refused to let him carry it on board. After much negotiation, it finished up in the captain's cabin.

He has had an extraordinary life, and he has just as many stories when he talks about the Co-op – "The only problem with the Co-operative movement is that they couldn't co-operate with each other" – about the charity Life Education Centres and about Radio City, the Liverpool-based commercial station he helped to found, how the decision to have a newsman on duty all night led to their breaking the news that John Lennon had been shot.

"There is so much chance in life," he says. "I left grammar school at 14 so that I could take up an apprenticeship in engineering. My father was a great believer in the Co-operative movement. He brought me up to believe that to help people was the natural thing to do. And all this has happened to me. It's been a wonderful life."

In late February, aged 94, he will be driving the 130-mile round trip from the Wirral to chair the annual dinner of Birch Vale Cricket Club where he will be starting his 55th year as President. The boy who batted valiantly to win those three penny coins in 1924. The engineer who saved *Wisden*.

Lord Nugent presents the Wisden Trophy to Frank Worrell
Ken Medlock is second left, behind Lord Nugent

119

WHO ON EARTH IS THIS BOY?

Neville Wigram

JULY 2009

Not for 75 years have England beaten Australia at Lord's. Not since that Monday in June 1934 when Yorkshire's Hedley Verity, exploiting a damp pitch, took 14 wickets in the day. A world ago it seems now – the newspapers full of alarm about events in Hitler's Germany, play at Lord's suspended in mid-morning so the teams could be presented to King George the Fifth.

It was the first Australian tour after the Bodyline crisis, and they lost only that one match in their five-month stay. Bradman was in his prime, 'Tiger' O'Reilly the leg-spinner was at his fiery best, and they won back the Ashes in style at The Oval. Only three men survive who played against the Australians that summer: Neil McCorkell of Hampshire, Hugh Dinwiddy of Cambridge University and Neville, now Lord, Wigram, who played for the North of Scotland in a two-day match at Forres on the Moray Firth coast.

The Forres match was the last of the tour. The Australians had arrived by boat on 25 April at Southampton, and by 11 September at Scarborough they had completed a schedule of 100 days' cricket in 19 weeks. Yet, before they sailed for home, they travelled by train to Forres and back to London, almost 1,000 miles, to play a two-day game against the North of Scotland.

Bradman was at his best at Scarborough, hitting a strong bowling attack – including Verity – for 132 in 90 minutes, an innings he later called 'one of the two most exciting I ever played in England'. So, when he led out his side in warm sunshine at Grant Park, Forres, the 6,000 Scottish spectators were alive with anticipation.

The game, indeed the ground with its magnificent pavilion, was financed by Sir Alexander Grant, a local boy who had started life in a bakery, invented the digestive biscuit for McVities and rose to be company chairman. With his childhood friend Ramsay MacDonald as Prime Minister, they were years of influence for the North of Scotland.

The side chosen to play the Australians consisted of local club cricketers – with two exceptions. One was Ian Peebles, the Aberdeen-born leg-spinner who had played for Middlesex and England and whose father was now minister in the nearby parish of Birnie. The other was the 19-year-old Neville Wigram, described in one local paper as 'a dark horse'.

"My father was Private Secretary to King George the Fifth," he explains. "We spent our summer holidays in a house on the Balmoral estate, and we were always invited by Sir Alexander to stay with him near Forres. That year we went across for grouse shooting soon after the 12th of August, and he told me about the Australian match and that he wanted me to play. I tried to say no, but he persisted. I was most embarrassed, worried what the team would think of an outsider like me."

He had just left Winchester College where, suffering from poor eyesight and sinus problems, he had only made the second eleven: "I was never very good, but I loved the game." By contrast, his father Clive owed his position in the Royal Household to his cricketing ability. Captain of cricket at Winchester, he had chosen a military career and been posted to India where, a Bengal Lancer, he dominated the English cricket scene. 'Of Wigram,' one paper reported, 'it has frequently been said by good judges of the game that he is unquestionably one of the finest all-round players we have ever had in India.'

"I'm sure he could have played county cricket," his son says. "The Viceroy at the time was Lord Elgin, and he liked his vice-regal staff to field a good cricket team. 'Young Wigram would be a good ADC for me,' he said."

Lord Curzon succeeded Elgin and, when the Prince of Wales, the future George the Fifth, made a state visit in 1905, Wigram was attached to the Prince – "and the two of them got on very well together." So much so that in 1910, when the Prince became King, the career soldier became his Assistant Private Secretary. "If I hadn't been a good cricketer," he always said, "I would never have got the job with the Viceroy."

The King liked horses and shooting, but his new Secretary exerted the influence of his own sporting interests. "My father was a great believer that the King should show himself to the public at as many sporting events as possible. The Cup Final, Lord's, Wimbledon. He even took him to watch greyhound racing."

In 1912 Clive Wigram married the daughter of the colonel who in an officers' mess in Jabalpur had invented the game of snooker, the name itself deriving from army slang for an incompetent – "They'd say, 'He's a real snooker' if he potted the wrong ball" – and in August 1915 the young Neville was born. It was a privileged birth: the King was his godfather and, in September, a month before the death of WG Grace, he was put down for membership of the MCC. He still retains a copy of the application. No wonder he was anxious what the club cricketers of Northern Scotland would think of him.

"Who on earth is this boy Wigram?" he recalls the crowd asking as he stepped out to bat on that warm Friday morning. The pitch had been over-watered, the Australian spinners had created havoc, and the scoreboard showed 44 for nine. But, according to one report, 'Wigram seemed less

The two teams
Neville Wigram: second left, back row   Ian Peebles: second left, middle row
Don Bradman: fourth left, sitting   Sir Alexander Grant: sixth left, sitting

nervous than the others and hit his first ball with gusto for a four.' Two balls later, he was bowled.

"Wait till Peebles gets you on that wicket," a spectator called out to the fielders as they came off. "It's a pity we can't bowl him at both ends."

In the summer of 1927, at the age of 19, Ian Peebles had gone down to London, plying his well-spun leg breaks and googlies for Chiswick Park and in Aubrey Faulkner's cricket school in Richmond. His first-class debut was for the Gentlemen against the Players, three festival matches followed, and in December he was bowling in the First Test in Johannesburg. In Bradman's great summer of 1930 he came into the England team for the Fourth Test at Old Trafford and, in the words of Wally Hammond, 'completely foozled Bradman with his first ball and so shook his nerve that he gave two chances before being out at 14.'

'I may as well admit,' Bradman wrote, 'that for the first time in my life I was unable to detect a bowler's leg break from his bosey.'

That was 1930, however. By 1934 Peebles' shoulder had become a problem, he was struggling with his leg break, and his two encounters with the Australians in May left him with figures of two for 224. He returned to Scotland, to the cricket of the country houses, and was astonished to discover himself selected for the all-important final Test at The Oval. 'The choice of Peebles in the circumstances is not surprising,' *The Times* declared, 'it is positively bewildering.'

Other newspapers were less complimentary.

'Many thanks,' he telegrammed the chairman of selectors. 'Will be there if not lynched en route.' The next day he chipped a finger bone so, when Bradman and Ponsford put on 451 at The Oval, he was watching from the balcony.

At Forres he bowled unchanged in the Australian innings, taking five wickets for 84 runs, but in circumstances far removed from Test cricket. Over lunch the visitors had each put five pounds into a six-hitting sweepstake and in a comical display of hitting O'Reilly, tailender-turned-opener, scooped the prize with four sixes. It was not quite what the crowd wanted to see and, when Bradman was caught at square leg for seven, there was a groan around the ground. Nevertheless, after the final wicket had fallen at 166, the local paper was proud to point out that only once on the tour – against Verity at Lord's – had Australia been dismissed for a lower total.

In the Scottish second innings Neville Wigram was promoted to number ten, going in at 69 for eight. By this stage Arthur Chipperfield was bowling his leg-breaks. At Lord's he had dismissed Sutcliffe, Hammond and Wyatt, but now the bespectacled Wigram cracked him for 16 runs in an over. "I remember hitting a long hop to leg and a nice cover drive along the floor. Then he bowled a rather attractive half-volley just outside off stump, and I drove it for six over cover point."

N Wigram, not out 28. A lusty innings, *The Times* called it. 'SCHOOLBOY SCORES OFF THE AUSTRALIANS' was another headline. He had made the highest Scottish score of the game, but it was not enough to prevent an innings defeat.

An exhibition match was staged the next day, at the end of which the Australians returned to London where Bradman went down with appendicitis. For some days he was – in his own words – 'hovering on the brink of eternity'. For recuperation he returned to Scotland, the guest in Perth of the whisky distiller Arthur Bell.

Eighteen months earlier, during the Bodyline crisis, Sir Clive Wigram had opened the Australian telegrams to the King. Now he received a happier communication: 'Your boy batted splendidly in the second innings,' the tourists' manager wrote. 'He is a fine lad.' His son had played the last strokes of a summer of restored goodwill.

Seventy-five years on, in July, he will be at Lord's, hoping to see that long-awaited English victory.

A REVOLUTION GLIMPSED

Alan Rayment at Lord's

Aug 2009

The ball was a half-volley outside off stump. Alan Rayment can still see it, fifty years on. "I was coaching in the next net, and the boy picked it up and hit it in the sky high over long-on, and it crashed into the mower sheds. 'Gee,' I thought. 'That's a great shot.'"

It was August 1959. The mini car and the transistor radio were on show for the first time. "The revolution had already started," is how Rayment puts it. "There was the music of Elvis – rock'n'roll. Young people had a bit of money to spend on records and style of dress. And I was quite radical in my thinking. I wanted to change things."

He was at Lord's for the summer, one of four assistants to MCC Head Coach Bill Watkins. The boy hitting the ball was on the ground staff, spending part of each day being coached, part bowling in the nets to the members.

"The next thing I saw was Bill Watkins walking down to the boy, waving his finger and remonstrating: 'No, no, like this", then demonstrating how to push the ball down the line to mid-off. 'What the bloody hell are you doing?' I thought. I was so incensed."

Watkins had played a little for Middlesex in the 1930s: "He was a small cockney sparrow, married to Lord's. A real professional of the old school. A lovely man. In the army he wouldn't quite make sergeant-major."

Rayment was a grammar school boy from Finchley. He had just left Hampshire after ten years, where he had combined his cricket with a prosperous second life as a ballroom dancing instructor. But all that had ended when, faced with family problems, he had had "a spiritual awakening". After an unsuccessful winter selling Aga cookers, he was in London, staying with George Cansdale, superintendent of London Zoo, and enjoying "a renaissance of the mind", reading Carl Jung and Teilhard de Chardin and yearning to go to university. "I'm a double Gemini. I'm always wanting to do something more challenging."

That day in August he had had enough. Few of the boys had real talent; he had watched them in out-matches "playing pretty strokes, not scoring runs". Who had chosen them? Why did they have to bowl to the members? What good was it all doing them? Angered by Watkins' wagging finger, he called for pads and bat and marched into his net.

"The coaches didn't normally bat. So there was quite a stir. I danced up the wicket, and I drove every ball out of the net as far as I could. The short balls I flat-batted tennis-style over the bowlers' heads. 'Get some more balls,' I shouted. There were balls all over the Nursery Ground."

"What was all that about?" the boys asked afterwards.

"This game is not about impressing coaches," he replied. "It's about hitting the ball, scoring runs, winning matches."

At Lilleshall, on the Advanced Coaching Course, he had scored the highest mark ever in the theory exam. "From my dance teaching I already had that analytical mind about movement. But I was always aware of the danger that coaching can drown the natural inner talent. You have to look for what is natural in a person."

A few days later he was summoned to see Billy Griffith, MCC Assistant Secretary, and Harry Altham, Treasurer and guru of the MCC coaching scheme. "It was a bit like going to the headmaster's study. I was expecting to be sacked."

"Well, Alan," Altham began. "We understand that you've been having some thoughts about the coaching we give to the boys. We'd like you to tell us what you think about your experience here."

Rayment spoke his mind with clarity and with passion.

"We have been informed of all this," said Billy Griffith, "and we've discussed it in committee. It's been decided to offer you the post of Head Coach from next season."

The shock produced a long silence.

"It might have been 30 seconds; it might have been a minute and a half. I was thinking like mad. It was a wonderful offer. Lord's to me was the Theatre of Dreams. I'd seen Patsy Hendren's last hundred there in 1937. I'd played there at the end of the war for Sir Pelham Warner's Lord's XI. But I kept thinking, 'What will happen to Bill Watkins?' Lord's had been his life. Also I had no inner sense that I wanted to be a cricket coach; I wanted to go to theological college – or university."

So he left Lord's, and there was no revolution. Bill Watkins remained, loyal and cheerful, eventually passing the baton to his assistant Len Muncer.

Alan Rayment, meanwhile, continued his picaresque journey through life: in turn teacher, estate agent, community worker, postgraduate student, property developer and psychotherapist. At the age of 81 he is still full of life.

"Coaching is about enabling and encouragement, about fun and enthusiasm," he says. "You're not doing a PhD in Molecular Science. Cricket is a game. So, more importantly, is Life."

A HUGE DISAPPOINTMENT

David Allen at Old Trafford 1961

Sept 2009

It was approaching noon on the final day. Australia were nine wickets down, only 192 runs in front, and David Allen, the Gloucestershire off-spinner, was preparing to bowl his tenth over of the morning. Forty-eight years have passed, and he still wonders if he did the right thing.

"Decisions were made," he says, "and I do question them in hindsight. But that's being clever. At the time I didn't question them."

The Australians were back at Old Trafford, where five years earlier Jim Laker had tormented them on a broken pitch, taking 19 wickets for 90 runs. "There was definitely a legacy from that game," David Allen says. "The Australians didn't enjoy playing off-breaks on a turning wicket."

Now Allen himself carried the legacy on his shoulder. The pitch had not broken up as it had in 1956, but there was rough at the Stretford end where Fred Trueman had been bowling and, coming round the wicket to the left-handed Alan Davidson, Allen was posing plenty of problems.

The Australians had battled through the previous day. With three slip catches going down, they had taken their score to 331 for six, a lead of 154. But in the opening minutes of the final day Allen had taken three wickets for no runs: the left-handed Mackay poking a turning ball into the hands of Brian Close at second slip, Richie Benaud playing back and departing, lbw, and Wally Grout caught at mid-off, trying to counter-attack.

"When he did that, I thought, 'Our luck's in. We're going to win this.' Then, of course, came the hour of the match."

Only the Australian number eleven, the 20-year-old Garth McKenzie, stood between England and a probable 2-1 lead in the series. "Just play straight down the line," the experienced non-striker Alan Davidson instructed. "We'll see what we can do." But, with Davidson manipulating the strike, Allen hardly got to bowl a ball at the youngster.

"If only Tony Lock had been playing. He was a super bloke to bowl with. If he ever had the good batsman down his end for the fifth and sixth balls, he'd make sure you'd have the tail-ender next over."

Brian Statham bowled five overs from the Warwick Road end, then came the first of the decisions that went wrong.

"Fred Trueman decided to have his say. 'Why don't you try Closey?' he said to Peter May. 'He's got a knack of getting wickets when you want them.'"

Close's two overs of off-breaks included five full tosses, and the score rose by 15. "That released it a bit," Allen says. Then Ted Dexter had a go. Still David Allen was bowling at Davidson.

His nine overs had conceded two runs, giving him figures of 37 overs, four wickets for 38.

"Peter May came up to me. 'Let's encourage him to play a shot or two at your end,' he said. He was the captain, I admired him a lot. And I was still young. I said, 'Yes, right.' Perhaps Davidson was already thinking, 'This over's got to go.' Unfortunately the two went together. And he played beautifully."

No longer bowling a tight line, Allen varied the deliveries, and the ball flew four times in the arc between extra cover and mid-off, twice for four and twice for six, the last one landing near the top of the terraced crowd. 'They were not wild, slogger's swings,' John Arlott wrote, 'but superbly made, measured strokes of immense power and perfect timing.'

"Thank you, David, that will do," May said, and he asked Trueman to bowl instead.

"I walked away, and I thought, 'A pity, that,' as you do. In hindsight I think we got it wrong. If he was going to go after the ball, let him do it when you're bowling tightly.'

'Such is the lot of the spin bowler!' Jim Laker wrote acerbically. 'I might be a little biased, but I felt certain Allen should have been allowed at least another over.'

The runs continued to flow. Trueman was not at his best, certainly not living up to his contribution at the pre-match team talk in the hotel: "He went through the Australian team, how we would get them out, and 'George' Statham sat back. 'Fred's got all ten, lads. Let's go to the bar and have a drink.'"

By the time Jack Flavell, the third seamer, bowled McKenzie, Davidson was 77 not out, and a target that might have been 158 in five and a half hours had become 256 in less than four. Only once in England, in 1902, had England scored that many in a fourth innings to win.

Yet this was all forgotten by 3.55 when they were 150 for one and Dexter, at his imperious best, was 76 not out. "He played magnificently," David Allen says. "One of his great innings. He'd already taken Benaud apart at Edgbaston, and he was doing it again."

The Australian captain was at rock bottom: three runs in his last four innings in the series and two wickets for 295 runs in his last five bowls. As a final throw of the dice he had taken to bowling his leg-breaks from round the wicket.

Afterwards he explained that he had discussed the idea the previous night with Ray Lindwall, the former Australian fast bowler. It was not a common ploy at that time, but he had seen the opportunity presented by Trueman's rough.

"Richie was the greatest captain I played under," David Allen says, experiencing him some years later on a private tour of Pakistan. "He was such a great public relations man. He was a press man; he had a smell of that world, and he worked it out wonderfully well. He'd come straight off the field, and he'd be talking to the press in the corridor outside the dressing room. Why he'd bowled when he did, why he went round the wicket. And I'm not sure. I'm really not sure. I personally believed at the time that it was a desperate, negative move. He'd tried everything else, and he was being hammered around. But he said it was his last attacking move. He was a great captain. Sobers was the greatest all-rounder, Benaud the greatest captain."

Yet how would history have judged Benaud if he had failed? The South African writer, Charles Fortune, recalled his thoughts at the time: "Poor chap. He's been a fine cricketer and captain, but this time it's gone. No wickets, no runs. Sad this should happen when he's captain, but that's the way it goes."

Then Dexter, attempting a cut, edged the ball into Grout's gloves, and Peter May swept at his second ball and was bowled behind his legs. "Like all the university boys he didn't lap. Nobody had ever bowled like that at him. He didn't even get down on one knee."

Peter May is bowled behind his legs by Richie Benaud

Close took up the challenge, sweeping repeatedly and with little success, even after Benaud had put in a fielder behind square on leg. "At the start of the next over he took a pace down the wicket and hit him over long-off for six. I thought, 'Brian, what a beautiful shot. We're on our way again.' Then he had two or three more goes at the sweep shot, and hit it straight to the fielder."

It was, according to John Woodcock in *The Times*, 'an innings best talked about in whispers', but David Allen is kinder. "There was no plan. We all went out and played as individuals. And Brian was going to take Richie apart. Give him marks for trying, I suppose."

150 for one became 171 for seven, and Allen himself was at the crease. He was on a high with his batting – a maiden century in the previous county game and a vital 42 in the first innings. "We got so that we only needed 60-odd to win, and I still thought we could do it. I played one of my flowing cover drives, which I wasn't very good at, and got a thick nick between Grout and Simpson. Simpson was stood so wide, he was almost second slip, and it was past him when he dived to his left and caught it one-handed."

"He was the best slip fielder I ever saw," Benaud says, "and that catch, I reckon, was the perfect example of that."

A few minutes later it was all over. Australia had won by 54 runs, with Benaud taking six for 70.

"You can talk about Peter May's shot and Brian Close's innings," David Allen says, "and the bowling changes. I think what lost us the match was our catching. They caught magnificently, we caught badly."

Benaud held his improvised press conference, the Ashes retained, and David Allen – his moment of glory snatched from him – packed his bag and embarked on a five-hour train journey to Pontypridd. "A wonderful Test match," he says. "It swayed one way and then the other; that was the beauty of it. But it was a huge disappointment to lose. And I'll tell you what. Sat on that train, going down to Pontypridd on my own, it got worse."

ONE OF TWENTY-NINE

Malcolm Scott of Northamptonshire

MARCH 2010

It was two to a peg in the second team dressing room at Northampton in 1959. "Down in the hutch, under the stand," recalls Malcolm Scott, who had come down from County Durham, where he had played football in the Newcastle United first team. "Everything at Northampton was very run down. I'd been used to much better facilities at my club in South Shields."

They were hard years for county cricket. The post-war attendance boom was over; the television money had hardly begun. Northamptonshire was the Cinderella county, but they had an ambitious new Secretary, Ken Turner. As Assistant Secretary he had built up a thriving football pool, with 79,000 weekly subscribers. That year it was responsible for almost 60% of the club's income.

As Secretary he wanted to recruit a team for the future. In an unpublished memoir he recounts his thinking: 'I asked myself the questions: "Where do cricketers come from? And where do you start looking for them?"' He sat with his *Wisdens*, checking the origin of every cricketer to tour with England since 1900. He was startled by the answer he found: 'Something like 50 per cent were originally from the Minor Counties.'

So there, in the cramped dressing room, where – according to Malcolm Scott – "only the pushy ones got a peg of their own", they came from far and wide: Durham and Staffordshire, Shropshire, Suffolk and Bedfordshire. "There were so many dialects in there. It was like National Service. When Ivan Bell arrived, a broad Northumbrian, I had to translate what he was saying."

It was the largest playing staff in the country, 29 of them in 1959. In the new second eleven championship they undertook 20 fixtures, twice as many as some of the counties. "You could get a fifty and find you weren't playing in the next game. They wanted to look at somebody else." Scott was one of five slow left-arm bowlers.

Colin Milburn arrived the next summer. "He nearly went to Warwickshire, but I think with me and Gus Williamson he felt at home with the Geordie humour in our dressing room."

There was big David Larter from Suffolk, little Brian Crump from Staffordshire – and later Crump's cousin David Steele. They won the second eleven trophy in 1960, then in 1965 they came agonisingly close to winning the championship itself. Their captain was the Lancastrian keeper Keith Andrew, who ran a happy team and whose air of absent-mindedness concealed a shrewd brain: "He reminded me of Stan Laurel sometimes."

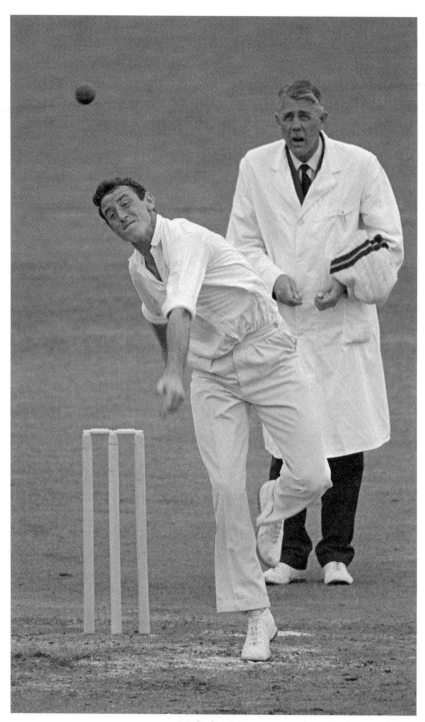

Malcolm Scott

At the end of that summer, the greatest in the county's history, the eleven contained only one player – Brian Reynolds – from Northamptonshire and eight from the minor counties.

'In due course,' Turner wrote, 'our methods were copied by other clubs, which led to greater competition.' His response was to scout among the under-15s, and next to arrive in Northampton were Durham's Peter Willey, making his first-class debut at 16, Wayne Larkins from Bedfordshire and Geoff Cook from Middlesbrough.

During Ken Turner's reign nine Northamptonshire cricketers made England debuts, a figure bettered during those years by only Yorkshire, Middlesex and Lancashire.

Scott from South Shields joined the staff in 1959, after completing his National Service. "I was offered a contract back in 1955, when I was only 19. I remember Ken Turner saying to me, 'You've got to get into this game when you're young, get used to playing in front of the crowds.' But I had an apprenticeship in the shipyard, and my father had come up through the '20s and '30s. He knew what unemployment was like."

Scott learnt about the crowds at St James' Park, playing for a Newcastle side on the way down after the glory years of Jackie Milburn. "Show us a wee bit of your magic, Scotty," someone called out from the crowd. Then came another voice: "Yes, make yourself f***ing disappear."

It was never that cruel at the County Ground, Northampton, not even when you fielded in the rough at the football ground end – or were trying to fill the gap that had been left by the great Australian slow left-armer George Tribe. "He was just mesmerising. I saw him and I thought, 'Follow that!'"

Scott was never in Tribe's class, but in 1964 he took 113 wickets and the following year he was a key member of that unfancied team who finished as runners-up. He still possesses his reward: a little Parker pen, inscribed 'M SCOTT 1965'. "I don't think it was even from the county. It was from the Wellingborough Supporters' Club." Ken Turner might have wanted a staff of 29, but he certainly did not believe in spending unnecessary money on them.

Scott's star gradually fell, leaving him with thoughts of what might have been: "I do look back and wonder whether I should have taken Ken Turner's advice. There's not a shipyard working on the Tyne now."

But the regrets are fleeting. He played county cricket and first-division football, and there are not many now who can say that. Later he did hard, patient work with maladjusted children, and he has just written a charming memoir of his life. "I don't know who'll be interested," he says with typical modesty. "But I was in the bookshop and I saw Victoria Beckham, *My Autobiography*. And I thought, 'Bollocks. If she can write one …'"

SIXES INTO THE ALLOTMENTS

Blackwell Colliery Ground

Aug 2010

They were an unlikely pair: Arnold Warren, the hard-drinking fast bowler from the Derbyshire mining village of Codnor, and Jack Chapman, his amateur captain, who learnt his cricket at Uppingham School and worked for a while in Russia. Yet their ninth wicket partnership one Tuesday in June 1910 set a new world record, and it is still standing 100 years on. It is the oldest batting record in first-class cricket.

The scene was the ground of the Blackwell Colliery, owned by the Derbyshire committee member John Todd. He was a hard, determined man, used to getting his own way, and the previous year he persuaded the county to add Blackwell to Derby, Chesterfield and Glossop on its fixture list. He sold tickets at the pit – a shilling for the three days – and he made it clear to off-duty pitmen that they were expected to support the venture.

The ground was laid in 1900, Cumberland turf on top of pit ash, and to this day it drains well. He employed a full-time groundsman who prepared pitches for cricket in summer, rugby union in winter. He introduced rugby to the area, hiring Welsh miners so that his Blackwell team could take on the likes of Wasps and Blackheath. He also built a rifle range in the corner.

Derbyshire were not a strong side in 1910. When they arrived at Blackwell in June, to play Warwickshire, they were bottom of the table without a win to their name; they had won only twice in 1909. Chapman was a somewhat reluctant captain, and his own form with the bat was poor. Twelve months earlier he had hit a thrilling 198 against Warwickshire at Coventry, but since then he had batted 39 times without another fifty and in the Derbyshire second innings at Blackwell he came in at number ten.

The game was all but lost. Midway through that Tuesday morning Derbyshire, following on 242 runs behind, sank to 131 for eight. With the train service from Blackwell patchy, the visitors were anxious to wrap up the victory and get back to Birmingham. But Warren and Chapman put bat to ball, and in 40 minutes before lunch they scored a carefree 73 runs.

The Derbyshire scorer, Will Taylor, later to be Secretary, recalled a lunchtime conversation with Frank Field, the Warwickshire bowler. "Well, Frank," he said, "you look like catching your train all right." "I don't know, Mr Taylor," Field replied. "These chaps are pretty good bats."

One hundred years on, the Derbyshire team are back at Blackwell, this time for a celebratory Twenty20 evening game against the village, organised by Bolsover District Council. The pit has long gone, the colliery office is a garage and the old Brigade Hall, where a doctor was on duty for pit accidents, is now the Cottage Inn. The cricket pavilion has been pulled down, and they change in the old rifle range. But the allotments, where Chapman drove a great six, are still there, and Loots Bosman is soon landing balls among the potatoes and runner beans.

On a bench the old boys reminisce with pride about the village in its mining days: the thousand men working there, the close-knit community, the thriving sport. "There were bloody good cricketers here. They bred them down the pit." "There wasn't a weed on the square. Men from the pit used to come out and dig them up with their pen knives." "Fatty Foulke, the great goalkeeper, came from Blackwell, you know. And Percy Toplis, the monocled mutineer." "We had the finest school choir in the country. The headmaster was the choirmaster; he was a real tyrant." "The club had two mowers stolen earlier this year. Things like that didn't use to happen. People used to leave their doors open all day." "Children weren't allowed in the ground. There was a terrace of miners' cottages over there, and I'd watch from my bedroom window." "When I was fifteen I used to bring my cricket bag to every game, hoping somebody wouldn't turn up. I wanted to play for Blackwell cricket club like boys today want to play for Manchester United." "We had two teams on a Saturday, one on a Sunday, we had nets three nights a week and a junior section. We did the league and cup double one year when we were in the Derbyshire Alliance."

Times have changed. There are no miners now: a draftsman, a window fabricator and some office workers. The captain, Robert Williams, is a contract supervisor for a drugs company. He also does the ground in his spare time, and they run one just one eleven, a Sunday side in the second tier of the Mansfield and District League. The plan is to raise money for a new youth section, and they start their centenary evening with a Kwik Cricket tournament between local primary schools.

"Building sporting communities in a post-pit era has its challenges," says Wayne Hatton, the council's Sports Development Officer. "We no longer have the option of press-ganging local miners, but hopefully events like this will create enthusiasm."

"The club was looking at finishing three or four years ago," opening bowler Peter Clements says. "Age is creeping up on some of us. But now we're determined to build it back up by bringing on some youngsters."

Young Stefan Lomas catches Tim Groenwald in the deep off his father Kevin's bowling, the batsman departing to the cacophonous blare of the Bay City Rollers: "Bye, bye, baby. Baby, bye, bye."

There are three schoolboys in the Blackwell side. One of them, Steven Bunning, has got a Biology 'A' level paper at nine o'clock in the morning, but he's not thinking about enzymes and molecules tonight.

Back in 1910 Warren was batting in much the same spirit as these Derbyshire Twenty20 men. He might have had a drink or two in the interval. They say he once downed several whiskies at Ashby-de-la-Zouch, then skittled out Leicestershire with a fiery spell. At his best he was a great fast bowler, taking five Australian wickets in the first innings of his only Test, but his waywardness meant that he was not always at his best.

In the game at Blackwell Warwickshire's Frank Foster, an amateur with an aggressive streak, took to bowling leg theory at him, at one point hitting him sharply on the back of his knee. Warren came down the pitch with his bat raised: "If you don't stop that," he said, "I'll knock your bloody head off." Or words to that effect.

After that Warren was limping, and it was left to Chapman, in his quieter, almost apologetic way, to play the shots. Together they took their partnership past the 111 they needed to avoid the innings defeat, past the English ninth wicket record of 193 and the world record of 232. At four o'clock they left the field for refreshments: the stand 238, the lead 127.

Warren had scored his first and only century and, if drink was a factor in his success, it was also – in the opinion of Foster – the reason for Warwickshire's increasingly ragged performance in the field. They had gone at it hard the night before, even the amateurs. "If we had gone to bed early," he wrote later, "the game would have been won."

The pair put on 283. Warren scored 123, Chapman 165, and there was too little time for the visitors to score the required runs. Warren had wanted to return leg-theory at the Warwickshire batsmen, but he was still hobbling and the game petered out uneventfully.

There is no such malice in the air as the Blackwell batsmen set about chasing 154 to win. The Derbyshire bowlers serve up friendly deliveries, and captain Robert Williams cracks 72 in 16 minutes, ending the match with two sixes into the allotments off Charl Langeveldt, a leading bowler in the recent Twenty20 World Cup. In all, the match has got through eight cricket balls.

The closing ceremonies are performed, and the crowd disperses. As the sun starts to fall below Crich Hill, a group of half a dozen boys and girls improvise a cricket match without stumps. Perhaps they will be at the heart of the club's revival, remembering into old age the day the village beat Derbyshire. On the ground that boasts cricket's oldest batting record.

FROM THE DEPTHS OF HAMPSHIRE

Vic Cannings

On 4 April 2010, the day after his 91st birthday, Vic Cannings will celebrate 50 years at Eton College: 25 as cricket professional, several more working with the 'threepenny' juniors and now enjoying a contented retirement in the same terraced house where he and his family took up residence in April 1960. He does not look or sound a day over 75 – "If it weren't for my knees, I could still be bowling" – and the stories tumble out with as much vigour as ever.

There cannot be many alive who can say that they have bowled at Jack Hobbs – as he did in 1934, for Farnham against Surrey Club and Ground. A farm worker's son from Hampshire, he was 15 years old and had been playing for the little village of Dippenhall. Now, in front of 3,000 spectators, he was running in to bowl to The Master. "Our umpire, a hairdresser in Farnham, reckoned I had him lbw and I didn't appeal. But I don't think I did."

Nor will there will be many left who played in the wartime 'Test' matches between England and Australia in Palestine. Cannings was in the Palestine Police, and among several Australian cricketers at the anti-aircraft battery in Haifa was Lindsay Hassett, who made a century in one two-day game in Jerusalem: "In the evening we took him down the Police Club, tried to get him drunk. It made no difference. He got 60-odd the next day."

Cannings was recommended to Warwickshire by a major who had been in Nazareth, and he spent three years at Edgbaston, starting in 1947. "Good luck," was the greeting of the captain, Peter Cranmer. "We're all mad up here, and I'm the maddest of them all."

It was mad when the groundsman dried the square with a flame thrower: "I got two pairs that week." It was also mad, but brilliant, on a dusty pitch at Brentwood when Tom Dollery persuaded Cranmer to send out two tail-enders, Charlie Grove and Tom Pritchard, at the start of their second innings. "The Essex team were walking out and they looked round, as you do, at the batsmen. I can still see the startled look on their faces. Then the ball started flying in all directions." The pair put on 107, and Warwickshire won by 34.

Then came ten golden years at Hampshire, bowling in tandem with Derek Shackleton, neither of them fast but both unerringly accurate. "We used to say, if Shack bowled more than one half-volley a summer, they would sack him. I was allowed two."

He rates Peter May the best batsman of that era, followed by Jack Robertson of Middlesex: "I used to think it would be an event to get a ball past Jack.

Vic
Cannings

Harry Altham, the Hampshire President, was an important man at Lord's. We'd say to him, 'Why isn't he playing for England?' He said, 'He can't hit the ball through the covers.' 'Well, he hits the bloody ball somewhere because he gets 2,000 runs every summer.' And he was a nice bloke, Jack."

One who rarely scored runs against him was Denis Compton: "He was known as my rabbit. I simply watched his feet when I ran up to bowl."

Cannings coached each winter: in South Africa, Pakistan, the Argentine and Trinidad. And there are stories aplenty there, too: "The High Commissioner in Karachi said, 'It would be nice, Mr Cannings, if you could improve relations between the two countries.' 'It would improve relations,' I said, 'if I could be paid some money.'"

Such was his stock as a coach and a happy, outgoing cricketer that in Trinidad he received two letters: one from Tonbridge School, where Colin Cowdrey had recommended him, the other from Eton. "We like to win matches," the Eton cricket master David Macindoe told him, "but we want you to make the boys enjoy the game." And Cannings certainly did that – in his own way.

"My predecessor, Jack O'Connor, used to call the boys sir. I said, 'I'm not going to call any boy sir.' I called them a lot of other things but never sir."

Soon enough his Hampshire burr was a familiar part of Eton life – "The mothers used to say to me, 'We've heard about you, Mr Cannings'" – and he developed many cricketers, none keener than John Barclay, the future Sussex captain. "Johnny used to spend half the winter in my cubicle in The Bat Shop. I'd get a bit of paper. 'Left-handed batsman, off-spinner, what's your field?'"

"When Johnny was captain, we had a system of signals. If it was time to change the bowling, I'd put my hands on my head, and he'd take his hat off to show he'd seen me."

No one else ever noticed – except when it went wrong one day at Marlborough. "I was trying to signal for a leg slip, and I slid down the bank. It's a hell of a bank there. I nearly broke my bloody leg."

Four hours after my arrival he was still going strong, telling me of the tied match at Eastbourne when he put on 55 for the ninth wicket with Peter Sainsbury: "There was a big tower with a clock that boomed out every quarter. I said to Robin Marlar, 'You'll hear that bloody thing a few more times before I'm gone.'"

But it was Monday afternoon, and he had a meal to cook for his son and grand-daughter, who were due for their weekly session of cards and mah-jong. "I can't grumble," he says. "I've done more or less everything I've wanted to in my life. Who would have thought that a ragged-arsed bloke like me, from the depths of Hampshire, would finish up at Eton?"

HANDSOME IS AS HANDSOME DOES

Arthur Booth of Yorkshire

June 2010

He was a little man, five foot four inches tall, a canny slow left-arm bowler who had long since lost his ambition to play for Yorkshire. Yet in 1946, in that makeshift post-war summer, Arthur Booth found himself at the age of 43 inheriting one of the great roles of English cricket: the slow left-arm bowler of the White Rose county.

He had been groomed for the role back in the mid-1920s, when Wilfred Rhodes was nearing retirement. But Rhodes played on till 1930, to the age of 52, and by then a better successor than Booth had arrived: the great Hedley Verity. In 1931 Booth played twice for Yorkshire, when Verity was away with England, then he departed to Northumberland and to a successful career in the leagues and in Minor County cricket. If it had not been for the war, and for Verity's death, he would have been remembered simply as 'not quite county standard'. Yorkshire only wanted one slow left-armer.

England was a struggling country in 1946. Food rations were tightening, coal supplies short, and our national sports had a make-do quality, never better illustrated than football's play-to-a-finish cup tie between Stockport and Doncaster in late March. In a spring heatwave three of the Doncaster team came straight from overnight shifts in the pits to play for almost three and a half hours before railway smoke combined with declining light to force an abandonment.

Yorkshire's cricketers began their season's preparations with twice-a-week nets in a shed in Huddersfield. They were seven years on from their last championship programme, with few young recruits, and they were looking to a 43-year-old to carry forward the flame of Rhodes and Verity. Booth, to his irritation, was nicknamed 'Grandad' by the skipper Brian Sellers, though Sellers himself was 39 and Barber, Leyland and Turner all well into their 40s.

John Arlott wrote of Booth's 'old face, bearing the marks of strain or worry … a man used to settling his own problems, self-reliant and neat with his fingers.' But he was not stern. He had a philosophical temperament, a happy humour and a fund of lovely stories.

He had learnt his craft through long years of practice, none more important or enjoyable than his summers in the north-east, and he took the field for Yorkshire in 1946 in his green Northumberland cap. With almost unerring accuracy he could pitch the ball on a length, though this was not enough for one filling Verity's boots. Terence Prittie in the *Manchester Guardian* talked of his 'jerky, hip-hopping run and mechanically rotating action', dismissing him as 'a tail-enders' terror, playing on untutored minds and tethered feet'.

Yet he was an intelligent bowler, and week after week through that summer he tied batsmen down and took wickets. His method was to set a six-three field and to bowl at off stump, sometimes with in-drift, sometimes away. He was not a great spinner of the ball, but he kept his arm behind his back till the point of delivery and he often accompanied its release with a canny click of the fingers on his right hand. He gave the ball air, and he knew how to torment the patience of batsmen.

At Bristol, while the great Wally Hammond was hitting 143, he bowled 45 overs for 49 runs. Then at Edgbaston, limping badly with a pulled thigh muscle, he bowled 42.5 overs in the match and took nine wickets for 40 runs. Yorkshire won the championship, in no small part because they had three bowlers in the top six in the averages – and top of them all was 'Grandad', with 111 wickets at 11.61, conceding his runs at just 1.4 an over. Only three times since the Victorian age has a bowler taken 100 wickets at a lower average – and none at such an economical run rate.

Booth came close to being selected for the winter tour of Australia. If he had gone, he could have been England's oldest debutant since Southerton in the very first Test in 1877. As it was, he endured the bitterest of English winters, developed rheumatic fever and played only four times in 1947, yielding his place to the young Johnny Wardle. He was a one-season wonder, and he returned to the leagues. As late as 1953, at the age of 50, he was topping the averages in the Birmingham League.

For some years he coached at Manchester Grammar School, where his protégés included Lancashire's David Green. In 1959 the 19-year-old Green scored 1,049 first-class runs, yet the previous summer, facing the 55-year-old Booth in the school nets, "It was an uneven contest. He used to throw the ball up, because he was small, and he had wonderful flight. He didn't turn it much, but just enough to do us all."

His coaching consisted of quiet advice: how to bring down the bat to play between the bowler and mid-on, how to build an innings. "He didn't believe in orthodoxy for orthodoxy's sake. He had this saying: 'Handsome is as handsome does.'"

Booth was not handsome to see. He did not have Verity's rhythmic grace and beautiful ease of movement. But, my word, for that one summer of 1946, he did not let Yorkshire down.

THE WORST DEAL

John Manners of the Royal Navy

Nov 2010

"I think I had the worst deal of any cricketer," the 96-year-old John Manners says, reflecting on a first-class career that spanned 17 years and took in only 21 matches.

In 1936, at the age of 21, he topped the Hampshire batting averages, coming into the side for the last four games of the summer and scoring 212 runs in six innings. *The Cricketer* called him 'a bold and aggressive batsman who should go a long way if his early promise is fulfilled'.

He faced Yorkshire's great slow left-armer Hedley Verity – "I was leaving my ground to play him; on a hard wicket he was no trouble" – and the Indian fast bowler Jahangir Khan: "He bowled me with one of the best balls I ever faced, a fast off-break after he'd been bowling out-swingers."

These games were the last that the great Hampshire stalwarts Phil Mead and Alex Kennedy played for the county. The 49-year-old Mead, the most prolific scorer in the history of county cricket, made a fifty in his final innings, and John Manners was at the wicket with him for much of it. "He waddled in the field, he couldn't throw and he was a most unattractive batsman, prodding ones and twos. But he did score his runs at a reasonable pace, and you couldn't get him out."

In his next appearance for Hampshire, against Kent at Canterbury, Manners hit a free-scoring 121 in 160 minutes – with 'perfect stroke play', according to *Wisden*. Doug Wright, the Kent leg-spinner with the bounding run and fast delivery, was at his most testing, and Manners and his fellow amateur, the Reverend John Bridger, were the only two to play him with confidence: "We played forward to him, and the pros all played back."

But that century against Kent was in August 1947, eleven years after his previous appearances. A naval officer, often at sea, he had gone ten summers without a first-class game.

In 1936 he was lucky, serving on the Royal Yacht – "I played as much cricket as I wanted" – but in 1937 he was on a motor torpedo boat in the Mediterranean, and in the following two years he was in the Far East. "I was saving up lots of leave to have a summer of cricket in 1940, then war was declared."

He spent the war at sea in destroyers, a busy war that ended with his commanding a ship protecting West Coast convoys. "The highlight was sinking a submarine." But there was little time for cricket. It was not till

John Manners

1947 when he was appointed Naval Liaison Officer at Sandhurst that he was able to play again with any regularity. Even then it was mostly two days a week, here and there for different sides.

His century at Canterbury was his only innings that summer for Hampshire, and he played just twice more the next year. "I was going to play against Warwickshire. I'd just got 120 and 80 not out against them for the Navy, but they asked me, would I mind not playing? Jimmy Gray had just come into the team, and they didn't want to drop him."

Thereafter he played his first-class cricket for the Combined Services. He hit 147 against Gloucestershire in the game that saw Tom Graveney, after a lean run, score his first century. The next summer Manners scored 123 against the New Zealanders; two years later he hit 75 against the South Africans.

He played with all the young National Servicemen, Trueman, Close, Parks and Illingworth among them. Some were in the Army, others in the RAF which under Alan Shirreff's captaincy "went out of their way to recruit cricketers and were thoroughly professional, playing to win where we were amateurs."

But the Navy did have one good young cricketer – Peter May. "It was amusing playing against the professionals who'd never heard of him and were looking to get some easy wickets. At Worcester he was caught on the boundary, trying to hit a six for his hundred. Then in the second innings he got 175."

Manners returned to sea in August 1953, missing to his great regret the match against the Australians, and he played no more first-class cricket. After the Navy he became Bursar at Dauntsey's School, then a photographer producing several books on country crafts.

He is now the second longest-standing MCC member, joining in 1937. "I was supposed to play twelve MCC matches before election but, as I was in the Navy, they said I could play them afterwards. I think it took me till the end of the '40s to complete them."

If he had had more time for cricket, could he have played for England? His record suggests so. But it's not a question that bothers him. "The Navy was my career," he says. "I only played cricket for enjoyment."

In September 2018 John Manners became the first
first-class cricketer to reach the age of 104.

THE LAST DAY

Hove, 1 September 1939

Oct 2009

The sun shone on English cricket on Wednesday 30 August 1939. Hitler and Stalin had agreed a non-aggression pact, and German troops were massing on the Polish border. Only 21 years had passed since the signing of the 1918 Armistice, and Europe stood on the brink of another war.

The previous Friday the West Indians had abandoned their tour, heading to Liverpool to sail home while they could, and their decision was greeted with dismay. They were due to play at Hove the next day, and the Sussex captain, Flight-Lieutenant 'Jack' Holmes, beseeched them in a telegram: 'Essential to play tomorrow. Keep the flag flying.' The Mayor of Brighton went further: "The failure of the West Indians to keep their engagement will certainly give the impression that we are not putting up a united front." Cricket was determined to go on.

On Wednesday the last full round of matches in the county championship began. Already the War Ministry had commandeered The Oval so Surrey versus Lancashire was rerouted to Old Trafford. The Surrey team arrived so late they had to sleep in the pavilion, but they scored 350 for eight and, in the words of the *Manchester Guardian*, 'As the sunshine of the evening fell on the field, most of us felt that the world had grown a little less stupid than at breakfast, when the barrage of newspapers challenged our nerve and philosophy. A day on a cricket field can be extremely sanative.'

War might be imminent, but the old gentlemen in the pavilion preferred to discuss 'a good stroke, a swift piece of fielding or the general condition of one's lumbago'.

It was the same scene at Hove. Yorkshire, already champions for the third year running, were the visitors. The match was being played for the benefit of the Sussex all-rounder Jim Parks. And, wrote Jim Kilburn in the *Yorkshire Post*, 'a considerable number of guests broiled upon the benches, sheltered in the stands, or lay scattered on the grass to watch cricket of unfailing interest, cricket for cricket's own sweet sake, with championship cares dead and buried.'

More than 4,000 were present, watching 499 runs in the day: Sussex – thanks to a sparkling 198 by George Cox – made 387, Yorkshire 112 for one. According to the *Brighton Gazette*, the 'carry-on spirit of England' was well illustrated by the group of women volunteers, led by Lady Eva de Paravicini JP, who ran the tea tent at the far end of the ground.

It was the last fine day of the summer. Thunder storms were drifting north across the channel, and the players at Hove did not take the field till 3.30 the next afternoon. 'All that morning, in the hotel,' Yorkshire's Norman Yardley wrote, 'we were feverishly discussing the cables from Poland and Germany. None of us had much attention to give to cricket.'

When play began, the wet pitch was treacherous, aiding the left-arm spin of Sussex's James Langridge, but Hutton, using his feet, 'changed the principles of his batsmanship and was as superbly master of the proceedings as ever.' His century was his twelfth of the summer, and Yorkshire closed on 330 for three.

Elsewhere the matches at Worcester, Taunton and Lord's were finished in two days, leaving three matches still in progress as Friday 1 September dawned: at Leicester, Old Trafford and Hove.

Around 6 a.m. German forces broke into Poland at four points. The games at Old Trafford and Leicester were abandoned. So, too, were September's festivals at Folkestone and Scarborough. But the Yorkshire team, concerned that their game at Hove was for Jim Parks' benefit, insisted on carrying on. It would be the last day of first-class cricket that England would see for six years.

In the early hours of that morning, as if to underline the passing of a world, the last Brighton tram returned to its depot, to be replaced by 'trolley-buses and heavy oil engine buses'.

Trees and kerbs were being painted white, shelters were being dug, sandbags delivered. At the railway station 14 trains full of London children, 'all labelled and with gas masks in containers round their shoulders', arrived. 'Whatever else may be said about them,' wrote the *Brighton Gazette*, 'the young Londoners are certainly not lacking in energy and animal spirits.' The trains also delivered 1,000 stretcher cases from London hospitals, many of them needing treatment on the platforms.

The cricket at the County Ground was almost as frenetic. 'Never within memory,' wrote Sir Home Gordon, the Sussex-based author, 'had a wicket at Hove been so unplayable, for it had completely "gone" with a nasty place at one end.' Yorkshire scored quick runs to take a first innings lead of five, then at 12.15 Sussex began their second innings. Jim Parks took first strike from the summer's leading bowler, slow left-armer Hedley Verity.

The rosy-faced Parks was a popular cricketer. Two years earlier, following the death of his wife, he had thrown everything into his summer's cricket and had achieved the unique 'double' of 3,000 runs and 100 wickets. But 1939 had not been kind to him: his benefit, affected by the onset of war, would raise only £734, and his 50th and last innings of the summer would not add to his meagre total of 1,108 runs. He was lbw, second ball, to Verity.

The lowest score of the summer was Derbyshire's 20 at Sheffield, and one Sussex batsman – perhaps it was Parks himself – told Home Gordon they would struggle to avoid getting out for less. 'Verity,' Kilburn wrote, 'bewildered, confused and confounded the enemy so swiftly and completely that no batsman had time or opportunity to make double figures.'

Jim Parks junior, the future England cricketer, recalls what George Cox used to say about the match: "I top-scored in both innings: 198 and 9."

Some said that Sussex's collapse was caused by their preoccupation with war, but their opponents had no such problem. 'While Yorkshire are in the field,' Yardley wrote, 'in war or peace, there will always be concentration enough to finish the game in hand.'

"This was the real Drake spirit," declared Arthur Gilligan, the former Sussex and England captain. Time enough to finish this game of cricket and beat the Germans too.

Within 45 minutes the innings was over. In six eight-ball overs Verity took seven of the first eight wickets, including that of the Sussex captain Holmes, comically bowled when he left a ball that pitched outside leg and hit his off stump. With Stainton unfit to bat, the innings ended when Nye drove Robinson into the deep and, with the ball already in Hutton's hand, started in vain for a second run. Sussex were all out for 33.

The 23-year-old Hutton was the brightest hope in English cricket, only 118 runs short of being the youngest man ever to score 3,000 runs in a season, but he scored just one when Yorkshire batted again. The 12-year-old Jim Pegg, later a local journalist, saw all three days of the match. "He was caught behind. I can still remember the appeal. There was a great cheer in the crowd. It was the big event of the day."

At 2.30 Yorkshire completed a nine-wicket victory, and within the hour their 16-strong party were making their slow way home in a hired charabanc, passing first through glorious Sussex countryside, then on through crowded roads towards Winchester and Oxford. They were supposed to reach Leeds at midnight, but they finished their day's journey in the blacked-out streets of Leicester where they had one last team meal.

'The farther we got from Brighton,' Hutton wrote, 'the deeper was our conviction that we would be lucky if we ever played cricket again.'

It would be seven years before Yorkshire would return to Sussex, winning the 1946 championship at Eastbourne. Hutton, after a wartime injury, had a left arm two inches shorter than his right. Jim Parks, a policeman in the war, had retired from the first-class game. So too had Flight-Lieutenant

Holmes, now Group-Captain. In 1939, an England selector himself, he had been chosen to lead MCC in a three-Test tour of India, but – like his fellow Sussex tourists Hugh Bartlett and John Langridge – he would never now play for his country.

They all returned to peacetime England, except Hedley Verity. A Captain in the Green Howards, he died from wounds sustained when leading his men through heavy German fire in Sicily. On the Saturday after his death the Yorkshire captain Brian Sellers took the field for the Army at Lord's and, when he reached into his blazer pocket, he found a piece of paper. '6-1-9-7,' it read. They were Verity's bowling figures at Hove, given to him by the scorer.

Seventy years on, on Wednesday 16 September, Sussex and Yorkshire will start a four-day match at Hove. Bobby Parks, grandson of the beneficiary Jim, will be there, and Douglas Verity, Hedley's son. Commemorating that last day of summer, 1939.

The morning of Friday 1 September 1939
Evacuated children boarding trains at Clapham Junction

MISCELLANY

Keith Andrew

Bomber Wells' Gloucestershire

Bill Owen's farewell

Three club stalwarts

Mated!

Jim Kilburn

KEITH ANDREW

This is the address I delivered at Keith Andrew's funeral. I was asked to adapt it into a written obituary for On The Up, the magazine for elite coaches, but I reproduce it here as I spoke it at the Church of St Botolph's at Aspley Guise on 11 January 2011.

I have only known Keith for the last 12 or 15 years. Many of you have known him much longer – known him as a magnificent wicket-keeper, as a gifted county captain, as a passionate champion of English cricket below the professional level.

But I speak as I find. I thought he was one of the nicest people I've ever met in cricket. Kind. Warm. Generous. Modest. Thoughtful. Intelligent. In his quiet, unnoticed way he was, in my opinion, one of the greats of post-war English cricket.

We wrote a book together. Eight or nine years ago. Every three or four weeks for a year or more I would drive here from Bath, settle into the armchair in his front room and listen to him talking.

He wasn't always the easiest person to interview. As you know, he could be absent-minded and forgetful. I was writing a book with Bob Appleyard at the same time, and he was quite different. You'd talk about the Second Test at Sydney, you'd cover all the key points, then you'd move on to the Third Test at Melbourne. It wasn't like that with Keith. He'd be at Brisbane, keeping to Alec Bedser, then five minutes later you'd be hearing how he'd signed up Mushtaq in a Karachi bazaar or how his cousin Les used to analyse football matches for Terry Venables. Eventually I would guide him back to Brisbane, and he would start again as if it were a new subject. It was hard some visits to know where I had got to.

But I always looked forward to the sessions. There was this great warmth about him – and an original mind that really fascinated me. Once you got beyond the outward vagueness, you realised what a deep thinker he was. Able to grasp the broader picture. Perceptive. Independent.

I interviewed Don Robson about Keith's time as chief executive of the NCA at Lord's. And this is what he said to me:

> Keith often appeared as a bit of a joke, he had this light-hearted approach and he could talk, sometimes without quite getting to the point, but his reports were superb. He had a very clear mind, and his analysis was usually spot on. I was Chairman of the NCA for twenty years, and we had all sorts there. There

Three keepers: George Duckworth, Keith Andrew, Godfrey Evans

were poseurs, people who weren't workers, people who were full of their own importance, and Keith was none of those. He was the best.

Keith didn't have an easy start in life in Oldham. His father left when he was eight, his mother had to work hard in the local mill to provide for him and there was no discipline in the first school he attended. But he had a determination to succeed, and after years in night school he became a graduate of the Institute of Mechanical Engineering. He never spoke as if the studies came naturally to him – but wicket-keeping did. He kept for Werneth in the Central Lancashire League, and he found himself selected to play for a league eleven against Lancashire, when he had to keep to the awkward chinamen of George Tribe. That day set him on a path that led via National Service to Northampton.

Those of you who played with him know how good he was. He was the best in the country for years. But, true to his Oldham roots, he did it all without show. He never made it look difficult, and maybe that counted against him when it came to picking the England team. He talked a lot to me about the skills of keeping, how so few people in the game know how to assess them.

Sometimes, when we played exhibition matches on Sunday, I'd stand back and throw myself about. But if you think about it, the tell-tale sign of a poor keeper is that he's late on the ball. He is making excessive late movements instead of anticipating – and that's almost the opposite of what the crowd sees.

He holds a world record. In 1965, across seven matches, nearly 900 overs and 2,132 runs, he did not concede a bye. 45 hours of concentration, at the same time as skippering the side. Keith never dwelt on it, though. Instead, he gave the credit to the bowlers. "It's no wonder I don't concede any byes," he told them. "You guys can't get the ball past the bat."

I know Keith was the early inspiration for Bob Taylor. I'm in no position to judge these things, so I will simply read you the words of 'Tiger' Smith, the great Warwickshire and England wicket-keeper and coach, written shortly before he died in 1979.

Alan Knott and Godfrey Evans gave England great service, yet neither had the class of Keith Andrew or Bob Taylor behind the stumps.

Then there was Keith the county captain. Some of you played under him. I've heard the stories. How David Steele took a career-best eight for 29 against Lancashire. How he seethed in the outfield as weeks went by before he bowled

Neale, Joyce, Keith and Clare, packing for a tour of the West Indies

again. How Keith then came up to him one day. "It's Steele, isn't it? You haven't had a bowl for a while, have you?" Had he forgotten, or was it his idea of a joke? The great thing about Keith was that you never quite knew.

But, as always with Keith, appearances were deceptive. He inherited a team at the very foot of the championship table, a team without stars, and he took them in 1965 to within one freak declaration of what would have been Northamptonshires's one and only championship. They were the best years in the county's history. As Colin Milburn wrote in his book, "He had a way with every member of the side, and he could read a match as well as any skipper I played under." Or, as Brian Crump put it to me, "He did everything quietly, and everybody respected him. They were the happiest years of my cricketing life."

I think the toughness of Keith's own early life gave him a feeling for people who came from humbler backgrounds. It brought out a fatherliness in him. I loved listening to him talking about Colin Milburn: his happy memories of great innings, his anger that people outside cricket led him astray, his regret that Colin never became a father himself.

> I spent years in the world of coaching, and the one thing I will take credit for is that I never, ever gave Colin Milburn any real advice. I knew I had a genius on my hands, and I wasn't going to tell him how to quell that genius. It would have been a sin.

It's not quite true, of course. He did give Colin one famous piece of advice. He told him to cut down on his drinking. "Why don't you drink halves instead of pints?" The next time Colin made a big hundred, Keith asked him what he wanted to drink. And back came that lovely reply: "I'll have two halves, please, guv."

Much lesser captains, blessed with all-star teams at the big counties, have been praised to the skies. But I wonder. How many of them could have led that Northamptonshire team as successfully as Keith?

Then there were the years at the NCA. Again an unfashionable corner of cricket, away from the headlines. Through years of passionate dedication he oversaw the development of a structure of coaching for the non-professional game. He wrote a wonderful book: *The Skills of Cricket*. He even supervised a set of films, one of which – on spin bowling – won a BAFTA.

Another of the films, on batting, featured Graham Gooch. The first showing was set for one afternoon at Lord's, and Keith told me how Sir Gubby Allen, the Grand Old Man of Lord's, suddenly announced that he'd like to come along. Keith was full of foreboding – what on earth would the great traditionalist think of Gooch's bat-up stance? – but all turned out well. Keith bought Sir Gubby a hamburger and a beer for lunch and, by the time the film was under way, he had nodded off.

So there you are. A lifetime of achievement – with the wicket-keeping gloves, as county captain, at the NCA. But that only tells part of the story.

What I shall remember most about Keith is his warmth. His sense of fun. His kindness.

His family was so important to him. He talked so often about his luck in having married Joyce, and he was very proud of Clare and Neale and their children and all their achievements. And if I could say this, what a great sculptor Neale is. His Larwood and his Redgrave, they're magnificent. And how like his father. He's so self-effacing, he doesn't get anything like the recognition he deserves.

A part of me wants to finish by performing Keith's great magical trick, the one he learnt from Jack Mercer. Sticking a postage stamp up on the ceiling. He did explain to me how you do it. But it's a long way up there. I think perhaps I'd better not try.

Keith loved the game of cricket with a real passion: its skills, its personalities, its great history. And, for all the rambling and the superficial vagueness, I loved listening to him. So I would like to finish by reading you something that he said to me.

> I wish we could put a greater warmth into cricket.
>
> We've put so much emphasis on the excitement of the result. We try to manufacture that in a short time through limited overs cricket. And there is a role for that. It has added something to the game. But cricket is about more than just the excitement of the occasion. It's about going home and carrying the memories with you, both that night and in years to come.
>
> Being successful is one thing, but we want to enjoy our lives as well – and part of that enjoyment is friendship between sportsmen. If people are cheating, they don't respect one another, and the feeling for the game disappears. You don't go home at night feeling half so well.
>
> Cricket is a game. You play to win. You play to be top of the pile. But that's not *why* you play cricket.
>
> We have to play cricket and to foster its playing everywhere. And we have to look after what is special about it, what makes people love it.

You did all of that, Keith.

BOMBER WELLS' GLOUCESTERSHIRE

This foray into ghost-writing, when I sat on the sofa in Bomber's front room transcribing his thoughts on Gloucestershire cricket, appeared in the 2002 publication '100 Greats – Gloucestershire County Cricket Club'.

Glorious Gloucestershire. Is there another county of such beauty? The stone-built cottages snuggling in the Cotswold hills. The magical villages hidden in the ancient Forest of Dean. The mighty River Severn with its elvers. The town of Cheltenham – "poor, pretty and proud," as my dad used to say. And my own beloved Gloucester – with its majestic cathedral and its throbbing industrial heart. The Wagon Works, Moreland's Matches, Fielding and Platt. And overlooking the city, Robinswood Hill, where we used to picnic on a Sunday. A bottle of water, a few sandwiches, and we were away and happy the whole day long. Oh, the hours we spent sliding down that hillside.

The city of Gloucester, from Robinswood Hill

I remember how, in springtime, we used to clamber onto our bicycles and head out to Newent and the fields around Dymock Woods. What a sight we must have been at the end of the day. Hordes of children pedalling home with daffodils filling our baskets and tied to our cross-bars. I used to sell them for a penny a bunch.

Glorious Gloster. We grew up with our own Gloucestershire Regiment, camped on Robinswood Hill. They were the only ones to have back-badges, a second badge on the back of their caps, awarded for their brave rearguard action at the Battle of Alexandria. And we had our own Gloucester rugby club, the cherry-and-white Elver Eaters of Kingsholm. They were all heroes to my boyish mind – but even they shrank beside the great Gloucestershire cricketers.

Wally Hammond. Surely the most magnificent batsman who ever walked to the wicket. My dad was always talking about his 300 on the Wagon Works ground. It would have been 400 if Notts hadn't put every fielder on the boundary.

Charlie Parker. The doyen of all left-arm bowlers. Quick, slow. You name it, Charlie bowled it. He got Bradman twice at Bristol in 1930, and never again did the Aussie put himself down to play against Gloucestershire.

Tom Goddard. He had hands as big as a bunch of bananas, and he used them to spin the ball like a top.

My father and his brothers would sit in the front room with a crate of beer, talking about them all, and I sat on the lino floor, soaking it all up. They would pick their best England side and the more they drank the more Gloucestershire players would be in it.

Hammond, Parker, Goddard. Before them was Gilbert Jessop, 'The Croucher'. The fastest scorer of them all. If he was still there at tea, he'd have 200 to his name – and that was in the days when you had to hit the ball out of the ground for a six.

And before Jessop were the Graces. Doctor WG and his brothers. They say that everything the great doctor did, he made look easy.

Grace, Jessop, Hammond. What county could match such entertainers, such personalities? To me, a little boy in the back streets of Gloucester, they were gods. They *were* cricket.

Then one Friday evening in July 1951, almost without warning, I found myself chasing about the city on my girl friend's bike, borrowing kit to take down to Bristol the next morning – to play for Gloucestershire in the county championship. Alongside the little maestro George Emmett and the elegant young Tom Graveney. There was Arthur Milton – what a talent! Football and cricket for England. You couldn't even get the better of him at bar billiards. Then there was Andy Wilson, the pint-sized keeper, and the immaculate Sam Cook.

A week later – how can I ever forget? – I arrived at the ground for my second home match. It was August Bank Holiday Saturday, we were playing Somerset and there were queues on both sides of the pavement, from the Nevil Road gates all the way to the Gloucester Road. I walked through them with my brown paper carrier bag, and I asked Bernie Bloodworth the groundsman, "What's going on?" And he said, "Wally's playing."

And there I was in the dressing room at Bristol, with George Emmett introducing me to my new team mate, the idol of my childhood. What a man! He had all the physical attributes of a prize fighter. I remember Sam Cook telling me how he'd borrowed Wally's blazer and how it almost went down to his knees.

I had nine wonderful years with the county. Whatever team I was on, it was always a joy. George Emmett was the greatest captain I've ever known, always on the attack. He instilled in all of us his great love of the game. We were its caretakers; it was our duty to look after it. And heaven help anyone who didn't walk when they knew they were out!

The years have rolled on since I last bowled a ball on Bernie Bloodworth's sandy pitches, but the entertainment has continued.

Zaheer Abbas. A lovely stroke player. A wondrous stylist. He took chances with his shots, and I could see the memory of Hammond in his drives.

Mike Procter. An attacking batsman, an attacking bowler. An exuberant personality. He had it all. He might have been South African, but he played in the Gloucestershire tradition.

Jack Russell. Mister Effervescence. A great servant to the county and a great favourite with Gloucestershire folk.

Robinswood Hill still looks down on the Wagon Works ground, but now the county plays in the shadow of Gloucester Cathedral – at the Archdeacon Meadow. When I was a boy, I used to pick bulrushes there, when it was just scrubland, and now it maintains the tradition of county cricket here in the city of Gloucester. How many runs Hammond would have scored on its placid surface, I can't imagine.

The County Ground in Bristol is no longer the open field it was in my day. It is a modern cricket stadium with all the facilities. But for the true cricket lover there can be nowhere like Cheltenham College on a Festival day – with the sun shining, Matt Windows cutting his way to a hundred and the folk around the boundary reminiscing about days gone by.

Reminiscing about Emmett and Zaheer, some even about Hammond and Parker, where once they sat and reminisced about Jessop and Grace. One day they will reminiscence about Russell and Windows.

Generation upon generation of great Gloucestershire cricketers. Long may they keep coming – as long as the sun shines over the River Severn.

BILL OWEN'S FAREWELL

This article was published in The Cricketer in November 2017.

On 17 September, at an autumnal Hinton Charterhouse ground south of Bath, one of the West Country's best-loved Sunday teams – Bill Owen's XI – took the field for the last time. After 47 summers and 774 matches, they have decided to call it a day – with Bill, at the age of 73, retiring. No one could countenance the club without him.

In every year he has undertaken all the functions of the club: captain, secretary, treasurer, fixture organiser, team raiser, kit supervisor, statistician and, above all, the ever-dependable guardian of their happy spirit. He only ever missed 31 matches, almost all because of injury. There could not be a Bill Owen's XI without Bill Owen.

It began on a Wednesday evening in June 1971. Bill, a young solicitor and no great cricketer, never got much of a game when he was selected for Portishead's 2nd XI, "batting from eight downwards and not bowling", so he got up his own side – friends, fellow lawyers, kindred spirits from Portishead – for a 20-over game against the staff of nearby Gordano School. If he had sat at home, he would have learned on the news of a major breakthrough in the government's attempt to join the Common Market. Instead, he came back to his wife Sue with a glow he had not known at Portishead, and he organised a second fixture – against the Post Office Regional HQ.

It was not many years before he had built up a fixture card of 20-odd games – not only evenings but alternate Sundays – and the team attracted decent cricketers with their infectious *esprit de corps* and their family-friendly atmosphere. "There's always been such a good camaraderie," says Bob Cornish. "Bill knew the right people to ask." "It was a wonderful mix," says Colin Sara. "At one time the team didn't change for ten years."

Never has Bill failed to raise a side for a fixture, though in recent times it has become harder, as evidenced by the two Pakistani postgraduate students guesting in this final outing. Overnight rain has left the Hinton pitch and outfield damp but one of the newcomers, Mushtaque, gets the game off to a blazing start with a flurry of violent cuts and lofted drives.

At 91 for four Bill steps out for the final time, and his stay is brief: bowled for one. His wife Sue joins the sad applause as he makes his way off. At least she was there to see that last run – unlike his only fifty, against the Exeter Geriatrics at the Devon County Hall ground, when she and their daughter Sally had gone into the city centre for tea. "When we came back, I thought they said he'd scored 15. I said, 'Fifteen? That's good.'"

They have played in so many special places, even on the County Ground at Bristol, and the tree-lined Hinton Charterhouse ground is as attractive as any, with its beech hedge and the tall lime tree next to the pavilion. The club is enjoying good times; its three league sides have all won promotion this year, and there is talk of a new pavilion. As the sun finally appears, Scyld Berry flights his leg breaks teasingly, and the Owens are all out for 143.

The tea is a magnificent spread. Then Bill, ever attentive to detail, produces a new ball for Hinton's reply, and it is soon struck into a thicket of trees

Bill Owen (right) at the toss

where it takes some time to find. This prompts one veteran to recall the day at Moretonhampstead when Bill, trying to lob the brand-new ball to the opposition, threw it into a stream where it floated away.

For many years Bill Owen's XI provided their opponents with friendly but competitive cricket, the skills of the two teams well matched. "As captain Bill always played it seriously," Colin Hawkins, a regular for forty years, says, "but not too seriously."

Anno domini has caught up with them now. In the field more catches are dropped than taken and, as the sun drops low behind the lime tree and the shadows lengthen, the Hinton fifth-wicket pair make light work of the last 80 runs. With three to win, Hinton's long-serving Everton Griffiths, named by his Barbadian father after Everton Weekes, pulls the ball high and hard over the hedge, the final moment of the Owens' 47-year venture.

A guard of honour is formed for Bill, followed by speeches, with Bill paying special tribute to Sue. They met as students at Manchester, when an early date involved a trip to Sheffield in his Austin A40. He was playing for the university's 2nd XI, for whom he did not bat or bowl.

For Bill and his team, it was always about so much more than batting and bowling, as the best of friendly cricket is. As he says, looking back on all the lovely venues, the thrilling finishes and the lifelong friendships, "I really have had the best career ever of any talentless cricketer."

THREE CLUB STALWARTS

These are taken from a series of articles I wrote for The Wisden Cricketer in 2008 and 2009, spotlighting people who had given long service to a single cricket club.

Ivor Chaplin of Brentham Cricket Club

It was a second eleven fixture that did it – back in 1963, nine years before league cricket came to Middlesex. The 25-year-old accounts clerk Ivor Chaplin was scoring for Turnham Green at Brentham, when his colleague in the box said he would be playing the following summer. "I looked out across the ground to the trees on the other side," Chaplin recalls, "and something seemed to gell inside me. I've been here ever since."

At the start of 1968 he was promoted to first eleven scorer, and he hasn't missed a game in 41 summers: completing 600 league matches last August as well as over 1,000 Sunday and midweek fixtures, including – he tells with pride – a Wednesday afternoon in 1992 when he had to hurry back from his mother's funeral in Brighton. "The funeral was at 11, and I was on the train at 12. I only missed two overs."

The big wheels of numbers, with the ladder for putting up the 100s, have given way to an electronic system, and fellow scorers no longer smoke: "Thank God for that!" With his Jewish background, he used to be the odd one out, negotiating an alternative to pork at lunch, but now he looks after the dietary needs of all the Muslim players. "Have you tried halal chicken? It's much better than Tesco's, I'll tell you."

You argue with his scoring at your peril. "All the people starving in the world," he'll say, "and you're worried about one run."

"He's eccentric," says young club member James Overy, "but he's a great guy to have around. A dying breed, especially on Sundays when he's often alone in the box. He's got so many wonderful stories."

"You've got to talk," Chaplin says. "You're in the box for six or seven hours."

In mid-April a hastily arranged fixture started his summer, forcing him to cancel his short mat bowls. He is a man with many interests – theatre, gardening, square dancing, philately, scrabble – "but cricket comes first," he says. "The rest has to fit in. You're in the fresh air, with all the wild life, and it keeps your brain active, keeps you in contact with the young. I'll do it as long as I can."

In July 2017 Ivor completed his 2,000th consecutive match. In 2014, to mark his 700th league match, the Brentham scorebox was named after him.

Mike Ashton of Barry Wanderers Cricket Club

It began in 1970. A group of friends in South Wales, students mostly, thought it would be fun to get up their own cricket team – Barry Wanderers. They arranged three fixtures, though only one was played: a Wednesday evening game against Barry NALGO. A second was rained off. And the third? Founder member Mike Ashton smiles. "Suffice to say, it was the day after my 21st birthday."

"When I started playing, I was useless," he says, but the flame was lit. The next year there were eight fixtures, then twelve, and he relished the adventure, even when he was teaching 150 miles away in East London. "I was always looking for nice places to go: good grounds and good teas." When the early members began to drift away, "I was determined to keep it going. I was secretary, treasurer, everything."

The breakthrough came when they persuaded Sully Hospital to let them create a cricket field out of its disused vegetable garden. For 18 months they laboured, and in May 1985 they were wanderers no more. They became one of the strongest non-league sides in South Wales, with a second and sometimes third side and a thriving junior section. "I played 64 games one year," Ashton says, by then groundsman as well. "One lad played 66, but his wife divorced him at the end of the season."

The peaceful tree-lined field sits beside the Bristol Channel, with a view across the sparkling water to Minehead and Weston. When the old hospital social club burnt down, they raised funds to erect a traditional wooden pavilion.

A happy family, the first team is now full of young men who started in the Under-11s, some of them sons of former players. They play league cricket – "That changed the whole ethos of the club" – and they no longer relish the travel. "Our season used to start at Worcester Norton Taverners. It was a long drive, but I knew some nice pubs on the route. Now, if I said we're going to Bristol next Sunday, they'd all start complaining."

Mike Ashton is the last of the founder members still playing, soon to bring up his 1,500th appearance. In the 1990s he took over 1,000 wickets with his slow bowling – "off-spinners when they turn" – but his pride is in the club's development: how that one Wednesday evening match turned into such a fulfilling part of so many people's lives. "I can't imagine we ever thought it would be that permanent."

At the club's annual dinner in 2009 Mike received a standing ovation when I presented him with a framed copy of this article. He died in September 2014, aged 64.

Cliff Bastin of the Bath Exiles

For 57 years 'Cliff' Bastin has been at the heart of the Exiles (Bath). Treasurer, fixtures secretary, team co-ordinator, groundsman, president, he has done all the jobs – and, at the age of 79, he is still doing most of them. "This is the Exiles Communications Centre," his answer phone says in summer, his neat availability book the hub of the operation.

"If it wasn't for Cliff, we would have folded long ago," club member Ed Collacott says. "But he never expects recognition; he just gets on with it."

Bastin was present when the Exiles were founded in 1951, at an extraordinary general meeting of the Oldfield Park Methodist Cricket Club. "The church objected to one of us playing on a Sunday for a Bath and District XI so we became the Exiles."

Their 1952 card had 19 fixtures, but "the shackles were off" and the next year they ventured into Sundays and played 35. "Other church sides were doing the same. St Philips called themselves R Wheeler's XI." It was friendly cricket, played without over limits on council pitches: "If you batted first and scored 110, you'd never lose."

A civil servant, he was posted to Aden in the 1960s; when he returned, the club was near collapse. "Only three of us turned up to the AGM, and I found myself secretary, fixtures secretary and captain by default."

The club became the focus of his energy: "The civil service is soul destroying; I never found anything in my working life that was worth any untoward effort." They found a regular ground, joined a league, started second and third elevens, and by 1984 there were 133 fixtures on the card. In 1992 the first team won the North Somerset League.

Bastin has never been more than a moderate player, an obdurate batsman prouder of his 413 not outs than his 10,000 runs, but he has worked tirelessly to sustain a happy club. "We enjoy the company in which we play," Ed Collacott says, "and Cliff is central to that. When anybody has a problem, it's always Cliff they phone."

"We've had some right old duffers at times," Bastin says. "But we are a cricket club, and the purpose of a cricket club is to provide cricket for people who want to play. If you want a game, you're on the list."

He works every Friday on the square – "You can score 200 now and lose" – and every Saturday and Sunday he scores. "And if we get there and we've only got ten players, I've got my kit in the boot of the car."

Ten years on, at the age of 89, Cliff is still at the heart of the club – secretary, president, scorer, assistant groundsman – but his playing days have ended, with a final not-out tally of 415. A recent eye operation now allows him to score without the use of binoculars.

MATED!

This appeared in the Hornsey Journal's chess column in May 1988, long before I took up writing about cricket.

Wednesday is my evening for cricket practice, when I eat at the same restaurant that Wil Ransome uses on his way to Muswell Hill Chess Club. I have been getting some fun out of showing up with corrections to his chess column. I think it's starting to get him down.

"Why don't you dig out one of your old games?" he challenged me. "The one when you were a queen up against Bruce maybe."

Ten years ago I played chess at Muswell Hill, and Wil's weekly column brings it all back. I fancied I could make myself into a good player but, with long hours of staring at the board in smoky rooms, it was becoming an obsession.

Chalke v Baer, 1977. Can White play R-K3?

I had a friend who had been a schoolboy champion, and I'd never understood why he wouldn't play. His wife got him back to it. "I had no idea, I thought it would just be an evening out for him," she told me. "Not all this playing over the game when he gets home, lying awake all night justifying each move."

Bruce was only eleven years old, and a win would put me in the lead in the club championship with only two rounds to play. Me, a second-teamer. I relished the prospect of glory, especially when I put together a nice combination to win his queen.

But Bruce never gave up. Not for him the early resignation, the irritation with a losing position. When we reached the illustrated board, I was the one who was getting irritated.

I played R-Q3, looking to simplify down, and Bruce obliged with RxR. Suddenly I saw what I had overlooked, my stomach turned over, and my brain went into a scramble. KxR would be met by N-N6ch. After that there would be only two places for my King. K-Q4 would allow P-K4ch, losing Queen, so I played K-K3. Bruce played R-B6ch, forcing K-Q4 anyway, and now it wasn't the Queen that went. N-K7 was mate, and a great hubbub ensued around me.

It had all lasted barely a minute, and it was as much as I could do to say "Well done" and head for the bus stop.

I spent the night reliving the horror and, when I got to work next day, my nerves still jangling, I knew it had all gone too far.

"I don't think you played much after that, did you?" Wil joked.

But wait! R-Q3 is rotten, but it doesn't lose. I could have afforded not to take the rook. Even after N-N6ch, N-K4 holds, e.g. BxNch, QxB NxQ, KxR and I am still ahead. I should have stepped away and calmed down before playing.

Who knows? I might have won that championship.

But then ... I might still be playing chess, lying awake after other disasters. There's more fresh air playing cricket.

It was not long before young Bruce was the best player at the club.

JIM KILBURN

This was my contribution to the 2007 book 'Sweet Summers – The Classic Cricket Writing of JM Kilburn', edited by Duncan Hamilton.

When I interview former cricketers about matches played years ago, I like to counterpoint their speech and the press reports of the time, to set the vernacular of the participant's voice against the formal prose of the reporter. It only works when I can find good copy in the old newspapers. I open them up, in bound volumes or on microfilm, with a sense of anticipation. Will the writer have an observant eye and a lovely turn of phrase, or will the report be a bare and lifeless summary of events?

The sight of certain reporters' names makes my heart leap, and chief among those are Alan Gibson of *The Times* and Jim Kilburn of the *Yorkshire Post*. People talk of EW Swanton as the doyen of cricket writers in the 1950s and '60s, but for me he does not create atmospheres or bring to life human character and passion, nor does he write prose to relish, as these two do.

I love the formality of Jim Kilburn's prose. The vocabulary and the sentence structures, the elaborateness of it all, tell me that cricket is important, Yorkshire cricket especially, and it must be written about properly. I love his insights into technique and character, his sense of occasion, his eye for the little detail – and, most of all, his feeling for the game and its traditions. The *Yorkshire Post* has been blessed with a long line of great cricket correspondents, a newspaper always keen to honour the passion with which the county plays its cricket, and Jim Kilburn was as good as any of them.

Here he is on a batting cameo by Gloucestershire's ever-cheerful Bomber Wells:

> Wells is a skilful and enthusiastic bowler of off-breaks, and it is the enthusiasm rather than the skill that he carries into the sideline of batting, but 25 minutes of survival meant 32 invaluable runs for Gloucestershire and lively entertainment for the spectators who could appreciate a willing spirit and the humour of the game. Tail-enders do not customarily drive Trueman through the covers in the midst of a running conversation.

Here on Len Hutton's approach to his 100th hundred:

> His batting in the morning had the calm and concentration characteristic of his approach to any important occasion. His

habitual touch of the cap before he takes up his stance, his constant examination of the pitch between overs, his refusal to play any but the strokes of his choice or run any but the most carefully judged singles, always betokens a Hutton on business bent.

Here on a tense, low-scoring day's play between Yorkshire and Surrey:

> This was one of two or three days to be found every season that build the memories of a lifetime and transmute a game from an entertainment to an experience. It was a day of recreation exhausting as a week of work, an occasion of restless anticipation, tautness of nerve and passionate opinion. It was filled with joy and shock and dream and doubting. An evening interruption was probably essential as a sedative.

The memories of a lifetime will die with the passing of the last participants and spectators, but Jim Kilburn's prose will survive, a reminder of an age when cricket was 'more than anything else a way of playing a game, of thinking a game, of caring for a game'.

> It is not a livelihood, but a living; not an exercise or an entertainment but an experience. ... Cricket should see its line of development not as a commercial enterprise, not as a political weapon, not as a synthetic concern of ulterior motivation, but as a form of stability linking a way of life through yesterday, today and tomorrow in practical idealism.

They are still words worth reading.

OBITUARIES

David Allen

Alec Bedser

John Clay

Stan Cray

Martin Horton

Brian Langford

Eddie Leadbeater

Peter Loader

Mervyn Mansell & Ted Jackson

Neil McCorkell

Arthur McIntyre

Frank Parr

Peter Roebuck

Reg Simpson

Jeffrey Neilson Taylor

Fred Titmus

Allan Watkins

Peter Wight

Don Wilson

WRITING OBITUARIES

I don't know what it says about me, but I have always been an avid reader of obituaries. I can't throw a newspaper away till I have read the obituary pages, whoever the subjects are. There is something about the format – celebrating the wholeness of a person's life at its conclusion – that appeals to me.

The first obituary I wrote was of Ken Biddulph, the former Somerset bowler whose tales of his days as a county cricketer gave me the idea for my first book, *Runs in the Memory*. By the time he died in 2003 I was writing a regular column for *Wisden Cricket Monthly* and I offered to write his obituary for the magazine. Later that year the cricket administrator Geoffrey Howard, with whom I had written a book, died, and I also wrote an obituary of him. I had been close to both men so it seemed fitting to write these pieces, but I had no thought for becoming an obituarist.

The turning point came in the spring of 2005, by which time the magazine had amalgamated with *The Cricketer* to become *The Wisden Cricketer*. The editor John Stern rang one morning to ask me to take on the magazine's tribute to the Reverend David Sheppard. "Why me?" I responded in shock. "Surely there are bigger names who can do this much better than I can." I had not interviewed David in depth, and his work outside cricket was intimidatingly important. To say that I was overawed by the request would be an understatement.

John prevailed on me – I think he had had several refusals and was getting desperate – so I set to work. I spent a long day in research, reading David's two autobiographies, but at the end of the second day, when I planned to complete the piece, I had written only one sentence. 'My, this is a tough task,' I wrote that night in my diary, 'and it is churning me up having to do it. The canvas is so large, his life's work so immense, that it is difficult to focus on the cricket appropriately.'

As so often happens, I slept on it, let it take shape in my subconscious, and by lunchtime next day it was in John Stern's inbox. Was it any good? I was not at all sure, but John seemed to like it and next month he printed a reader's letter commending it, saying that I had fused the cricketer and the Christian in 'a complete obituary'. Most of the newspapers, it seemed, had dealt with the two strands in separate tributes.

The following year John landed me with an even greater bombshell: would I write the main obituary of Fred Trueman? Again others had turned down the task – Frank Keating and John Woodcock were mentioned – and again I found myself gasping at the enormity of the challenge. My book *The Way It Was* included these two obituaries, of David Sheppard and Fred Trueman, and the enlarged paperback edition added Alec Bedser, the third major obituary that John landed on me.

In 2010 I agreed to take over the writing of cricket obituaries for *The Independent*. Unlike with a monthly magazine the turnaround time was short, especially when the cricketer was famous, and that added to my anxiety. I am not a fast writer; I like to do my research and mull over how best to put it all together: the high points of the career, the descriptions of playing style, the little humanising stories, the sense of the man at the heart of it all. Each obituary had a strict word limit and, as the deadline neared, I always seemed to have 50 or 100 words too many.

Fred Titmus was a challenge. In mid-morning I told Chris Maume, the obituaries editor, that Fred had died, and he wanted my copy for the edition next day. To make matters worse, it was Budget Day and the obituary pages were going to press early. Could I submit by three o'clock? I was in a panic, unable to see how I could do Fred justice with so little time, but relief was at hand. Late in the morning, news came through that Elizabeth Taylor had died. She took priority over Fred, and I was given another 24 hours.

I liked working for Chris. He seemed to appreciate my efforts and was always happy to go along with me when I offered off-beat subjects such as Jeff Taylor and Frank Parr. He rarely altered my copy, though on one occasion he did balk at the inclusion of a crucial quote: "What do you want to play that fucking nigger music for?" After reflection he made his decision, "You can have the nigger but not the fucking," and, in the interests of historical accuracy, I opted to drop the quote.

The Independent had pre-written copy on Don Wilson so there was no conflict of interest when the *Daily Telegraph* asked me to write his obituary. My favourite story in the piece was one Don had told me about Peter O'Toole in the Lord's nets facing the bowling of Imran Khan but, for some reason which I never understood, when the piece appeared in the paper, a sub-editor had changed the story so that it was Don facing Imran. I rang to complain, saying that *The Independent* never altered my copy like this, only to get the reply: "That's because they can't afford sub-editors."

Two years later, when the *Telegraph*'s cricket obituarist, the delightful Robert Gray, stood down, he recommended me to take over from him. Remembering the episode, I stayed loyal to *The Independent*. As things turned out, it proved an unwise loyalty.

I have written almost forty obituaries. In this collection are some that did not appear in *The Way It Was* – plus one of Jeff Taylor that was in the paperback edition. I include it because it is my personal favourite.

DAVID ALLEN
(1935-2014)

The end of the Lord's Test of 1963 was one of cricket's most dramatic moments. England, wanting six runs for victory, lost their ninth wicket in the final over, and, in an atmosphere of high excitement, out of the pavilion came Colin Cowdrey, with his left arm in plaster. The West Indian Wes Hall, the fastest bowler in the world, had two balls left, and England survived for the most heroic of draws.

In fact, the batsman required to face the two balls was not Cowdrey at all but David Allen, the Gloucestershire off-spinner. "I had to fend off Wes Hall," he would say with wry amusement, "while Colin just stood there, watching me with a smile on his face. Not only that but, for years afterwards, he got fan mail for his brave knock, and no one ever mentions DA Allen."

The son of a Bristol bus driver, David Allen learned his cricket at the Stapleton Club where, as a boy among men, he was encouraged to give the ball plenty of air. "I used to get slogged out of the ground. 'That's all right,' they'd say. 'Pitch it up, he'll get out in a moment.' They had that lovely optimistic attitude. But then there wasn't the fear of losing."

From Cotham Grammar School he progressed to Gloucestershire where in 1953, in his fourth game, he took six wickets for only 13 runs to win a famous last-over victory over the champions Surrey. His friends from school carried him shoulder high from the field.

At another county his progress would have been rapid, but Gloucestershire already had two off-spinners, John Mortimore and Bomber Wells, and for the next five summers Allen played only intermittently, becoming so frustrated that he decided to call it a day in the autumn of 1958.

The saving of him was the appointment of Tom Graveney as captain. Graveney was less tolerant than his predecessor of the overweight Bomber Wells, with his rustic batting and comic antics, and Allen finally got his chance. It was the summer when England were looking for someone to replace Jim Laker, and such was Allen's success that at the end of it he was picked to tour the Caribbean, as the third spinner behind Ray Illingworth and Tommy Greenhough.

On the boat the manager Walter Robins took him aside. "You're not going to be playing much cricket on the tour," he said. "And I'll have a lot of speeches to make. So I'd like you to look after my briefcase. That'll keep you busy."

Greenhough struggled with sweaty hands, and in the early matches Allen, with his higher flight and greater spin, out-bowled Illingworth. So, within a year of nearly giving up cricket, he became England's number one spinner.

David Allen

Between 1960 and 1966 he played 39 Tests, taking 122 wickets and hitting five fifties. An outgoing character who, in his own words, "loved the pomp and ceremony of Test cricket", he was a popular tourist, achieving many of his best performances overseas. He did well in the Indian sub-continent and, in tandem with fellow off-spinner Fred Titmus, he bowled England to victories in Durban and Sydney, both under the captaincy of MJK Smith, whose straightforward approach to the game he welcomed.

His finest performance, and his greatest disappointment, came early in his Test career against Australia at Old Trafford in 1961, in a game that he might have won for England. Bowling with superb control he had taken four for 38 off 37 overs when, with one wicket to fall, Peter May instructed him to tempt the batsman Alan Davidson to have a whack. Davidson duly did, hitting 20 off the over, and May fatally took Allen off. With England's batsmen then collapsing against Richie Benaud, Allen's glory had been snatched from him, and he departed for a five-hour train journey to Pontypridd for Gloucestershire's match next day. "It was a wonderful Test match," he said. "It swayed one way and then the other; that was the beauty of it. But it was a huge disappointment to lose. And I'll tell you what. Sat on that train, going down to Pontypridd on my own, it got worse."

His Test career ended in 1966, at the same time as MJK Smith lost the captaincy, but he played for Gloucestershire till 1972, taking in all 1,202 wickets and scoring 9,291 runs. In 1961 he did the season's double of 1,000 runs and 100 wickets.

After retirement he worked for Harvey's, the Bristol sherry merchants, and he gave an immense amount back to cricket. He might have loved the glory of the Test arena, but he was also at home among club players. Right up to his death he held many positions in local cricket, and always he put in the hours, whether entertaining guests as Gloucestershire President, sitting thanklessly on the disciplinary committee of the West of England League or teaching spin to the young boys and girls at his local club, Thornbury. For many years he organised the fund-raising Old England XI where his short end-of-day speeches, delivered in his lovely deep voice with its mellifluous West Country ring, perfectly captured the warmth of each occasion.

He grew up in an age when, as he put it, "We played for the love of the game, not the money", and he never lost that love.

David Arthur Allen: born Bristol, 29 October 1935; died Thornbury, 24 May 2014. Gloucestershire (1953-72), 39 Tests for England (1960-66).

ALEC BEDSER
(1918-2010)

Sir Alec Bedser was a big man: with a big frame, big hands and a big, big heart. For several years after the last war, when England's bowling resources were at their thinnest, he carried the attack. He was a strike bowler and a stock bowler, all in one. He would test the batsmen when the ball was new, and he would bowl long, accurate spells in the heat when the going got tough.

He was never frightened of hard work, never overawed by a cricketing challenge. Growing up in Woking in hard times, he and his twin brother Eric spent summer holidays working unpaid on a local farm and digging their father's allotment. "If you do that," he would say, "you don't get a bad back." Then in the war, serving in the RAF Police, the twins were caught up in the evacuation at Dunkirk. In a cornfield they flung themselves down as a German plane flew low over them, and they felt the spray of bullets all around. "It was bloody frightening," Alec said. "After that I was never nervous playing cricket."

Alec and Eric were inseparable all their lives but, to help their joint progress at Surrey, Eric was turned into an off-spinner, allowing Alec to become the great fast-medium bowler of his era. He was nearly 28 when cricket resumed in 1946, and he made his England debut against India at Lord's, taking eleven wickets. Rations left him hungry, he was carrying a groin strain, yet he took another eleven in the Second Test at Old Trafford.

His approach to the wicket was not long, but he had a powerful body action and follow-through and the ball hit the pitch hard. His natural delivery was a late in-swinger but, in Australia in 1946/47, he discovered how to use his enormous fingers to bowl a leg-cutter. At its best the ball would swing late into the batsman, pitch on middle-and-leg, then cut away like an eighty-mile-an-hour leg-break to hit off-stump. At Adelaide, in one of the great moments of all Test cricket, he bowled Bradman for a duck with one such delivery. Len Hutton called it 'the deadliest ball I've ever seen'. The Don reckoned Bedser the most worrying of all the England bowlers he faced, losing his wicket to him six times in Tests.

"He didn't have a long run-up," Tom Graveney says, "but he had beautiful timing when he released the ball, with his arms up high and his great hands like bananas. He was so accurate, and he had fielders all around the bat, with his keeper stood up to the stumps. It was misery batting against him."

He reached his peak in the early 1950s. In Australia in 1950/51, when England's strangely selected side lost 4-1, he shouldered the main burden,

Alec Bedser

taking 30 wickets at 16.06. Then in 1953 in England he took 39, a new record in Ashes cricket, at 17.48.

At Surrey, with Laker, Lock, Loader and brother Eric, he was part of the greatest bowling attack in the history of county cricket. Surrey won seven consecutive championships from 1952, the bowlers so accurate that the catchers could stand closer to the bat than any other county's fielders. Micky Stewart was in the bat-pad position: "I came into the side in 1954," he says, "and the first time I recall a horizontal bat shot played past me off Alec was Reg Simpson at The Oval, August Bank Holiday 1956."

In those years of six-day-a-week cricket, Alec Bedser worked as hard as any bowler, regularly getting through more than 1,000 overs a summer. His greatest year was 1953 when, in 19 weeks, he bowled 1,253 overs and took 162 wickets. It was Coronation Summer, England were striving to regain Ashes lost in 1934, and he played as important a part as anyone in the success. At Nottingham in the First Test he took seven wickets in each innings, and only rain prevented an England victory.

He had seen hardship and war, and he was not one to get carried away with sporting success. "We've overdone it now with adulation," he would say. "It's nice for kids to aspire to do these things, but not for grown men to get so worked up. Mum wouldn't speak to the press. After I got 14 wickets at Nottingham, some one got through. 'What do you mean, he took a lot of wickets?' she said. 'He's a bowler. I thought that's what he was supposed to do.' And she put the phone down."

The Ashes were won back at The Oval. On the first day Alec bowled 29 crucial overs, having bowled 21 the previous day for Surrey at Loughborough. "I was getting a bit tired by then," he would say in that matter-of-fact way of his, but it did not lead him to approve of the modern practice of resting bowlers. "To me they're not match hardened. It takes them half a day to get used to playing in a match again." His rest after that long summer was to join his brother and father, building the house near Woking where he and Eric lived for the rest of their lives.

His Test career ended sadly. On Len Hutton's tour of Australia in 1954/5 he developed shingles and was not at his best in the disastrous First Test at Brisbane. He was rested at Sydney, when Tyson exploded onto the stage, but he was expecting to play at Melbourne, his favourite ground. He was the leading wicket-taker in all Test history, and he never forgave Hutton that he only learned of his omission by reading the team sheet on the dressing room wall. For all his caustic comments about amateurs, he was not comfortable with a fellow professional as captain.

He played once more for England, in 1955, but by then a new generation of quicks had emerged: Tyson, Statham and Trueman. He was starting to lose pace, yet even in 1957, at the age of 39, he took 131 wickets, one of five Surrey bowlers in the top ten in the national averages. He played till 1960, captaining capably whenever Peter May was absent, and he never let slip the high standards he set for himself.

His brother Eric and he established a successful stationery business, and that allowed Alec to remain involved in cricket. He toured Australia in 1962/63, quietly doing all the chores as assistant to the manager, the Duke of Norfolk, and twice he returned as the manager. From 1962 he was a Test selector, serving for a record 24 summers. In 1969 he became the first professional cricketer to be appointed Chairman of Selectors, holding this post till the end of 1981. In the words of fellow selector Alan Smith, "He was as complete a selector as you could get. He was conscientious, dedicated and a very sound judge of a cricketer: temperament as much as technical ability. He knew how players thought."

They were not easy times. He coaxed Geoff Boycott back to Test cricket after a three-year absence, and he picked up the pieces after Tony Greig, England captain, had defected with several key players to Kerry Packer. One of his first decisions as chairman, to give the captaincy to the new Leicestershire skipper Ray Illingworth, was inspired – as was one of his last, to recall Mike Brearley in the golden summer of 1981. "He was supportive," Brearley says, "and he always gave room to people to speak. He liked cricketers though he found some modern ones, even those who thought they were modern in the late 1970s, rather puzzling."

Alec was not enamoured of modern ways, and his conversation could be wearing to those who did not hear the wry humour beneath the moaning. He represented a strand of English life – honest, principled, hard-working, without fuss or self-aggrandisement – that is not so much valued in the razzamatazz of our fast consumer society. Yet we will be poorer without men like him. He gave great service to the English game, both on the field and off, and his knighthood was much more than an act of sentiment by John Major. It was richly deserved.

Sir Alec Victor Bedser: born Reading, 4 July 1918; died Woking, 4 April 2010. Surrey (1939-60), 51 Tests for England (1946-55).

JOHN CLAY
(1924-2011)

John Clay played for Nottinghamshire from 1948 to 1961. He grew up in West Bridgford, close enough to Trent Bridge to hear the five-minute bell and to run to the ground before the players had reached the middle. In those pre-war years he loved to watch the exuberant stroke play of the amateurs, though his own batting in the 1950s was less glamorous. He was keenly aware of his limitations, often unsure of his place in the side. "The crowd weren't interested in watching me," he said of the years he opened the batting with the fast-scoring Reg Simpson. "If we were 100 for none and I'd got 20, they were happy and so was I." For all that, he scored 1,000 runs in a summer six times, and he was a capable slip fielder.

He hit 11 centuries, though none gave him as much pleasure as the 89 and 58 he scored against Surrey in 1953. Few visiting batsmen prospered at The Oval, but in that match he transcended his usual workaday concentration to achieve a rare freedom of stroke play, his joy heightened by the belly-aching all around him: "Stuart Surridge was giving Locky some terrible stick, Locky was getting redder and redder, and the Bedsers were niggling each other in their mardy way."

Clay ceased to be a regular in the Notts side after 1957. Then, for the summer of 1961, with a year to fill between Reg Simpson's retirement and the arrival of the Oxford amateur Andrew Corran, the county broke with tradition and asked Clay, a professional, to captain the struggling side. He was not at ease in his hired dinner jacket, he could barely afford the hospitality he had to dispense at the bar, and the team finished in last place. Nevertheless he was a popular captain, he ran a happy side and for the following seven summers, ever patient and helpful, he nurtured the young players in the second eleven.

In old age, still living in West Bridgford, he walked more slowly to the ground, where he sat at mid-wicket, well away from the politics of the pavilion. He never lost his love of the game.

John Desmond Clay: born West Bridgford, 25 October 1924; died West Bridgford, 11 February 2011. Nottinghamshire (1948-61, captain 1961).

STAN CRAY
(1921-2008)

Stan 'Chick' Cray, who died in October, was the last survivor of the Essex side that finished fourth in the championship in 1939. He was just 18 years old, an orthodox right-handed batsman with a sound defence, and he showed great promise, never more than at Sheffield in August. In an innings of which he was always proud, he put on 109 for the seventh wicket with Ray Smith, setting up a famous innings victory over the champions.

He had had two frustrating years on the ground staff at The Oval, but now his career was blossoming – till the following week, when war stopped play. He joined the Honourable Artillery Company and served as a radar operator in India where, in January 1944, he once more held a cricket bat. Stationed in Assam, he was summoned to play in a charity match in Bombay, making a gruelling, 12-day journey to get there.

By the time he returned to England, he had missed Essex's first season back, and he was nearly 26 years old. But in 1947 he hit three centuries, scored a fine 98 against the touring South Africans and finished with 1,339 runs.

In winters he coached in South Africa, and it was there after the 1950 season that he received with shock the letter from the county, dispensing with his services. The club chairman was MP for Chelmsford, and Cray wrote to him at the House of Commons, enclosing his batting statistics. It did not save him.

He moved to Devon where he played for several years as professional for Paignton. He had only taken one wicket for Essex, but his off-breaks proved handy in the club game. One summer he scored 2,000 runs and took 100 wickets.

He was a good coach, patient and undogmatic, and he took the game into the state schools. Then in the 1960s he spent eight summers as coach at Wrekin College.

A lifelong bachelor, he remained in Devon, working as a postman and a kitchen assistant – and still coaching. He never went back to Essex and, in retirement, he increasingly became a recluse, his greatest friend his beautifully toned music centre and his superb collection of records, both classical and jazz. Only six mourners attended his funeral.

Stanley James Cray: born Stratford, East London, 29 May
1921; died Torquay, 10 October 2008. Essex (1938-50).

MARTIN HORTON
(1934-2011)

As a county cricketer Martin Horton was in the first rank. A busy, intelligent all-rounder with Worcestershire, he combined the specialist roles of opening batsman and off-spinner so effectively that in 1961 he did the 'double' with 1,808 runs and 101 wickets, the only opener since the war to perform the feat. County cricket was a relentless circuit of three-day matches, 35 in little more than four months of that long, hot summer, and between the gruelling coach journeys Horton, a strongly built man of average height, batted 66 times and bowled almost 900 overs.

He was a cricketer's cricketer, popular with team-mates and opponents alike. His cheerful disposition and easy sense of fun were part of what made Worcestershire one of the happiest county sides in those years, and that spirit turned to glory in 1964 when they won the championship for the first time in their history, repeating their success a year later.

The son of a Worcester publican who had once been the heavyweight boxing champion of the Midlands, Horton made his first sporting mark at the age of nine – in the pub skittles team. Three years later, in May 1946, he fell in love with cricket when he was taken to the beautiful ground at New Road, Worcester to see the Indians, and such was his progress that within another three years, nearing his 15th birthday, he joined the ground staff there. For ten shillings a week he fetched tea from the local café, rolled the outfield and sold scorecards. The following summer he topped the Second XI batting averages.

His progress was slowed by two years of National Service, but he could hardly have made a more eye-catching return in 1955. By tradition the summer's tourists opened their programme at Worcester, with a good turnout of pressmen in attendance, and on the last afternoon the South Africans were caught on a wet pitch that suited Horton's off-breaks. He took nine wickets for 56 runs, inflicting on the Springboks their only defeat outside the Tests. He stayed in the team all summer and completed the 'double'.

He was not quite a cricketer of Test class. As a bowler, although he had an easy rhythm and a sharp brain, he lacked penetration on hard, true pitches. As a batsman, although he scored an exceptional 2,468 runs in 1959, he had a short backlift and a punchy, bottom-handed style that was not what the purists at Lord's favoured.

It was therefore something of a shock – both to the commentators and to Horton himself – when he was selected to play for England against India in the First Test of 1959. England had returned from a disastrous tour of Australia and were looking for fresh faces, not least an off-spinner to take over from the ageing Jim Laker. Horton scored 58 and in the Second Test took two cheap wickets, but he had not convinced the cognoscenti and he returned to Worcester. "I thought I was very lucky to play," he said in later life, "but perhaps unlucky not to play a little longer."

The following summer a skiddy ball from Kent's fast bowler Fred Ridgway cracked his kneecap. The aftermath of the injury led to some loss of mobility, with a few of his team-mates nicknaming him Jake the Peg. For all that, his opening partnership with Don Kenyon was as solid as any in the country and his bowling continued to take wickets, both vital elements in the championships of 1964 and '65. His last game was at Lord's in September 1966, losing to Warwickshire in the final of the Gillette Cup, an appearance that they owed to his century against Hampshire in the semi-final.

He was blessed with a happy marriage. With their daughter he and his wife Margaret emigrated to New Zealand where for 17 years he was the national coach, bringing forward a generation of cricketers who raised the country to an unprecedented level of success. "In those years," Jeremy Coney says, "New Zealand cricket was run out of a garage, and he just got on with the job, calm and relaxed, with no ego. Everybody liked him." His grassroots work was little noticed, but in due course the Cinderellas of world cricket turned into a team that went twelve years without losing a home Test series.

Returning to Worcester, Horton became cricket professional at the Royal Grammar School. Dean Headley was his star protégé, a thin lad who could bowl with real pace. One night, on a tour of Zimbabwe, the locals in the bar asked Horton about the boy's prospects. "He's going to be a really good bowler," he replied. "All he needs is plenty of beef, plenty of beer and a good woman." Across the room the barman's voice boomed out: "My Christ, you're the manager for me."

Horton joined the Worcestershire committee. His was a voice of calm wisdom, though the committee room was not his natural habitat. While others tut-tutted about modern youth, he would sit with a quiet smile, recalling his own playing days – like the time they persuaded the club to let them travel to away matches by car. One team-mate had a drink too many and demolished several bollards in London's Oxford Street. 'County cricketer spends night in jail,' screamed the newspaper placards when they arrived at Lord's. As Horton put it, "It was back to the coach for a few years after that."

From the age of twelve he had been besotted with cricket – "If I could have," he said, "I'd have been happy to play for nothing" – and he retained that love.

In retirement he enjoyed his Wagner and his skittles, and he stayed at the heart of Worcester cricket, running the Old Players' Association. In summer he was a regular at New Road, and in winter, at the local Cricket Societies, his cheerful face was ever in evidence. In the community of cricketers he was as popular as they come.

Martin John Horton: born Worcester, 21 April 1934; died Worcester, 3 April 2011. Worcestershire (1952-66), 2 Tests for England (1959).

BRIAN LANGFORD

(1935-2013)

In another era, even perhaps with a county other than the unfashionable Somerset, Brian Langford would almost certainly have played cricket for England. He was an outstanding off-spin bowler, accurate at all times, with teasing flight and, on responsive pitches, probing turn. His county career spanned 22 summers, during which he took 1,410 first-class wickets, but in an age of great English finger-spinners his path into the Test team was blocked first by Jim Laker, then by Fred Titmus, David Allen and Ray Illingworth.

Growing up in Bridgwater, he would regularly catch the bus to Taunton to watch Somerset, queuing up outside the pavilion with his autograph book and playing lunchtime cricket on the outfield with a glass bottle and tennis ball. He left grammar school at 15 when his father died, going to work at the local Cellophane factory, pursuing his cricket at the Bridgwater club where he opened the batting and bowled medium-pace. As the result of entering a talent competition in a local newspaper, he was taken onto the Taunton ground staff in 1952. There the coach Harry Parks turned him into an off-spinner, and he stayed through the winter where his tasks included cleaning the toilets and weeding the field by hand.

In early June 1953, still in awe of the first-teamers whose autographs he had collected, he was told to report to Bath where the county would be playing Lancashire. He thought he was going as twelfth man – "I wouldn't have slept if I had known I was going to be playing" – but he found himself taking part in one of county cricket's most remarkable matches. The newly laid turves of the Bath pitch had not knitted together, and the three-day match, the takings from which had been allocated to the benefit fund of the long-serving Bertie Buse, was all over that evening. On the treacherous surface Somerset, dismissed for 158, won by an innings and 24 runs.

Langford himself bowled just three overs, taking the wicket of Brian Statham, but he stayed in the side for the remaining two games of the Bath Festival. While the groundsman rolled bull's blood from the nearby abattoir into the pitch, Langford was given a few shillings by Air Vice-Marshal Taylor, the Somerset secretary, to buy some better boots. "I had an old pair that were rather heavy. Some of the senior pros thought I might have a better chance with a decent pair."

They were right. In the next two matches he bowled 131 overs and took 25 wickets for 290 runs, figures which took him to the top of the national averages when they next appeared. He was a fresh-faced, fair-haired 17-year-

Brian Langford

old, and in later years he would say that he owed much of his success that week to the guidance of two older professionals: the great Harold Gimblett who set the field for each incoming batsman and Maurice Tremlett who told him what pace to bowl.

Two years of National Service disrupted his progress, but he re-established himself in 1956 where once more he found Bath to his liking, taking 28 wickets in the three games there. "The only way to enjoy county cricket is to be a regular in the side," he said later in life. "I was too young to know it at the time, but those games at Bath did take the pressure off."

Throughout his career he did well at Bath – and also at Weston-super-Mare where on a rain-ruined pitch against Lancashire in 1958 he achieved his best figures: nine for 26 in the first innings, 15 for 54 in the match. By contrast Malcolm Hilton, a Test cricketer, took five for 85 for Lancashire, and his enraged skipper, the hard-to-please Cyril Washbrook, chucked him out of the team. In those days of uncovered pitches, if the surface was helpful, the spinner was expected to take his wickets at a low cost, and Langford always had the calm temperament to do so. Sixteen times he took ten wickets in a match, more than either Illingworth or Allen.

He was a vital member of the Somerset side when in the 1960s they shook off their also-ran image and finished in the top half of the championship table six years running, as high as third in 1963 and 1966. But key players retired, and by 1969, when he was prevailed upon to take on the captaincy, they were back at rock bottom. "We don't expect you to win a game," he was told. "Just go and try your best." They finished in last place in the championship – and next-to-last in the newly created Sunday League. It was in one of these Sunday matches, against Essex at Yeovil, that Langford set an unbeatable record, bowling his eight allotted overs without conceding a run. Forty-over cricket was in its infancy, and Essex's Brian Ward decided Langford was the 'danger man' and should be played out.

He captained two more summers, when the county's fortunes improved with the arrival of Warwickshire's master-seamer Tom Cartwright and Yorkshire's larger-than-life Brian Close, who succeeded Langford as captain. At the end of 1972 he retired, but in an injury crisis he was summoned back and with no practice he dropped his off-breaks on a length straightaway. By this time a new generation, spearheaded by Ian Botham and Viv Richards, was emerging. In all, he appeared in 504 first-class games for Somerset, more than any other player in the county's history. "I played with both Gimblett and Richards," he would point out. "I'm the only one who can say that."

After retirement he stayed close to Somerset cricket, his one year as chairman of cricket ending with the tempestuous departure of Richards and Botham, a schism which proved beyond his conciliatory nature to prevent. People were always telling him he should have played for England, but it didn't make him bitter. "There's only one England side," he would say. "The greatest accolade is to be recognised by the players you played with and against."

He was a true professional. Up and down the land he was respected by everybody in the game.

Brian Anthony Langford: born Birmingham,
17 December 1935; died Taunton, 12 February
2013. Somerset 1953-74 (captain 1969-71).

EDDIE LEADBEATER
(1927-2011)

In two respects Eddie Leadbeater was a most unusual cricketer. He was the first and – until Adil Rashid recently – the only leg-spinner to play regularly for Yorkshire. Even more remarkably, he played twice for England without ever being awarded a county cap.

The youngest of six in a working-class family, he learned his cricket at the Almondbury club on the southern outskirts of Huddersfield. He was only thirteen years old when he made his first team debut in 1941, and he was still playing there, as captain of the second eleven, at the age of 68. A bubbling, cheerful character, he was a short man who flighted his leg breaks, scored useful runs and was lively in the field.

Yorkshire were traditionally suspicious of wrist-spin bowlers. They took wickets, but they tended to bowl bad balls as well – and the county was too parsimonious to tolerate that. "At Yorkshire," Leadbeater said, "when you ran in to bowl, always at the back of your mind you were thinking, 'I hope this isn't a full toss ... I hope this isn't a short one'." One time he slipped in an off-break, bowling Geoff Edrich in a Roses match, and all he got was a bollocking from the captain: "I've set your field for leg spin."

It was the same for the batsmen, especially those coached by the dour Arthur Mitchell. "Where's tha' come from, lad?" he would bark down the net. "Huddersfield? Well, leave that shot there then." "Freddie Jakeman were a good left-hand bat. He used to say, 'I had all the shots till I went in t' nets. When I came out, all I had were a forward push.'"

It was a harsh environment for a young cricketer, intended to separate the weak from the strong, and perhaps it did not suit Leadbeater's genial personality. His highest score came one day at Sheffield when he rebuilt the innings in a long partnership with Ted Lester. Lester completed his century, but Leadbeater fell just short of his, looking for quick runs before the declaration. "Well batted, Ted," the chairman said warmly in the changing room, but all the younger man got was "What were tha' doing, Leadbeater, getting out for 91?"

When he returned his best bowling figures, eight for 83 at Worcester, he found his partner Johnny Wardle demanding to bowl from his end in the second innings. Worse, Wardle started to offer him advice that, he later suspected, was intended to stop him taking further wickets.

At the end of his first full season, 1950, when he took 87 wickets, he was offered a contract by Hampshire, and in later life he came to regret that he did not head off to its more easy-going pastures.

In 1951 Leadbeater took 81 wickets, but he lost his place for the last three matches when the off-spinner Brian Close returned from National Service. Though nobody had said it, he always knew that he was filling in while Close was absent, and he was released at the end of 1952. Over the next four years he played a handful of further games, then moved to Warwickshire where in 1958, after the retirement of the veteran leg-spinner Eric Hollies, he played a full season. He scored a maiden century against Glamorgan and enjoyed his cricket greatly.

In his view he was bowling better than ever, but he retired in order to save his marriage. Unfortunately he lost not only his career but his wife as well, though his second marriage endured and was happy, which eased his bitterness.

In the winter of 1951/52, after his second full summer at Yorkshire, England sent a tour party to India. At that time it was a minor tour, from which the senior players were excused, and a month into the trip the leg-spinner 'Dusty' Rhodes came home ill. Several possible replacements were already committed for the winter or did not fancy four months on the Indian sub-continent. So it was Leadbeater who boarded the plane to Bombay. He was a welcome addition to the party, full of fun, but he did not do himself justice on the field. Pitched into the Second Test he dropped two slip catches on the first morning, then pulled a thigh muscle.

With Close back in civvies, Leadbeater spent much of the following summer in the Yorkshire second eleven – an England cricketer but never a capped Yorkshire one. He had begun an electrical apprenticeship, but after cricket he was a salesman for a multi-goods warehouse and he returned to Almondbury Cricket Club where he became a legend, still topping the league averages in his fifties. His final tally of 1,812 first-team wickets was for some years the league record.

He had an infectiously happy personality, and he loved his cricket. "It's a great game," he would say. "In good weather it's the best game there is."

Edric Leadbeater: born Huddersfield, 15 August 1927; died Huddersfield, 17 April 2011. Yorkshire (1949-56), Warwickshire (1957-58). 2 Tests for England (1951-52).

PETER LOADER
(1914-2006)

The success of the great Surrey side of the 1950s was built on a quartet of outstanding bowlers, the last of whom, Peter Loader, died this week after a long illness. The spinners Jim Laker and Tony Lock were household names, as was Alec Bedser, with his medium-pace cutters. But Loader was as important a part of the county's seven successive championship titles. He was fast, he could swing the ball to devastating effect, and he had the mastery of a lethal bouncer and a cunningly disguised off-break. He had a fast bowler's snarl, too. Few batsmen relished the prospect of facing him.

His potential was not spotted early. He was excused National Service on account of asthma, and his tall, wiry physique suggested a frailness that would not cope with the relentless six-day-a-week schedule of county cricket. In the summer of 1951, at the age of 21, he was a trainee dental mechanic playing for the Beddington club when Surrey, deprived of the services of Bedser (on Test duty) and Stuart Surridge (at his father's funeral), gave him a single game. His three wickets were expensive, but he impressed sufficiently to be offered a contract for the following summer.

That summer of 1952 was Surridge's first as captain, the start of Surrey's triumphant run, and Loader, whose asthma had now disappeared, played several times in July and August. Surridge, whose family ran a bat-making business, sent Loader off for a winter on one of their willow plantations, where the gruelling work broadened his shoulders and toughened him physically. The benefits were clear by July when in a golden nine days he took 34 wickets in three matches, twice taking eight in an innings and against Kent at Blackheath taking nine for 28, the other wicket falling to a run out. His winter programme this time was five months in India with a Commonwealth team where in unhelpful conditions he topped the tour averages.

There was a dearth of fast bowlers in England in the immediate aftermath of war, but by this time a new generation of quicks was emerging, spearheaded by Brian Statham and Fred Trueman. The selectors, influenced by events in the Caribbean the previous winter, were keen not to have to pick Trueman for the 1954/55 tour of Australia, and their prayers were answered in the showcase Gentlemen-Players match at Lord's when Loader destroyed the Gentlemen's batting with seven wickets for 37. His bowling, now controlled and accurate, had come of age.

In Australia it was another young bowler who gained all the headlines, the lightning-fast Frank Tyson, and Loader was an outsider in Len Hutton's Ashes-winning party. He reckoned Hutton only spoke to him once off the field of play, asking him in the gents after the Ashes had been won, "Did you have a good tour, lad?" Hutton was an enigmatic introvert, deploying the strategy of a slow over rate to keep his fast bowlers fresh, and that was not how they played at Surrey where Surridge was loud, aggressive and always impatient to get on with it.

Loader played just 13 Tests for England, mostly when Trueman was out of favour or Statham injured. He bowled well without luck in South Africa in 1956/57, but his moment of glory came at Headingley the following summer against the West Indies. He took three early wickets, the illustrious trio of Sobers, Worrell and Weekes, and he returned in the evening to finish off the innings with a hat-trick. It was the first by an Englishman in England for 58 years, and it would be 38 more before Dominic Cork would repeat the feat. It was an age when the fall of a wicket was greeted with little show of emotion but, when his third ball demolished Roy Gilchrist's stumps, Loader went on a wild celebration. 'He danced a fandango,' wrote one reporter, 'and his curls stood on end.' Trueman, by all accounts, was less ecstatic. "That Gilchrist, he bowled me a bloody bouncer. I were gonna nail 'im to t' sight screen."

Most of Loader's great days were with Surrey, though. In five summers from 1954 to 1958, some of them wet and unhelpful to fast bowling, he bowled almost 4,000 overs and took 563 wickets at an average of just 16. He was in his prime, and he enjoyed the sense of menace that came with being a fast bowler. "Wife and kids?" he snorted when the Gloucestershire opener Martin Young enquired after his family's health. "I'll give him wife and bloody kids."

His courage did not extend to batting, however, not when the bowling was quick. On one occasion, going out in a crisis, he provoked his veteran team-mate Bernie Constable to threaten him: "One step to square leg, and you'll have this bat round your head. And I tell you, it'll hurt a lot more than a cricket ball." They scraped home by one wicket.

As a bowler he lost a little of his fire at the same time as Bedser turned forty, Laker left and Lock had to remodel his suspect bowling action. Surrey's dominance was over, though Loader played till 1963, passing on his knowledge to the emerging Geoff Arnold before emigrating to Perth where he ran a transport business and did cricket commentaries on television.

His Surrey team-mate Micky Stewart remembers Loader above all else in the evening time at The Oval. "If we declared half an hour before the close, he always seemed to knock two or three over that night. He was quick and he was accurate, and he would bowl them out or have them lbw. He was a crucial part of our success."

Peter James Loader: born Wallington, Surrey, 25 October 1929; died Perth, Australia, 15 March 2011. Surrey (1951-63). 13 Tests for England (1954-59).

MERVYN MANSELL & TED JACKSON

Two stalwarts of North London cricket have died in recent months: Mervyn Mansell of Ealing and Ted Jackson of Brondesbury.

Mansell grew up in Rhodesia, for whom he played as an 18-year-old in 1936. His younger brother Percy, making his debut in the same match, went on to represent South Africa in 13 Tests, but Mervyn emigrated to England. He trained as a pharmacist and volunteered for wartime service in the Royal Navy, during which he won a Distinguished Service Cross for 'bravery, daring and skill' in combating German E-boats.

He joined the Ealing club in 1952. Playing in glasses like his brother, he was a classical batsman whose strength was on the off-side. Ealing was a top team at that time, but Mansell was among those who saw problems ahead. "Cricket in schools was declining," he recalled, years later, "so we had to start producing our own youngsters."

In 1955 a Colts side was formed, and Mansell became its driving force. He had a young family and a pharmacy business but, with his wife June's support, he always found time for youth cricket, extending his influence when he helped to found the Middlesex Colts Cricket Association in the 1960s.

The population of Ealing steadily changed, and many of his youngsters went away to university. But he stayed at the heart of the Ealing club, running the colts with quiet dedication for more than fifty years. He took an especial pride that three of his 1955 side were still playing for the club in the summer of 2009. Even as he lay dying in hospital last August, he wanted to know that week's results.

Ted Jackson learned his cricket at Charterhouse and Cambridge University, playing as a fast bowler in the 1943 wartime fixture against Oxford. By the time he was captain of Brondesbury, however, he had turned himself into a top-order batsman and medium-paced leg-spinner.

A man of great intellectual energy, he worked as a barrister for the Inland Revenue, loved literature and music and threw himself with passion into cricket coaching. When the 11-year-old Mike Gatting arrived at Brondesbury, Jackson quickly recognised his potential. With evangelical zeal he nurtured the youngster, championing his cause so relentlessly that Gatting was playing in the Middlesex second eleven before his 15th birthday.

"My mother saw an advert in the *Willesden Chronicle*," Gatting recalls. "'Brondesbury Cricket Club: Colts Required.' It was two bus rides, but I went along. It was probably the best thing that ever happened to me. Ted was there, barking his orders; I'm sure he frightened some of them off.

But he had so much energy, and his enthusiasm made most of us want to go back. It was never going to be boring. He was six foot two, bowling in-swingers and out-swingers and quick leg breaks that bounced up on the concrete surface. 'Hit it down, Gatting,' he'd shout when I played the pull shot or the cut."

Jackson became a leading light in the developing world of coach education, describing his week at Lilleshall on the Advanced Course as "the happiest of my life – and I've had three honeymoons."

He held strong views on the skills of cricket, despatching long, densely written letters to all and sundry. One I received denounced the ECB's latest publication on Mental Skills: 'They have the chutzpah to mention WT Gallwey in their bibliography but advocate rubbish like "Positive Thinking" and "Self-slaps on the Wrist".' Another began: 'I'm in utter despair over ECB's obstinate stupidity over (1) the STANCE and (2) TRIGGER MOVEMENTS.' Diagrams and quotations were enclosed, in various coloured pens, and a scribbled note on the bottom about a game he played in India in 1944.

"He was always writing to me," Mike Gatting says. "Amazing epistles, with bits of books about the great players – 'just in case you haven't seen this'. He had this thing about 'gapping', angling the bat to play into the gaps. He had so many ideas. In many ways he was ahead of his time."

He was a visionary, full of life, a passionate man who cared deeply about the game, and he left his mark on many – as did Mervyn Mansell, who was awarded an MBE for services to youth cricket in Middlesex. Ted Jackson's CBE was for services to the law – though it could just as easily have been for his coaching work. Without such men, always giving generously of their time, the game would not pass so well to future generations.

Arthur James Mervyn Mansell MBE:
born Bulawayo, 19 January 1918; died London, 26 August 2009.
Edward Oliver Jackson CBE:
born Calcutta, 3 December 1922; died London, 5 October 2009.

NEIL McCORKELL
(1912-2013)

Neil McCorkell was a regular in the Hampshire cricket eleven from 1932 to 1951, a quiet man of no great height who kept wicket and, for much of his career, opened the batting, a demanding combination in the six-day-a-week schedule of those years.

He was born near the harbour mouth in Portsmouth in March 1912, leaving school at 14 to work at the Officers' Sports Ground of the Royal Navy. With little coaching he played his cricket for local church teams before being selected for a district eleven against a visiting Hampshire side. His efficient, no-fuss keeping caught the eye, and in 1931 he joined the county staff, earmarked as the successor to the former England keeper George Brown who by then was well into his forties.

He made his debut in May 1932, establishing his place immediately and winning his county cap at the end of the summer. Hampshire's captain, the ageing Lord Tennyson, had become portly, and the other great stalwarts, Phil Mead and Alex Kennedy, were also way past their prime. Nevertheless they were legends of Hampshire's history, and the young McCorkell was in quiet awe of them. In later years he referred to that first summer as "a world of wonder".

As a batsman he had an unorthodox grip, with his hands far apart, and in the early years he lacked attacking strokes. However, he had a calm temperament and great powers of concentration, and by 1935 his repertoire of shots was beginning to expand. In July that year, in two games in the same week against Lancashire, he hit 150 at Southampton, then 154 at Liverpool. In all he scored 1,319 runs, the first of nine times he passed 1,000 in a season. The following summer Les Ames, the England keeper, was out of action with a bad back, and McCorkell was a strong contender to take his place on the boat to Australia. He kept wicket tidily in the prestigious Gentlemen versus Players match at Lord's, but in the end Ames, after an operation, was fit.

He lost the years of his prime to war, which he spent as a firefighter at Vickers aircraft factory in Newbury. However, he was back to his best in the golden summer of 1947, averaging 40 with the bat. In 1951, in his 40th year, at Gloucester's Wagon Works ground, he hit his only double century, sharing a large partnership with a young Alan Rayment who remembers him as "a lovely man, quiet but kind and really helpful to me". McCorkell had started out as an awe-struck boy, almost lost for words in the great Lord Tennyson's side, and he ended up as a highly respected senior player, full of tales of his happy life on the circuit. In his last match he was given the rare honour of captaining the side, among whom was the 17-year-old Colin Ingleby-Mackenzie, who ten years later would lead Hampshire to their first championship title.

McCorkell's kindly helpfulness was ideal for coaching, and after Hampshire he took up a position, which he held for thirty years, at Parktown High School in Johannesburg, where he settled permanently.

Neil Thomas McCorkell: born Portsmouth, Hampshire, 23 March 1912; died Uvongo, South Africa, 28 February 2013. Hampshire (1932-51).

Neil McCorkell in 1935

ARTHUR McINTYRE
(1918-2009)

Arthur McIntyre was the wicket-keeper in the great Surrey side that won the championship in seven consecutive summers from 1952 to 1958. He was the consummate professional, the best 'day in, day out' keeper on the county circuit, standing up to the stumps not only to the Surrey spin twins Jim Laker and Tony Lock but also to the awkward medium-pace of Alec Bedser, all of them bowling on lively, uncovered pitches.

Unfortunately he played in the same years as the more spectacular Godfrey Evans, and he won only three Test caps. Evans was a showman, lacking the dedication necessary for the six-day-a-week routine, but he could turn on the style on the big occasions.

McIntyre grew up in Princes (now Cleaver) Square in Kennington, a quarter of a mile from The Oval. His father was a Scottish bricklayer, often out of work, but he managed to buy his five-year-old boy a cricket bat, shaving off the bottom. In the middle of the square were disused allotments and, in the games that were played there, the boy who had the only bat was soon making progress. His schoolmasters at Kennington Road encouraged him, he watched his idol Jack Hobbs whenever he could, and in June 1932, at the age of 14, he opened the batting at Lord's for the London Elementary Schools. His partner was Denis Compton, they put on 100 together, then "he hit the ball straight at cover point and ran me out."

He joined the Oval groundstaff, where he supervised members' bicycles, turned out for the Young Players of Surrey and was sent one winter to Maidstone to develop his leg-breaks under the tutelage of the great 'Tich' Freeman. McIntyre, a 'tich' himself at five foot five, was seen as a leg-spinner who also batted, and he progressed into the first team for a few games in 1938 and 1939.

Then came the war. He was posted to North Africa, then to Italy where a large piece of shrapnel had to be extracted from his hip. It was there that he met up with the Bedser twins, who were in the RAF police, and he experienced the rare joys of "clean sheets, lovely ham sandwiches and cricket talk". The pre-war Surrey keeper George Mobey was in his forties, and the Bedsers suggested to McIntyre that keeping might be his best route into the side. So 'Mac' turned himself into a keeper.

In fact, he played the summer of 1946 as a specialist batsman, scoring 791 runs including a century and winning his cap. All the while he was working with the great Herbert Strudwick, England keeper before the first war, to improve his glovework, and the following summer the position became his.

Alec Bedser liked his keepers standing up, and the slow left-armer Tony Lock became a testing bowler to keep to, particularly with his faster ball. But it was the off-spin of Jim Laker that McIntyre found hardest. On a dusty track at Chelmsford in 1947 Laker's deliveries bounced over his left shoulder and he conceded 33 byes.

With the England fast bowler Peter Loader emerging in the early 1950s, it was arguably the best county bowling side of all time – and by then Mac was taking them all with a calm unobtrusiveness. 'He was never acrobatic,' Peter May wrote. 'There was no need, as he was always in the correct position on his two feet.'

He was a wristy, attractive batsman, keen to get on with it. Though he did not make the runs he might have done as a specialist batsman, he scored seven centuries and completed 1,000 runs in a summer three times. He played the lap shot well and what we now call the slog-sweep, but his running between the wickets was not popular with one or two of the older, heavier players, notably Jack Parker whom Mac described as "like an old ship going down the wicket".

McIntyre was chosen as the reserve keeper for the 1950/51 tour of Australia, captained by Freddie Brown. On the way out he scored a century in Ceylon and was picked as a batsman for the First Test at Brisbane, taking part in the most extraordinary day's cricket.

On Saturday Australia made 228. Then came two days of rain, followed by a tropical sun that made the drying pitch an unplayable sticky dog. England struggled to 68 for seven, then declared. Australia reached 32 for seven and also declared, setting England to score 193 for victory. Survival till morning, and a calmer pitch, was paramount, and Hutton and Compton were held back.

It all went horribly wrong, and at 23 for five Mac joined Evans at the wicket. It was the greatest opportunity of his life, and he immediately hit the mystery spinner Iverson for a leg-side four. The next ball lived forever in his memory:

> I hit Iverson down to square leg, a fair way. A chap named Johnson chased it. We'd run three easy runs. And we went for the fourth. This chap threw the ball in. It missed the stumps by quite a bit. Don Tallon, their keeper, backed away from the wicket, took the ball, threw it at the stumps and it hit them. And I was out. Run out, going for a fourth.
>
> Christ, if I could have walked off the ground the other way and not had to face Freddie Brown, I would have done. It was

such a vital time. If I could have stayed there … To have got run out of all things … Crikey, did I get some stick?

Hutton batted superbly the next morning, but they lost by 70 runs.

Back in South London, Jack Parker was sitting downstairs in the early hours, listening to it all on the radio, and he greeted the run out with a series of expletives: "The ****, he's **** done it again." Unknown to Parker, his young daughter was sitting on the staircase, and she went up to her mother's bedroom to ask what the words meant; for days the house was filled with frosty silence.

McIntyre returned to Surrey and to the seven championship titles, his last season coinciding with the last of them. He then did 18 years as county coach, upholding the traditional values of the game – the discipline, the smart appearance, the fair play – and proving a shrewd judge of up-and-coming youngsters. He worked closely with the local schools, and ten of his recruits, among them Bob Willis and the New Zealand captain Geoff Howarth, went on to play Test cricket.

In 1963, five years after retirement, he played one last time. The Surrey keeper had appendicitis, and McIntyre did not want to expose the young deputy to the intimidating atmosphere of Bramall Lane, Sheffield. He scored an unbeaten 50 and took three catches, the last of them the young Geoff Boycott.

He and his wife Dorothy retired to Lymington, enjoying 57 years of marriage before her death. He lived another six years, always happy to share his love of cricket with visitors. Nobody had ever batted better than his idol Jack Hobbs, nobody bowled better than Shane Warne. And nobody had ever set off on a run more disastrous than his at Brisbane.

At the time of his death he was England's oldest Test cricketer. That mantle now passes to his old friend, Sir Alec Bedser.

Arthur John William McIntyre: born Kennington, London,
14 May 1918; died Lymington, 26 December 2009.
Surrey (1938-63). 3 Tests for England (1950-55).

.

FRANK PARR
(1928-2012)

If things had worked out differently, Frank Parr could have been one of the great characters of post-war English cricket. An acrobatic wicket-keeper, he caught the eye almost as soon as he appeared in the Lancashire side. At The Oval in 1952, in only his second county match, he was tipped by *The Times* to be Godfrey Evans' successor in the England side. Herbert Strudwick, England keeper in the 1920s, thought he was very special. A fortnight later he caught the headlines again, this time as a batsman when, with nine wickets down, he resisted Fred Trueman and Johnny Wardle to save a Roses match at Old Trafford.

The following May, with word of his great promise spreading, the selectors invited him to play for MCC at Lord's, then enquired about his availability for that winter's tour of the Caribbean. A slight weakness when keeping to the off-spin of Roy Tattersall became apparent, but he remained a regular in the Lancashire side through 1953 when, with more luck with the weather, the county might have won the championship.

Parr, however, was an eccentric on the county circuit. A grammar school boy from Wallasey, he combined his cricket with playing trombone in the semi-pro Merseysippi Jazz Band and, to the distaste of some at Old Trafford, he brought too much of the anti-establishment scruffiness of that world to his daytime job. On one occasion, at a House of Commons reception, he turned up – horror of horrors – in a blue shirt.

'Frank was a fine wicket-keeper,' the fast bowler Brian Statham wrote, 'but he was an arty, untidy type who looked what he was, a spare-time musician. Even in flannels, walking onto the field, he still managed to look anything but a cricketer.'

As long as the easy-going amateur Nigel Howard was captain, these eccentricities were no problem. But in 1954 the 'no nonsense' professional Cyril Washbrook, a narrow-minded snob, took over, and Parr had no chance. He was dropped after five matches, never to return. In the second eleven he kept superbly – "I was at my best at that time," he reckoned – and Worcestershire offered him a job. Then Washbrook wrote to them – 'I should inform you that he can be a grave social risk' – and his days as a professional cricketer were over.

He was distraught – "I thought it was the end of the world; it's probably why I took up serious drinking" – but soon he found himself in London where he joined the Mick Mulligan Band, with its lead singer George Melly. For several years he lived a wonderfully chaotic life on the road, letting out all his inner

demons through his trombone. "All jazzmen are kicking against something," he said, "and it comes out when they blow. If they knew what they were kicking against, they wouldn't blow nearly so well."

Melly devoted six pages of his autobiography *Owning-Up* to Frank: his untidiness, his lack of personal hygiene, the dark sweat-ridden holes that appeared under the armpits of his sweaters and the dramatic speed with which he would pass through the stages of drunkenness: 'wild humour, self-pity and unconsciousness, all well-seasoned with the famous Parr grimaces.'

In his early days with the Merseysippis his trombone playing had been, by his own admission, "more attitude and enthusiasm than skill. I shudder to think what my standard was." Yet, as the surviving CDs of the Mulligan Band testify, he was a gifted performer by the late 1950s. Unfortunately their revivalist jazz went out of fashion, as they discovered one night in a South London cinema. They played their set to an unenthusiastic teenage audience, who then screamed the house down when the young rock-and-roller Tommy Steele appeared. In the bar Parr knocked back whiskies in utter despair. "I remember declaiming, and one did declaim in those days, 'He'll put us all on the breadline.'"

They finished in 1961 and, after a brief spell with the Clyde Valley Stompers, he put away his trombone. For ten years he was Acker Bilk's manager, then he worked for a company that sold advertising space for charities, a job which – despite his lunchtime drinking – he did better than any of his more conventional colleagues.

He lived for some years in the 1970s with an actress Christine Dunbar, railing against the 'bourgeois pretentiousness' of her dinner parties, occasions when he defiantly insisted on eating a plate of bacon and sausages. He never gave up his own flat, though, eventually returning to life on his own, determined to the end to make no concession to cleanliness or tidiness.

He had many friends in the jazz world, regularly attending London clubs, but it was cricket that was always closest to his heart. He played till the age of 60 for a team of jazzmen – "just piss-artists" – called The Ravers, and he occasionally walked down the road to Lord's. Mostly, though, he sat with the curtains drawn in his council flat, watching the games on television.

The Ravers – Frank seated in the centre

He would have been a wonderful breath of fresh air in English cricket in the 1950s, an entertainer with a bohemian streak, but it was not to be. Jazz and cricket did not make easy bedfellows, certainly not with a conventional man such as Cyril Washbrook in charge. On one occasion, at Oxford, Parr played his trombone in the dressing room, with team-mate Bob Berry beating time with a stump. "Much to Washy's disgust." Washbrook's vitriolic words, on the racial origins of jazz music, were never forgotten.

He was not bitter, though. He was too intelligent, too independent for that. "I've been extraordinarily lucky," he would say. "I've done the two things which I loved most. I made a living out of both of them, and I had a good time. I wouldn't swap my life for anything."

*Francis David Parr: born Wallasey, Cheshire, 1 June 1928;
died London, 8 May 2012. Lancashire (1951-54).*

PETER ROEBUCK
(1956-2011)

Peter Roebuck was a very good cricketer, an opening batsman who gave great service to Somerset and who was unlucky not to play for England. He was not a great stylist, preferring to bat within his range and to leave the entertainment to those who followed, notably Viv Richards and Ian Botham. As a writer on the game, however, Roebuck was quite different: a sparkling intellect with an easy way with words, a true original who loved nothing more than to play all the shots. The slow pace of cricket lends itself to endless comment and analysis, but Roebuck could be relied upon to say something fresh. For many he was the best cricket writer in the world.

Roebuck, one of six born to schoolteacher parents, caught the cricket bug as a young boy in Bath. He applied for a scholarship to Millfield, the sports-centred independent school run by the eccentric Jack Meyer, a former Somerset captain whose greeting to the 13-year-old entering his study was to throw an orange at him. "Well caught," he said. "But you should have thrown it back." Roebuck was in, so were both his parents as teachers, and they were given a house in nearby Street. Meyer, ever an unconventional thinker, appealed greatly to the youngster.

Success in schools cricket led to a contract with Somerset in 1974. The new coach, the former Warwickshire all-rounder Tom Cartwright, had persuaded the committee to pay six youngsters £1,000 each for the summer, and Roebuck's fellow recruits included Botham, Richards and Vic Marks. Living in Wells, the socialist Cartwright regularly drove the youngster to Taunton, spending every journey in intense conversation about the game. Roebuck, the searching intellectual with left-wing sympathies, lapped it up.

The county captain, in the twilight of his career, was the Yorkshireman Brian Close, and Roebuck related to him, too: his streak of madness and his inspiring courage. In an early game Roebuck was felled by a bouncer from the lethally quick West Indian Andy Roberts, returning after a visit to hospital to have his cap knocked off by the same bowler. His response was to sit in a darkened room, where he played a Joni Mitchell record and resolved to improve his technique. It was not what Close would have done, but the same determination was there.

Close and Cartwright: Roebuck called them the Churchill and Attlee of Somerset cricket. The results of their influence became clear in the golden years from 1979 to 1983 when Somerset, perennial losers, won five one-day trophies. Roebuck's batting was now mature and effective, and he was also starting to write. His first book, *Slices of Cricket*, was a series of entertaining essays; his second, *It Never Rains*, was a profoundly honest diary of the 1983 summer, revealing his inner demons. Last year a poll of cricket writers in *The Cricketer* voted it the third best cricket book of all time.

Somerset cricket imploded in the years that followed, with the Botham-Richards circus growing too big for the West Country dressing room. Roebuck, appointed captain in 1986, thought the unthinkable and decided to replace Richards with the New Zealander Martin Crowe. The registration rules meant that the West Indian Joel Garner had also to be sacrificed; Botham walked out in solidarity. Meetings of outraged members were held, and Roebuck took great flak. The glory years never returned, some including Botham harboured lifelong grudges, but Roebuck's unflinching courage was admired by many.

He retired from the first-class game at the end of 1991, by which time he was third in Somerset's all-time list of run-scorers. In all, he scored 17,558 runs, with 33 centuries. He wrote a superb history of Somerset cricket, *From Sammy to Jimmy*, then captained Devon for ten years. He led them to four successive Minor County Championships, the most successful captain in the competition's history.

Following a 2001 court case that revealed his bizarre regime of caning young overseas cricketers, a case that some saw as the revenge of Botham's mates, he left England, deeply out of love with its culture. He shared his time between Australia, where he wrote for the *Sydney Morning Herald*, and South Africa, where he promoted the cause of young black cricketers.

A highly intelligent man, winning a double first in Law at Cambridge, he could be other-worldly. He was untidy, was awkward with women and spoke at high speed, the ideas tumbling out of him with insistent clarity. The tragedy of his early death, by suicide in South Africa, will mean that he is remembered as a tortured soul, which to an extent he was, but his achievements in cricket – as player, captain and, above all, gifted writer – should not be clouded by that. As his mentor Cartwright put it shortly before his own death, "I feel the world hasn't treated Peter as well as it should have done. He doesn't get the recognition he deserves."

"Do tell Tom that I'm fine," was his reply to that. "My life is rich and varied, and I am highly regarded in many places." Alas, it was not the whole truth.

Peter Michael Roebuck: born Oxford, 6 March 1956; died Cape Town, South Africa, 12 November 2011. Somerset (1974-91).

REG SIMPSON
(1920-2013)

In the post-war years of austerity there were few more attractive sights in English cricket than the Nottinghamshire batsman Reg Simpson. With a quick eye and the natural gift of timing, he developed a back-foot technique that seemed to give him more time than anyone else against the fast bowlers. If they bowled bouncers, he swayed effortlessly out of the way. If they pitched it up, he drove them elegantly. Always he played with a positive spirit, prepared to embrace risk in pursuit of victory.

A grocer's son from Sherwood Rise, north of Nottingham, he fell in love with cricket at primary school, visiting Trent Bridge where for him there was no more thrilling a sight than the hawk-eyed Indian prince Duleepsinhji of Sussex playing with graceful artistry the lightning-fast bowling of Harold Larwood. In the back garden at home it was Duleep he wanted to be.

At Nottingham High School he broke the record in the 100-yard sprint, scored dashing tries at rugby and attracted the county cricket club's attention. He joined the Nottingham Police, becoming a cadet detective in the Special Branch. Then, when he was 19, war broke out, blocking his path into first-class cricket. At first he remained a policeman, scoring big runs in wartime matches at Trent Bridge; then he joined the RAF, learning to fly in Arizona and finishing up in India. "Don't fly too high," his mother beseeched him, but it was not advice Simpson was ever going to take. At the controls of a plane or car, or with a bat in his hand, he was not temperamentally inclined to caution.

In India he flew more than 1,000 hours, but he found time for cricket, making his first-class debut for Sind against Bombay at Karachi. Late in his life, to his great amusement, *Wisden* took to listing him as RT Simpson (Sind & Notts). He got back to England in the middle of 1946, and within a month of his county debut he scored 201 against Warwickshire.

He was determined to play his cricket as an amateur, and this became possible when the bat-makers Gunn & Moore took him on. It was only a pretence of amateurism, but Simpson, unlike some with such jobs, took his work seriously, becoming in time managing director. He was offered the captaincy of Northamptonshire, but he stayed at Trent Bridge, where he skippered the side from 1951 to 1960.

He toured South Africa in 1948/49 where he sorted out his weakness against spin bowling. Gloucestershire's Jack Crapp told him how the great Wally Hammond had concentrated on the ball in the air, not the hand delivering it. "The funny thing was," Simpson said, "when you did that, you actually saw the different action of the hand more clearly." The following summer, against Leicestershire, with their deadly chinaman bowler, the Australian Jack Walsh, he hit two hundreds in a match, the second in a sensational run chase in which Notts scored 279 runs in 35 overs. That summer, against New Zealand at Old Trafford, he hit his maiden Test century.

Simpson played 27 times for England, scoring four centuries, the most memorable of which was at Melbourne in the last Test of the 1950/51 series. England had lost the first four games, making their post-war record against Australia: Played 14, Drawn 3, Lost 11. But Simpson finally raised the nation's spirits with a match-winning hundred in the first innings. He stood up to the pace of Lindwall and Miller, he mastered the mystery spinner Iverson, and in a crucial last-wicket partnership of 74 with Roy Tattersall, when he took his score from 92 to 156, he manipulated the strike so that he could face six out of eight balls each over. "The situation really suited me. I could take some calculated risks and play my shots."

'He could be one of our great modern players,' the former Australian Test cricketer Jack Fingleton wrote, and Simpson underlined the verdict with a dazzling 137 in the first Test of the summer against the South Africans. Yet even in that innings the warning signs were there in the reaction of the more conservative Len Hutton, soon to become England captain. "I hit Athol Rowan over the top to the pavilion for a near-six and, as we crossed, he said to me, 'This is a Test match, you know.'"

By the Fourth Test Simpson was out of the side. "All the time I was playing Test cricket, I had the feeling I was fighting for my place, and it does make you over-cautious. If somebody had said to me, 'You're in for five matches,' I could have attacked in my own way as I did at Notts."

He never became a fixture in the England side, but he continued to entertain the crowds at Trent Bridge. As late as 1962, when he was 42 years old and only playing part-time, he topped the national batting averages. In all first-class cricket he hit 64 centuries, ten of them doubles.

For many years he was the driving force at Nottinghamshire, chairman of the club as they rose from the lower depths to win the championship in 1981. Though he disapproved of much in the modern game, he remained a great believer in playing positively.

Still playing at the age of 63, he was proud of his Man of the Match award in a Lord's Taverners game in which he hit a fifty off a bowling attack that included Paul Allott and Richard Hutton. At the time of his death he was England's oldest Test cricketer.

*Reginald Thomas Simpson: born Sherwood Rise,
Nottingham, 27 February 1920; died Nacton, Ipswich,
22 November 2013. Nottinghamshire (1946-63, captain
1951-60). 27 Tests for England (1949-55).*

JEFFREY NEILSON TAYLOR
(1930-2010)

In the early 1970s Radio Three broadcast a most unusual talk. It began with a Bellini aria, sung by Maria Callas, which faded into commentary on a Bobby Charlton goal. "Whatever could be the connection?" Neilson Taylor, the well-known baritone, then asked. In an earlier life he had been Jeff Taylor, the quick-footed centre-forward for Huddersfield Town and Fulham, and for ten minutes he explored the affinities between the two activities: the muscular control, the self-discipline, the poise and balance. "Certainly for me," he concluded, "football and singing are not so far apart."

His was a rare combination of talents, and his younger brother Ken was no less remarkable. Also a professional footballer for Huddersfield in the old First Division, he played cricket for Yorkshire and England and studied fine art at The Slade. The two of them were like gentlemen amateurs from the Edwardian age, yet they came from the humblest of backgrounds in the Primrose Hill district of Huddersfield. Their father struggled to find work through the 1930s, and they lived in a small terraced house where, till he was fifteen, Jeff shared a bed with his younger brother.

Jeffrey Neilson Taylor was born in 1930 into a working-class community that valued music. "You were an outsider," he said, "if you didn't sing." Every Sunday evening after chapel the choir would gather around a piano at somebody's house, and as a boy soprano Jeff won a talent contest in Greenock Park with a rendition of the Victorian hymn 'The Holy City'. He also had a taste of popular entertainment when as a small boy he accompanied his grandfather to Blackpool beach for his Punch-and-Judy show. Jeff's task was to attract a crowd by performing a tap dance on a small mat.

He scored goals aplenty in junior football – 62 in nine matches in the local under-15 league – and, after attending Almondbury Grammar School, he was signed by Huddersfield Town football club. He scored on his debut against Chelsea in November 1949, and he used his wage of six pounds a week to support himself through a geography degree at London University, travelling each Saturday to meet up with his team-mates. In two years he played 71 matches, scoring 29 goals.

One football magazine tipped him for international honours. 'Taylor,' it wrote, 'is only of medium build but he moves like quicksilver, has good ball control and is very dangerous anywhere near goal with either foot or head.'

His university professor advised him to cut back on football in his final year but, instead, Jeff got himself transferred to Fulham, who paid him a ten-pound signing-on fee. The club was known for its show business atmosphere; the chairman Tommy Trinder was a popular comedian, and the board also included Chappie d'Amato, the band leader. "It was more of a Christmas club than a football club," Jeff said. "A fun club. Not at all like Huddersfield. I felt very much at home."

Fulham were relegated to Division Two, but they had a forward line of rising stars – the future England captain Johnny Haynes, the future England manager Bobby Robson and the ever-loquacious Jimmy Hill who would become the face of football on television. Jeff Taylor stayed with them for three seasons before moving to Brentford where he became club captain.

All the while he continued his studies. He trained to be a schoolteacher, but an unhappy placement at Chiswick Grammar School convinced him that he was on the wrong path. "They put me to teach a class of six sixth-form girls, and it frightened me to death. I didn't know anything about girls."

He remained an active amateur singer. Once, after a match at Liverpool, he hurried off to sing the baritone lead in 'Merrie England' with the Colne Valley Male Voice Choir, and he was prominent in the university's Music Society. So, when teaching no longer appealed, he applied to the Royal Academy of Music where he began training as an opera singer.

His football ended one Saturday in December 1956 when his cheekbone was fractured in a Cup tie against Crystal Palace. He stayed on the pitch, scoring a late goal, and was sent for plastic surgery to East Grinstead. "I had to go down on my own on the train, and nobody in the club got in touch till Tuesday." All his life he had a numb nerve from the operation, and he decided to call it a day as a footballer, resisting Brentford's offer of a pound-a-week pay rise.

The Brentford chairman Vic Oliver offered him work on his radio variety show 'Band Box', and this led to years with the Cliff Adams Singers, on 'Friday Night is Music Night' and 'Sing Something Simple'.

By now he was Neilson Taylor, his working life taking in both light music and opera. One time he was in Australia, training a backing group for Tommy Steele; another he was at Glyndebourne, playing Arbace in Mozart's 'Idomeneo' alongside a young Italian tenor on his first visit to England, Luciano Pavararotti. He spent a year in Mantova in Italy, studying with Pavarottis's teacher Ettori Campogalliani, and this led to opera work in Covent Garden and Rotterdam.

The promise of those early years was never fulfilled. When his performance as Montfort in Verdi's 'Sicilian Vespers' was re-released a few years ago, one reviewer wondered why, with such a fine voice, 'his tone so rich and secure', he was not a household name. Perhaps, as with his football, he lacked a little in self-belief, and he was not helped when his Yorkshire stubbornness led to a dispute with an influential impresario.

He found his calling in 1974 when he became Professor of Singing at the Royal Scottish Academy of Music in Glasgow, staying there for 18 years and coaching several singers, male and female, who went on to greatness, notably Anthony Michaels-Moore, Iain Paterson and Simon Neal. He was an outstanding teacher, a perfectionist who understood the technicalities of singing and the individual requirements of each of his students. Through his will he has established a fund to help young singers at the start of their careers.

Neither of his two marriages lasted, but he enjoyed many friendships in his final years which he spent amid the beautiful countryside of the Holmfirth area, south of Huddersfield. He despaired somewhat of the cynicism of modern football, but he never grew weary of the company of musicians. Several of them continued to visit him for coaching, even in his last months when he was very ill. For years Michaels-Moore, wherever he was singing a leading role, would fly him out to hear the final run-through.

From the terraced house in Primrose Hill to the roar of the crowd at Fulham's Craven Cottage, from the Methodist chapel choir to the opera at Glyndebourne, he moved far beyond the horizons of his parents' world. "But I'm still a Yorkshireman," he would say proudly. "Whatever I've done, nothing has knocked that out of me."

His brother Ken, a working artist, survives him.

Jeffrey Neilson Taylor: born Huddersfield 20 September 1930; died Holmfirth 28 December 2010.

FRED TITMUS
(1932-2011)

It was Fred Titmus's simple belief, both in his long career as a professional cricketer and later in a spell as an England selector, that the statistics of the game do not lie. "If you've got it, you'll get runs (or wickets)," he would say. "If you ain't, you won't." By such a measure Titmus had certainly got it. He did the classic double of 1,000 runs and 100 wickets in a season eight times, a figure bettered by only four men, and his 2,830 wickets place him in the all-time top ten of bowlers.

In some ways he was an unlikely character to achieve such success. As an off-spinner he had the advantage neither of great height nor of long spinning fingers. He was not, in fact, a great spinner of the ball. But he did have a shrewd cricketing brain, and he developed the great gifts of flight and drift, varying the point at which he released the ball and maintaining an accuracy that drove frustrated batsmen into error. Similarly with the bat he built a highly effective game, even opening the innings in a Test against Australia. Fred Trueman called him 'the most successful self-made player since the war'.

A railwayman's son, he was born close to King's Cross station in November 1932. He attended William Ellis Grammar School, where – despite his small size – he was in the first team at the age of 13. He was also a promising footballer, playing for Chelsea Boys, and for a while he was unsure where his greater ambition lay. Then he watched the young MCC professionals in the nets at Lord's, and with a confidence that he never lost he thought, "I can do as well as them." He had kept the statistics of all his performances, and he wrote for a trial in early 1949: "I said I'd scored about 1,200 runs the previous summer. I didn't bother to add that it had taken me 84 innings." In a net behind the ladies' refreshment room he bowled six balls and did not bat. "You'll do," they said.

"You'll do," they also said when they were looking for an eleventh man for the Middlesex side at Bath in late June. His whites were in the wash and, after a scramble to borrow replacements, he caught the train from Paddington. He had been due to sell scorecards at the Lord's Test, where five of the county's regulars were in the England eleven. Instead, he became the youngest Middlesex cricketer ever, joining a makeshift side which included the 46-year-old former England captain Gubby Allen and, in his second and last appearance for the county, the schoolmaster Horace Brearley whose son would also captain England. Titmus showed his steady temperament by scoring 13 in an eighth-wicket partnership of 34 with Allen, vital runs in a narrow victory that would lead to Middlesex sharing that summer's championship title with Yorkshire.

At this stage Titmus was a batsman who also bowled, mainly seamers, but in the following years he turned himself into a first-rank off-spinner. Middlesex, with an ageing team, encouraged his progress, picking him through most of the next summer and, after two years of National Service, he settled into an annual routine of cricket that continued till 1976. Sixteen times he took 100 wickets, with a best of 191 in 1955 when he also scored his maiden century and topped 1,000 runs for the first time. Still only 22 he was selected for two Tests that summer but, having little success and with Jim Laker in his prime, he was discarded. It was seven years before England turned to him again, by which time he had become a master craftsman.

He would stand at the end of his run-up, hitching up his trousers and surveying the field with a knowing smile. There was a calm, unhurried air about everything he did, a sense of control as he probed away at the batsman. "He was the best bloke I ever bowled with," the miserly England seamer Tom Cartwright said. "He bowled with the same philosophy as me, building pressure." Like Cartwright he loved bowling, always willing to shoulder the burden when conditions were unhelpful.

The last forty years, at least until the emergence of Graeme Swann, have seen a great decline in the potency of the traditional English off-spinner. The causes are several: the covering of pitches, the greater power of bats, the rise of the one-day game. It was so different in the 1960s, with Titmus one of a generation of fine exponents that included David Allen, Ray Illingworth and John Mortimore, all of whom were useful batsmen as well.

Australia, with its firmer pitches, has never been a happy hunting ground for off-spinners, but England took three in 1962/63 – Allen, Illingworth and Titmus – and Titmus confounded the critics by taking 21 wickets in the five Tests, including seven in an innings at Sydney. The Australian writer Tom Goodman called him 'the outstanding personality of the tour', describing his success as 'a triumph of character'. 'He gave himself precise tasks,' Alan Ross wrote, 'and he fulfilled them admirably.'

He had further success in the next two winters, in India and South Africa, holding his place in the England team till a tour of the Caribbean in 1967/68 when on a boat trip out of Barbados's Sandy Lane Bay his left foot got caught in the propeller and he suffered the loss of the four small toes. His fellow passengers thought he might never play again, but two months later he was bowling for Middlesex, on his way to another haul of 100 wickets.

In 1971 Mike Brearley took over the Middlesex captaincy. Titmus had had an unsuccessful spell in the post in the mid-60s, and he did not initially see eye to eye with the younger man's new ways. Nevertheless he remained a model professional, continuing to bowl with canny effectiveness well into his forties. Then, to general astonishment, the selectors plucked him back into the England ranks for the 1974/75 tour of Australia. He could not repeat the success of his first tour there, but he lifted flagging spirits with some gutsy batting against the ferocious pace of Lillee and Thomson. Underneath his equable temperament the competitive fire still burned strongly within him. In all, he played 53 times for England, taking 153 wickets and scoring 1,449 runs.

His last summer as a professional cricketer was in 1976, when for the first time Middlesex dropped him in favour of the young John Emburey. He took the decision without fuss, but he soon proved it wrong, returning to the side in August and ending his career with a harvest of wickets: six against Lancashire, six in each innings against Derbyshire and seven for 34 against Glamorgan at Swansea. With a late run of victories, Middlesex were county champions for the first time since the summer of his debut.

He had two years as coach at Surrey, where the club was going through an unhappy spell, then he left cricket to run a sub-post office at Potten End in Hertfordshire. Yet even that was not the end. With Emburey away with England, he was summoned out of retirement in both 1979 and 1980. Since the establishment of the championship in 1890, only he and Wilfred Rhodes of Yorkshire have played for their counties in five different decades.

There was one last and most extraordinary appearance, the stuff of fiction. One morning in late August 1982, nearing his fiftieth birthday, he came down to Lord's, popping his head into the home dressing room before start of play. "Fred, just the man," Brearley exclaimed. "We could do with a third spinner." Boots had to be found for him, just as whites had been 33 years earlier when he had made his debut alongside Brearley's father, and on the last afternoon, with time running out, he took three vital wickets. It was Brearley's last match at Lord's, and the victory led once more to the championship title.

Only five first-class cricketers have scored 20,000 runs and taken 2,500 wickets: Rhodes and Hirst of Yorkshire, Tate of Sussex, the great WG Grace and Fred Titmus. For a self-made cricketer, he ended his career in pretty good company.

Frederick John Titmus MBE: born London, 24 November 1932; died Long Mimms, Hertfordshire 23 March 2011. Middlesex (1949-82, captain 1965-68), Surrey (1978). 53 Tests for England (1955-75).

ALLAN WATKINS
(1922-2011)

When the great Australian batsman Donald Bradman walked to the middle for his final Test innings, at The Oval in 1948, he needed just four runs to complete his career with a batting average of 100, almost 40 more than any other cricketer has ever achieved. He was applauded all the way, by the England team as well as the crowd, and he played his first ball, a leg-break from Warwickshire's Eric Hollies, safely to the fielder crouched in front of him on the leg side. The next ball was a googly and, to the great shock of the packed ground, Bradman failed to read it and was bowled.

At short leg, and thus the last man to field a ball from Bradman in Test cricket, was Allan Watkins, who was making his England debut, the first Glamorgan cricketer ever to play in an Ashes Test. His captain Norman Yardley had told him to go in close – "See the whites of his eyes" – so he was better placed than anybody to answer the age-old question. Had the ice-cool Bradman been affected by the warmth of his reception? "I can't say that," he said shortly before he died, "but I can tell you he was dry-eyed."

Watkins had a bad game. An all-rounder, he made 0 and 2 and was hit so badly on the shoulder by a Lindwall bouncer that he bowled only four overs. After the match he stayed in London for treatment, missing his county's vital game at Bournemouth where victory would take the championship title to Wales for the first time. He spent an anxious Tuesday afternoon at Hither Green railway station, buying every fresh edition of the evening paper to keep up with the score in the Stop Press till finally the good news arrived.

Glamorgan, under the combative Wilf Wooller, were not a side blessed with star players, but they took fielding, particularly close to the wicket, to a standard not previously known in the game. Watkins was at the heart of this, his 40 victims in the leg trap making him the leading catcher, other than wicket-keepers, in the country. John Arlott wrote that he was 'without doubt the best close-to-the-wicket field in the world. He has caught the uncatchable so often as to have made the impossible his normal standard.'

That winter Watkins toured South Africa, playing all five Tests. He took one of Test cricket's greatest catches at Durban, hit a maiden century at Johannesburg and secured England victory in the final Test at Port Elizabeth when he and Jack Crapp scored 19 frantic runs in the final ten minutes. Yet he lost his place in the side the following summer, not regaining it till a tour of India in 1951/52 when the senior players were all

Allan Watkins

rested. There he headed the Test averages, saving the first match at New Delhi when in intense heat he scored an unbeaten, nine-hour 137. By the end his legs had gone. "I played one down leg side, I went to run, and I couldn't."

A labourer's son from Usk in Monmouthshire, he attended the local grammar school, but his interests were all sporting. He made his Glamorgan debut in 1939 and during the War, serving in the Royal Navy, he found time to play rugby union for Pontypool and football for Plymouth Argyle. Then in 1946, seven years on from his early county games, he returned to Glamorgan cricket, becoming a vital part of their side for 15 summers. He admitted in later life that he had suffered from anxiety all through his career, smoking heavily and taking "a lot of pills" to calm his nerves: "I walked bloody miles waiting to bat; I couldn't sit down." But he showed few signs of it at the crease, his adventurous left-handed stroke play in the middle order bringing him 32 centuries. Thirteen times he scored 1,000 runs in a season, twice he took 100 wickets with his left-arm medium pace, and he held 464 catches, second only to Peter Walker among Glamorgan cricketers. In those days of relentless six-day-a-week county cricket, not many reached such a standard in all the three disciplines of the game.

Struggling with asthma, he retired at the age of 39 during the summer of 1961. After a spell working in a borstal, he moved to the east of England where he became a hugely popular cricket professional, first at Framlingham School in Suffolk, then at Oundle.

He was 'old school', upholding the traditional values of the game in the nicest possible way, glad that he had played in the years he did when it was, in his words, 'a wonderful game of friendship'. He had a long and very close marriage, and almost to the end he stayed in Oundle in a house he called 'Ellis Park', after the Johannesburg ground where he hit his first Test century. "It was a strenuous life," he said, "but I wouldn't change a minute of it."

Albert John Watkins: born Usk, Monmouthshire,
21 April 1922; died Kidderminster, 3 August 2011.
Glamorgan (1939-61). 15 Tests for England (1948-52).

PETER WIGHT
(1930-2015)

Peter Wight was a shivering 20-year-old, a frail figure of only nine stone, when he arrived from British Guiana in the cold spring of 1951. He had been working for a warehouse on Georgetown docks. "If you want to go to England, there's a place on this boat," he was told. Three days later, with a new passport and a family in tears, he set off. "I didn't have any warm clothes," he remembered. "We passed the Azores, and I froze."

His family was of Scottish/Portuguese ancestry. His branch of it was poor, but there was sporting talent. His brother Leslie and cousin Vibert played cricket for the West Indies, while other brothers represented their country at hockey, tennis and soccer. He himself had just made his cricketing debut for British Guiana, and it was through a friend playing in the leagues that he found his way to Lancashire. The landlady where he was taken for lodgings was full up, but "We'll have him," she said. "He looks pathetic."

Wanting to be an engineer, he found work in a garage and attended night classes. He had chapped hands from the cold, rationing left him hungry and, when his employer refused to release him for his exams, he sailed to Canada, then came back to a factory job. He played cricket for Burnley and, when he visited his sister in Bridgwater in the summer of 1953, her husband said: "Why don't you play for Somerset? They've got no players." Next day they went down to Taunton by bus.

The county was at its lowest ebb and, after a good performance for the second eleven, he was pitched into the first team – to play the touring Australians. Out for a duck, he was in low spirits and lonely, shocked by the gambling, when the two teams played skittles in the evening. "Don't worry," the young Richie Benaud consoled him. "You'll get a century in the second innings." And he did.

There followed twelve summers when he delighted the Somerset faithful with his wristy batting, relying on his quick eye to drive the ball on the up, on uncovered pitches very different from the shiny surface of Georgetown's Bourda. He did not get his front foot close to the ball, and that led some to think he was frightened of the quickest bowling, especially when he backed to leg and flicked short-pitched deliveries through the off side.

Legendary were his battles with Surrey paceman Peter Loader, who liked to add verbal accompaniment to his menace, some of it about Wight's skin colour (though in Georgetown he had been a white man). "Even now it hurts to think of it," he said fifty years later. "It's unnecessary." He answered with his bat, never more remarkably than on an awkward track at The Oval

Peter Wight

in 1956. In the first innings he alone made runs with a valiant 62 not out. "I came in and sat down. We had to follow on, and they said, 'Don't take your pads off.' So I had a drink and a stretch and, blow me down, within minutes, 'You're in, Peter.'" Loader took seven wickets as Somerset were all out for 196. The waif-like Wight, at his majestic best, came off with 128 not out.

"There was always a lovely ring to his bat," team-mate Graham Atkinson said. "He seemed to middle the ball so well. If he'd gone out with an old chair leg, there'd still have been a nice ring to it. I used to stand at the other end and drool at the shots he played."

The only bowler he never mastered was Fred Trueman, but there was revenge of a sort at Taunton in 1962. Vic Wilson, Yorkshire captain, dropped the England star for not arriving on time, and Wight celebrated with the second double-century of his career. He passed 2,000 runs that summer, as he did in 1960 when he was first in the country to the landmark. In all, he scored 16,965 first-class runs for Somerset, more than any other batsman since the war, second in the all-time list to Harold Gimblett.

He even had days of glory with his off-breaks. Once at Chesterfield he came on, seventh-choice bowler, and won the match with six wickets for 29 runs.

For 30 years he was a first-class umpire. As in his playing days he retained a quiet independence, not getting drawn into the beery camaraderie, not afraid to give lbws or uphold regulations. In all, as player and umpire, he took the field in 895 first-class matches in England, more than anyone since the war.

After his playing days he set up a cricket school in Bath, where he spent his winters coaching. His favourite club was the Somerset Wanderers Ladies, whom he and his wife Joyce supported with great generosity. Never losing his high-pitched Caribbean accent, he infected the juniors' Saturday afternoon sessions with a great sense of fun. They all loved him.

It is hard to think of a cricketing immigrant who has given more to the English game – and he only came here to study engineering.

Peter Bernard Wight: born Georgetown, British Guiana, 25 June 1930; died Ross-on-Wye, 31 December 2015. Somerset (1953-65).

DON WILSON
(1937-2012)

Don Wilson bowled slow left-arm in the Yorkshire side which won seven county championships in the ten years from 1959 to 1968. An infectiously cheerful man, full of excitable reaction when bowling, he played six Tests for England and went on to become an immensely popular MCC Head Coach at Lord's.

Born in Settle in the Yorkshire Dales, he suffered from chronic asthma as a young boy. His father, an ambulanceman, saved up to take him for a consultation in Harley Street where, only seven years old, he told the doctor he wanted to be a professional cricketer. "That's the perfect job for you," came the reply. "Out in the fresh air."

In fact, when he left school at 15, he became an apprentice joiner, often working with asbestos, but the course of his life was altered when, in a Sunday benefit match at Settle, he bowled the great Len Hutton. This led to an invitation to attend nets at Headingley where his first session with the bat, facing the full pace of Fred Trueman, did not impress the gruff coach Arthur Mitchell. "What do you do for a living, lad? ... Well, forget the cricket. Fetch some bloody timber and board that end up."

The Dales had no tradition of producing Yorkshire cricketers but in 1957, aged only 19, he made his championship debut, filling in for Johnny Wardle who was playing for England. The role of slow left-arm bowler had always been crucial in Yorkshire's success: through Bobby Peel, Wilfred Rhodes and Hedley Verity to Wardle, who by this time was in his prime. The next year, though, the often cantankerous Wardle fell out with the newly appointed captain, the amateur Ronnie Burnet, and was sacked in mid-season. Suddenly the inexperienced Wilson had to maintain the great tradition, playing in front of Yorkshire crowds angry at the loss of one of their stars.

Wilson was not a great spinner of the ball, relying more on subtle changes of flight and pace, but, with the canny off-spinner Ray Illingworth at the other end, he was soon winning over the sceptics. Burnet brought in several players he had skippered in the second team, and a new youthful spirit brought the championship title back to Yorkshire in 1959, after ten painful years without success.

Wilson took 100 wickets in a season five times in the 1960s. "Wils had an easy run-up, a nice delivery stride and a high action," his team-mate Ken Taylor says. "And he was so enthusiastic. He expected a wicket every ball, throwing his arms up and widening his eyes. Even if the ball didn't penetrate the batsman, his eyes did."

Don Wilson

He was an outstanding fielder at mid-wicket, and as a lusty lower-order hitter he contributed useful runs, none more spectacular than his innings at Worcester in 1961 when, against all advice, he went out to bat with his left arm in plaster. With nine wickets down and 36 runs still wanted, his intention was to block out the last few minutes for the draw – but, true to the title of his autobiography, *Mad Jack*, he got carried away by the occasion. Holding the bat with only his top hand, he flailed six fours, three of them in an over off the fearsome Jack Flavell who was bowling at high speed with a new ball. Then he hit Len Coldwell, another England bowler, back over his head and strode off victorious with 29 not out.

He was the most convivial of team men, enlivening many an evening with his singing. He and his great friend Philip Sharpe were lovers of the 'Black and White Minstrel Show', spending one winter as dressers to the show in Scarborough.

He toured India in 1963/64, playing all five Tests. He also toured Australia with Ray Illingworth's Ashes-winning party of 1970/71, though his only Test that winter was in New Zealand.

His last years at Yorkshire, in the early 1970s, were unhappy ones. Brian Close had gone to Somerset, Illingworth to Leicester, and Trueman and others had retired. Geoff Boycott became captain, the team struggled and Wilson developed the yips, unable to run up and pitch the ball. He retired at the end of 1974, after which he had three happy years captaining Lincolnshire.

He spent several winters coaching in South Africa. For a time he was head coach at the Wanderers ground in Johannesburg. Then he was asked to promote the game in the townships and, with his infectious enthusiasm, his pioneering work was a great success. Nevertheless it was a shock to him when he received a telephone call from EW Swanton, the *Daily Telegraph* cricket correspondent, asking him if he would like to become MCC's Head Coach. It was a most unlikely appointment – "You're not mixing me up with the Wilson who played for Kent, are you?" he almost asked Swanton – but it was an inspired one.

He enjoyed working with the Test stars when they called at Lord's for help and, perhaps even more, he loved the days when he spread the joys of cricket to wide-eyed schoolchildren. Peter O'Toole became a friend, calling regularly for a net, and on one famous occasion O'Toole was the only batsman available when Imran Khan arrived, wanting to bowl at full pace ahead of a World Cup in Australia. "Peter was bruised from head to foot," Wilson said, "but he loved it. It was like he was Lawrence of Arabia all over again."

After 14 years at Lord's he returned to Yorkshire, to coach at Ampleforth College, where he introduced summer schemes for London schoolchildren. The game of cricket had given him the happiest of lives, and he was determined right to the end to pass on the joy.

Late in his life the breathing problems of his childhood returned. "If I were you, Don, I'd look at it this way," I told him. "You started your life with a chronic illness, and you're ending with it. And in between, against all the odds, you've had a wonderful life." That Christmas I received a card from him: "I often think of what you said to me. I've been a very lucky man." He was indeed lucky – as were all those who played alongside him or were coached by him.

Donald Wilson: born Settle, 7 August 1937; died York, 21 July 2012. Yorkshire (1957-74). 6 Tests for England (1963-71).

INDEX